Smart's Handbook
of Effective Writing

Smart's Handbook of Effective Writing

by

WALTER K. SMART, Ph.D.

and

DANIEL R. LANG, Ph.D.
Northwestern University

PUBLISHERS

HARPER & BROTHERS

NEW YORK *and* LONDON

SMART'S HANDBOOK OF EFFECTIVE WRITING,
THIRD EDITION

Copyright, 1922, 1931, 1943, by Harper & Brothers

PRINTED IN THE UNITED STATES OF AMERICA

L-V

Contents

v

CONTENTS

Preface

This Handbook is both a textbook for class use and a manual for theme correction.

I. As a textbook it covers the material ordinarily given in a freshman course in writing—including the whole theme, the paragraph, the sentence, diction, spelling, punctuation, and mechanics. Covered also are such subjects as the précis, the term paper, the library, and the use of the dictionary.

Punctuation is presented from a functional point of view, rather than as a set of arbitrary rules. The function or value of each punctuation mark and the relationship between the parts of a sentence are described. Effective punctuation means the choice of the right mark to indicate the particular relationship between the parts.

The chapter on Diction deals with common mistakes in the use of words and also with methods for increasing one's vocabulary. The purpose is to lead the student, first, to avoid the errors that he has been making, and then to broaden his acquaintance with words and cultivate an interest in them. It is only by a combination of these two kinds of study that an adequate vocabulary can be obtained.

In the present edition new and more extensive drill exercises have been provided. These include some of a constructive type which are to be filled in by the student, and others which require identification and correction of errors. At the end of various chapters there are also exercises in word study, and review exercises covering the work done in preceding chapters on sentence structure.

Much of the text has been rewritten, and a number of features have been added in the present revision:

1. A review of grammar in outline form—for students who require a systematic survey of fundamentals, and

also those who need a convenient manual for occasional reference.

2. A section on the dictionary—including exercises intended to familiarize the student with the scope of information to be found there.

3. A section on the library and its resources.

4. A section on writing habits and précis writing.

5. A section on the term paper.

6. A brief section on business letters.

II. For the correction of themes a system of reference numbers and a correction chart are provided. This system covers the points that commonly require attention, not only in sentence structure, diction, and punctuation, but also in the analysis of the subject, organization and writing of the whole theme, and structure of the paragraph.

Evanston, Illinois   W. K. S.
February 15, 1943   D. R. L.

To the Instructor

The arrangement in this book follows a commonly accepted plan, but it is not expected that this order will be best for everyone. Different classes require different emphasis on certain matters, and a different order of presentation.

Some instructors, for example, prefer to discuss the paragraph before taking up the whole theme. In other instances it may be advisable to begin with the chapter on Grammatical Correctness in order to give a preliminary review of fundamentals.

Preferably, the work in punctuation and diction should be spread over a considerable period—for one recitation hour, or part of an hour, each week—instead of being crowded into a number of consecutive recitations. With classes meeting several times a week, different phases of the work—diction, punctuation, sentence structure, and other subjects—can be carried on in parallel lines without confusion.

The corrections plan is simple, and easy to use. The different chapters are marked A, B, C, etc., and the principles or rules in the chapter are numbered A1, A2, A3, B1, and so on. These numbers are listed on a correction chart which is included in the book for ready reference by the instructor and the student.

Smart's Handbook
of Effective Writing

Chapter One

GOOD WRITING HABITS

THE IMPORTANCE OF
GOOD ENGLISH

Among the many who need to speak and write effectively, professional lecturers and writers constitute but a relatively small group. Business men, lawyers, engineers, doctors—indeed, men and women in all vocations—are called upon every day to communicate ideas and information to other minds. The success which they attain depends largely upon their ability to express their thoughts in correct and forceful English. To convey messages adequately, they must be able to speak and write in a way that is immediately clear. Without this ability, they are seriously handicapped in all their contacts, professional as well as social. For everyday expression, therefore, proficiency in the use of English is essential.

Since good English is a basic requirement, students should master the language before they leave college. After graduation, skill in expression will not appear magically when it is needed. It can be acquired only by forming the habit of using correct English both in and out of the classroom.

Too often, undergraduates assume that good English is to be practiced only in composition and literature courses. They should remember that it is also of prime importance for effective work in history, in biology, and in all other branches of the curriculum. Just as they use their knowledge of mathematics not only when working in that field, but also when dealing with problems in chemistry and in physics, so they should carry over the practice of good English into all their courses. Reports and class assignments should be written with the same care and attention to details that are given to themes for English instructors. In this way habits will be formed that will prove valuable to students when they enter their vocations.

THE DEVELOPMENT OF WRITING HABITS

Over-all efficiency in writing—efficiency in the use of language during college years and thereafter—is acquired through the cultivation and practice of good writing habits. Several of these are briefly discussed in the following sections.

Deliberately Apply the Principles of Effective Writing. Mere quantity of writing does not in itself make a good writer unless the principles of composition are intelligently applied during the period of learning. Whenever the student prepares a paper in any course, therefore, he should consciously use his knowledge of sentence construction, punctuation, and other technical matters. If basic principles are constantly practiced, they become a habit.

In his reading, however, the alert student will notice that established writers do not always follow the letter of all the rules. They may, for instance, make incomplete sentences, may use *which* and other pronouns without a definite antecedent, or may write paragraphs which, according to standard procedure, are not completely developed. Seeing these apparent violations, the student may ask why he should not have the same freedom.

Closer examination will show that these writers normally observe the standard principles, and make exceptions only when they want to secure special effects: that is, when they have an intelligent reason for departing from orthodox practice. This sort of deviation is vastly different from disregarding standards unknowingly. If one knows the proper forms, he can make intelligent exceptions without danger of going too far. Throughout this Handbook the emphasis is on standard principles. The student should follow these until he is sure that his judgment is sufficiently developed to warrant intentional deviation from them.

Plan Every Paper. Few writers are able to compose a well-organized article without first making a plan. If they do not actually formulate a complete outline, they do give considerable thought to the arrangement of material before they begin to write. Usually, however, they prepare a logically arranged outline of the topics which they want to cover. This provides a chart of the road that they are to follow, step by step, in developing the finished article; like a highway map, it serves as insurance against wandering into bypaths and making unnecessary detours.

Since established writers find this method helpful, students would do well to adopt it.

Prepare a First Draft. After the outline has been completed, the various topics should be developed into a preliminary draft. In preparing this first sketch, some writers proceed slowly and give each sentence approximately its final form before they go on to the next sentence. Others work rapidly without attempting to polish their style. At this stage of the work, they say, too close attention to matters of form interrupts the flow of thought and is likely to lead to the overlooking of important ideas. Both of these methods are used by good writers. The student will choose the one that seems better for him.

Revise the First Draft. The preliminary draft must be revised. The first type described above may need only a few changes. The second, however, requires careful attention. In either case, the task of revision should be approached in a critical frame of mind.

The whole paper should be tested to determine whether it treats the subject adequately. Examination of the individual paragraphs for unity, coherence, and emphasis might well be the next step in revision. Sentences should be checked for grammar and effective construction. The right punctuation marks should be used to point out the exact relationship between sentence elements. Whenever the student is doubtful about the spelling of a word, he should consult the dictionary. He will, of course, also use the dictionary to find words more precise than those which occurred to him while he was preparing his first draft.

This habit of careful revision not only helps to fix the principles of effective writing in the writer's mind, but also develops the faculty of self-criticism—the ability to evaluate one's own work.

Keep a Record of Errors. Keeping a record of the errors that he makes in his themes will help the student to improve his writing. For this record the following type of chart is convenient:

Theme No.	Correction Symbols
1	C 1 — E 6 — C 9 — F 5 — K 2
2	C 1 — E 6 — E 4
3	C 1 — E 6 — F 1 — H 5

The first column identifies the number of the theme; the second lists the symbols that the instructor marked on each paper to indicate the mistakes. Each symbol refers to the section of the Handbook where the error is discussed.

A glance at the chart tells the student what mistakes he is in the habit of making. To overcome the fault designated by C 1, he would have to master the rules governing the agreement of subject and predicate. The recurrence of E 6 shows that dangling participles still remain a problem for him. Having thus been made aware of his persistent errors, he should eliminate them by carefully reviewing sections in the Handbook specified by the symbols.

Analyze the Style of Reputable Authors. Analysis of the work of established authors is another aid to good writing. The student should concentrate once or twice every week on a few pages in a standard book. After a first reading to get the thought of the passage, he can very profitably go over the section three or four times, making a systematic study of various specific points.

On the first excursion he might confine himself to an examination of the author's handling of paragraphs, his use of topic sentences, and methods of developing the topics.

Attention to sentence construction might be the object of the second round. If the student finds difficulty in the use of participles, for example, or in the co-ordination and subordination of elements, he would concentrate on these points. In other words, he can use the reading as a laboratory exercise in which he works out problems that bother him in his own writing.

Study of the professional writer's use of punctuation will show how important this factor is in making clear the relationship between parts of sentences, and in expressing subtle differences in meaning.

Another rich field for study is the author's diction. The student will, of course, note and look up in a dictionary any unfamiliar words, but—even more important than this—he should observe the apt choice of words to fit a given situation.

Finally, reading passages aloud will help to cultivate a feeling for the rhythm of well-built sentences and an appreciation of the big difference in effect that can be achieved by small differences in phrasing.

PRÉCIS WRITING

Practice Writing Précis. Practice in making précis also improves one's writing. A précis is a brief statement in summary form of the essential ideas in a longer article. The procedure in making this summary may be outlined as follows:

1. The student should read the article carefully in

order to obtain a clear understanding of the subject as a whole.

2. Then he should reread it paragraph by paragraph. Each paragraph in the original is built around a definite topic or idea, which has been developed by means of details, specific examples, and other devices (see Sec. B 10). These supplementary data must now be eliminated and only the main idea retained.

3. After he has determined the main idea of the paragraph, the student should restate it clearly and concisely in his own words. This can usually be done in a single sentence.

4. The same process is repeated in the succeeding paragraphs. The complete précis will therefore consist of a series of sentences, each representing the essence of a paragraph, and all of them giving a compact summary of the entire article. It should be a finished piece of writing, with sentences properly constructed and smoothly connected.

Précis are useful in a number of ways:

First, they provide an economical method of recording notes.

Second, in term papers borrowed material may be effectively presented in the form of précis.

Third, by crystallizing the thought in a long article, the précis makes it easy for the student to remember essential points.

Fourth, and most important in a composition course, making précis offers valuable training in learning how to write. It helps undergraduates to form the habit of reading critically and of observing the various methods that are used in organizing, clarifying, and emphasizing ideas. Preparation of précis requires exact analysis and reflective thought—the bases of good exposition. Furthermore, condensing a longer composition to a brief summary that states precisely the essence of the original is excellent practice in clear, correct, and concise writing.

Example of a Précis

(Original Passage)

Fifteen or twenty years ago there were few summer camps for children. Because even those few were very expensive, only the wealthy could afford to send their sons and daughters to them. Within the past ten years, however, the number of camps has greatly increased. Those privately owned are still too costly for most parents; but the rates charged at many others, such as those operated by churches, by fraternal orders, and by the Boy Scouts and Girl Scouts, are not beyond the average family income. To underprivileged boys and girls, similar recreational facilities are offered free of charge by many civic organizations.

Parents, therefore, not only can but should send their children to a summer retreat, for there is no place of greater benefit to them. Camps provide peaceful living away from the danger, noise, and heat in the city. Good food, clean air, and proper rest make their bodies strong and healthy. Purposeful activities, carefully planned, teach them how to work, play, and live with others. These activities give them a better understanding of right and wrong than they could obtain in any other way. Through the training given in arts, crafts, and sports, children progress mentally and physically. Certainly, then, for the full development of their sons and daughters, American parents ought to give them the benefits of a summer in a modern camp.

(Précis)

All parents, whether rich or poor, can now send their children to one of the many private or free public camps established during the past decade. All children, therefore, should be given the advantages of the social, mental, moral, and physical development provided in safe and healthful modern summer camps.

Exercise

Make précis of the following passages:

1. The periodical literature of the English people contains a living record of their esthetic and intellectual progress. Half

sheets, essays, magazines, reviews—these afford an opportunity for the examination and appraisement of the cultural progress of Great Britain, from the seventeenth century to our own time. The periodicals are, in effect, the "score keepers"; from generation to generation they have marked the steps forward. More than this, they have rendered immense service to literature, both by direct contribution, and by the essential support they have given men and women in their younger days—who, perhaps through the very training they were thus able to obtain, achieved literary eminence.[1]

2. In its loosest sense, thinking signifies everything that, as we say, is "in our heads" or that "goes through our minds." He who offers a "penny for your thoughts" does not expect to drive any great bargain. In calling the object of his demand *thoughts,* he does not intend to ascribe to them dignity, consecutiveness, or truth. Any idle fancy, trivial recollection, or flitting impression will satisfy his demand. Daydreaming, building of castles in the air, that loose flux of casual and disconnected material that floats through our minds in relaxed moments are, in this random sense, *thinking.* More of our waking life than we should care to admit, even to ourselves, is likely to be whiled away in this inconsequential trifling with idle fancy and unsubstantial hope.

In this sense, silly folk and dullards *think.* The story is told of a man in slight repute for intelligence, who, desiring to be chosen selectman in his New England town, addressed a knot of his neighbors in this wise: "I hear you don't believe I know enough to hold office. I wish you to understand that I am thinking about something or other most of the time." Now reflective thought is like this random coursing of things through the mind in that it consists of a succession of things thought of; but it is unlike, in that the mere chance occurrence of any chance "something or other" in an irregular sequence does not suffice. Reflection involves not simply a sequence of ideas, but a *con*sequence—a consecutive ordering in such a way that each determines the next as its proper outcome, while each in turn leans back upon its predecessors. The successive portions of the reflective thought grow out of one

---

[1] Walter James Graham, *English Literary Periodicals,* Thomas Nelson & Sons. Reprinted by permission of the author and the publisher.

another and support one another; they do not come and go in a medley. Each phase is a step from something to something —technically speaking, it is a term of thought. Each term leaves a deposit which is utilized in the next term. The stream or flow becomes a train, chain, or thread.[2]

3. Has anyone considered the present plight of the dramatist? I do not mean his difficulties created by the competition of the talking pictures or the outrageous demands of the theatrical unions or the financial depression. I mean his plight when he sits down to think what he can write about and cannot find a workable theme in his head. During the autumn of 1940 play after play was produced on Broadway, each a little more vapid, more ineffective than the last, and there was general agreement that our theater had reached a new low. Many causes were assigned, including the War, and doubtless there are many causes. But there is one cause which may well be paramount—the failure of the dramatists to find themes which are practical.

What do we mean by a practical theme? Any drama, to succeed, must make a mass appeal, and make it instantaneously. It cannot appeal to one man here, and another there, who in time may spread its message. It must be intelligible and emotionally stimulating to a thousand people every night. If it isn't, it fails. To succeed, then, it must have a theme which wins general understanding and response— much the same response from all the audience. A theme which does that is practical. One which doesn't is, for theatrical purposes, of no use. Since all dramatists write to succeed in the theater (if they didn't they wouldn't be dramatists), a practical theme is to them of the utmost importance. Without it they remain dumb or else fumble into failure.

But why, with so much of intense emotional interest going on in the world, should the dramatist find difficulties in hitting upon practical themes? Again the answer is found in the nature of the acted drama, in the fact that it makes its appeal to the mass, and must make it instantaneously. The laugh or the tear must come to everyone as the word is spoken or the pathetic gesture made, and to accomplish that the dramatist must base his wit or his situation on habits of thought and

---

[2] John Dewey, *How We Think*, D. C. Heath & Co. Reprinted by permission of the author and the publisher.

feelings, on customs and taboos, which are more or less universally possessed and accepted by his audiences. Even if he pioneers into new habits or customs, as Ibsen or Shaw once did, his point of departure is known and accepted, and his hero or heroine gains dramatic stature by defying convention. An accepted custom is an obstacle we can all understand, and the defiance of obstacles is the essence of drama. So the plight of the dramatist to-day lies to a great extent in the lack of widely accepted customs and habits of thought, in the confusion of feeling, in the loss of ancient social taboos, and the absence of any new ones to take their place as obstacles. There is little sufficiently concrete for his hero to oppose, either for tragedy or comedy. There is only chaos.[3]

USE OF THE DICTIONARY

To anyone who would master words, a dictionary is an indispensable reference book. The student, therefore, should keep a reputable dictionary on his desk for easy and frequent reference. When he consults it, he should observe the following kinds of information:

Spelling
Pronunciation
Grammatical classification
Etymology
Definitions
Synonyms
Antonyms

An entry reproduced from the fifth edition of *Webster's Collegiate Dictionary* will show how this information is presented.

fic′tion (fĭk′shŭn), *n*. [F., fr. L. *fictio,* fr. *fingere, fictum,* to form, invent, feign.] **1.** *Obs.* Act of fashioning; hence, a device. **2.** *Obs.* Dissembling. **3.** A feigning or imagining; as, by a *fiction* of the mind. **4.** That which is feigned or imagined; esp., a feigned or invented story. **5.** Fictitious literature; specif., novels. **6.** *Law.* An assumption of a possible thing as a fact.

[3] Walter Prichard Eaton, "The Plight of the Dramatist," *Harper's Magazine.* Reprinted by permission of the author and the publisher.

Syn. Invention, fable, coinage, forgery, falsehood.—**Fiction, figment, fabrication** (in the sense of invention). **Fiction** suggests imaginative fashioning, whether with or without intent to deceive; it is opposed to *fact, truth, reality;* **figment** implies more irresponsible invention; it often suggests a somewhat transparent fiction, esp. to keep up appearances; **fabrication** commonly implies something made up to deceive.—**Ant.** Fact, truth.

Spelling. When more than one spelling is given, the first form is usually preferred. In addition to the spelling of the word, the student should observe its division into syllables. In the example above, a heavy accent mark (′) indicates the point of division. [Other devices used to show syllabification are: the centered period (·); the light accent mark (′); and the short, light hyphen (-). The light accent mark (′) is used to show where the secondary stress should be placed.]

Pronunciation. Pronunciation is indicated by the accent mark and the phonetic respelling in parentheses. A key to the phonetic symbols appears at the bottom of the dictionary page. For a complete explanation of the sounds, the student should consult the "Guide to Pronunciation" on pages vii–xix in *Webster's Collegiate Dictionary,* fifth edition.

Grammatical Classification. The abbreviation *n.* signifies that *fiction* is classified as a noun. [Symbols for other parts of speech (*adj.* for adjective; *v. i.* for intransitive verb, etc.) are explained in the list of abbreviations given in the forepart of the dictionary. Inflectional forms, such as the plurals of nouns, the comparative and superlative degrees of adjectives and adverbs, and the past tenses and participles of verbs, are listed in the vocabulary entry when they are irregular.]

Etymology. The bracketed item indicates that *fiction* was taken into English from French (F.), which had borrowed it from the Latin (L.) *fictio,* derived from the verb *fingere,* of which *fictum* is a participle. [Symbols for other languages—OF. (Old French); Gr. (Greek); Du. (Dutch); Heb. (Hebrew)—from which words in

English have been derived are listed among the abbreviations in the forepart of the dictionary.]

The etymology of a series of words formed from the same root is usually given only after the basic word. For example, the derivation is presented only after *depart,* the basic word in the group *depart, department, departmental,* and *departure.*

In most cases, the meaning of a prefix is explained only at the head of a list of words that begin with that prefix.

Definitions. Of the six definitions of *fiction,* the first two, marked *Obs.* (obsolete), are not currently used. The third, fourth, and fifth definitions refer to inventions of the imagination. The sixth defines the word according to its technical meaning as a legal term. [For other usage labels—such as *Alg.* (Algebra), *Biol.* (Biology), *colloq.* (colloquial)—see the list of dictionary abbreviations on pages xxv–xxvi in *Webster's Collegiate Dictionary,* fifth edition.]

Synonyms. The five words in the first group following **Syn.** (synonyms) are basically related in meaning to *fiction,* but obviously these terms are not always interchangeable. The three words in the second group are explained in detail to illustrate their various distinctions in meaning.

In the dictionary, synonyms are generally grouped under only one of the several words similar in meaning. For other members of the group, cross references are cited in their own particular entries. Thus, if the student looked up *figment,* he would find this notation: "Syn. See Fiction."

Antonyms. This last item includes two words opposite in meaning to *fiction.*

Other Dictionaries

In addition to the fifth edition of *Webster's Collegiate Dictionary,* other reliable abridged works suitable for desk use are: Funk and Wagnalls' *College Standard Dictionary; Macmillan's Modern Dictionary;* and the *Winston Simplified Dictionary.*

Frequently the student will want to consult an un-abridged dictionary for words not included in the abridged work that he keeps on his desk. For this pur-pose he may go to the Reference Room in his college library, where he will find one or more of the following unabridged dictionaries:

Webster's New International Dictionary. Published in 1934, the second edition of this one-volume dictionary is accepted everywhere as authoritative.

New Standard Dictionary. This is a thoroughly re-liable one-volume compilation.

Century Dictionary and Cyclopedia. This comprehen-sive twelve-volume work, published in 1911, is still use-ful though not up to date. Volume XI (*Cyclopedia of Names*) is a pronouncing dictionary of proper names from biography, literature, history, and other fields.

New Century Dictionary. Revised in 1938, this two-volume *Century* uses a simplified method of indicating pronunciation and includes many quotations to illus-trate definitions.

A New English Dictionary on Historical Principles (also called the *Oxford English Dictionary,* or *Murray's Dictionary*). In this notable work, consisting of twelve volumes and supplements, definitions are illustrated in phrases and sentences quoted from English books pro-duced from 1150 to 1928. It is the supreme authority for the history of the spelling, pronunciation, derivation, and meanings of words.

A Dictionary of American English. Two volumes and three parts of this important compilation have been published, and other sections will be printed as they are completed. When the work is finished, it will con-tain the histories of words as they have been used and as they are being used in the United States.

Since dictionaries compiled by various editors differ

in scope, in plan, and in lexicographical principles, the student should examine the introductory pages of a dictionary that he consults for the first time. In those pages he will find, in addition to a table of contents, a detailed exposition of the plan and scope, a key to symbols that indicate pronunciation, a list of abbreviations used in the work, and explanatory notes which will make clear the various devices employed in the presentation of vocabulary entries.

Exercises

1. Interpret all abbreviations and explain the kinds of information given under the following vocabulary entries in your dictionary:

abject	fillet	period	waif
bedlam	Mercury	tonsure	youthful
estate	off	trammel	zone

2. By referring to a dictionary, find the past tense and the present and past participles of:

be	burst	dive	lie
begin	hang	lay	swim
bid	forsake	lead	swing

3. Use a dictionary to find the plural forms of:

appendix	dogma	locus	précis
beau	echo	madame	spectrum
company	folio	memorandum	staff
curriculum	half	phenomenon	thesis

4. As applied to entries in your dictionary, what do the following abbreviations mean?

Anat.	Chem.	lit.	pron.
Arch.	dial.	OE.	sp.
auxil.	fig.	OHG.	subj.
Cartog.	her.	poss.	Sw.

5. Consult a dictionary for the standard present use of these words:

chief	humor	railroad	want
discourse	large	temper	warm
fellow	nice	that	watch

6. Refer to a dictionary to determine the part of speech of each word in the following sentence:

The fatally injured boy called feebly to his three companions on the desolate beach.

7. Look in a dictionary for the correct pronunciation of the words:

address	foyer	indisputable
arctic	genealogy	infantile
comparable	genuine	irrevocable
despicable	gourmet	mischievous
either	hegemony	municipal
exquisite	incomparable	vaudeville

8. According to the dictionary, what is the correct syllabification of these words:

business	guardian	nautical	precedent
departure	happiness	occasion	precision
discipline	irreparable	occurrence	production
emotion	medium	posterior	verdant

9. Compare the information given under the following entries in your abridged dictionary with the information given for them in an unabridged dictionary:

juxtaposition	labyrinth	quality
kaleidoscopic	liturgical	rest

10. In a dictionary find synonyms for the following words. Point out the different shades of meaning in the various synonyms.

calm	difficulty	great	recondite
careful	feeling	negligence	renounce
concise	gift	pay	transform

Chapter Two

THE ARTICLE AS A WHOLE

The process of writing involves four principal steps:

1. *Choosing the subject and limiting it* to a phase which can be handled adequately in the allotted space.

2. *Analyzing the subject* into its essential elements or topics, which are to form the framework of the discussion.

3. *Organizing the material:* that is, arranging these topics into a working plan or outline, which will serve as a basis for an orderly presentation of the subject.

4. *Writing the article:* that is, filling in the outline by means of a detailed discussion of each of the headings. This is the final step, for which the other three have been a preparation. It involves careful attention to the structure of paragraphs and sentences, the choice of the right words, correct punctuation, and other details.

CHOOSING THE SUBJECT

The subject for a short theme or article should preferably be one which is within the range of the writer's experience and interest. For some of his themes, the student writer will naturally turn to the activities with which he is personally concerned—his life and work at school, his work outside of school, and his hobbies. Available also is a wide choice of material in which he, as a student and as a citizen, should be interested—such as current events and contemporary movements in politics, sociology, the natural sciences, business, and the whole range of human activity. His classroom work should suggest other topics, perhaps some which are only touched upon in the regular assignment, but which arouse his interest and invite further study.

In developing some of these subjects, the student will have sufficient information for an adequate discussion. For others he will need to do supplementary reading in the library.

A Limited Subject

A1. **The subject should not be too broad.**

When a writer chooses and announces a subject, he virtually enters into a contract with his reader to furnish an adequate treatment of it. Obviously, it is impossible for him to fulfill this contract in an article of five hundred or seven hundred words if the subject is a broad one. A satisfactory discussion of *The Airplane*, for example, would fill a volume or several volumes; and similar space would be required for *Labor Unions, Rudyard Kipling, The American Government, Poetry*, or *Rubber*.

For a brief article, these general subjects must be narrowed to some particular phase. Thus *The Airplane* might be narrowed to *Across the Atlantic by Plane*; *Rudyard Kipling*, to *The British Tommy in Kipling's Poems*; or *Rubber*, to *A Brazilian Rubber Plantation*. The amount of limitation that is necessary will depend, of course, upon the amount of space at the disposal of the writer.

For a list of suggested subjects for themes, see the end of this chapter.

An Effective Title

A2. **An effective title should be chosen.**

The first requirement of a title is that it shall indicate the particular phase of a subject that is to be discussed— not the broad, general subject.

Thus, an article on improving one's writing through the reading of good literature should not be given a general heading, like *Good Reading,* but should have a limited title, such as *Good Reading—An Aid to Good Writing.* Similarly, *Immigration* is too broad; *A Proposal to Restrict Immigration* fits a particular phase of the subject. *Loyalty* is general; *Loyalty to Our Football Team* is definite.

For factual themes, a definite, matter-of-fact title of the sort described above is often sufficient. For articles of a popular nature, a more individualized and interest-catching heading is usually desirable. The two types are illustrated below. Those in the second column are taken from articles in well-known magazines.

DEFINITE AND MATTER-OF-FACT	INDIVIDUALIZED AND INTERESTING
A New Kind of Microscope	An Eye for Miracles
A Carrier of Typhus	Death Rides the Cootie
Bethune-Cookman College	A College Built on Faith
A Trip to the Mountains	Escape to the Wilderness
Gutzon Borglum, the Sculptor	The Man Who Carves Mountains
Vitamin B_1—an Aid to Morale	Morale in a Test Tube

Exercise

Limit the following subjects to a phase suitable for a theme of five hundred to eight hundred words, and select an appropriate title. *Tobacco,* for example, might be limited to the pleasures of smoking or to the evils of the tobacco habit. A suitable title for the first theme might be *Smoke Dreams;* for the second, *Smokers Beware!*

Tobacco	Fishing	Freedom
Candy	Chess	Honor
Flowers	Baseball	Morality
Candles	Hobbies	Beauty
Furniture	Parties	Leisure

ANALYZING THE SUBJECT

After the subject has been chosen and properly limited, it must be analyzed into its essential elements. This analysis means finding the points that need to be discussed.

Too often a student begins to write an article without making this preliminary survey. He starts with a topic which seems suitable for a beginning, and then proceeds through the rest of the article, relying upon his ability to find other topics as he goes along. This is a haphazard and wasteful procedure. Later he may find that his beginning is not appropriate, and he must therefore rewrite this part. Moreover, in the stress of writing he may overlook important material. A careful analysis, made before he begins the article, will help him to avoid later missteps.

Complete, Logical Analysis

A3. **The analysis should be complete and logical.**

In the preliminary analysis, certain points will occur immediately to the writer. If he is to tell about how a book is published, he naturally thinks of such steps as preparing the copy, setting the type, and correcting the proof. Again, in discussing a play that he has seen, he is not likely to overlook the stage setting and the actors. After jotting down these obvious topics he then proceeds to a more thorough survey to make sure that he has covered the field adequately.

a. All Essential Points Included. The analysis should include all essential points—all those that the reader must know about in order to secure a clear understanding of the subject.

Some points, though they are not important enough for a full discussion, may deserve brief mention. In the finished article these may be combined into a miscellaneous paragraph with only a sentence or two of comment; and in the outline the miscellaneous character of the group will be indicated by a heading such as *General Characteristics* or *Minor Features*.

If the writer finds that, as the result of his preliminary analysis, he has more material than can be handled adequately in the space at his disposal, he should make a closer examination to see whether all the points are really essential. If not, those which are comparatively unimportant may be omitted. If all are essential, then the subject that has been chosen is too broad, and must be limited (see Sec. **A 1**).

b. All Irrelevant Points Omitted. Any topic which is not definitely connected with the subject should be omitted.

The chief danger here is that the writer may include points which belong to *another* phase of the subject, but not to the *particular* phase which he has selected.

An article on *Historic Richmond*, for example, would not include the commercial and industrial activities of the city. These activities are essential in a comprehensive account of *Richmond*, but they are irrelevant in a discussion of *Historic Richmond*. Similarly Theodore Roosevelt's prowess as a big-game hunter has no place in *Roosevelt, the Statesman;* or the comic strip in *The Newspaper as an Educational Medium*.

ORGANIZING THE MATERIAL

As the result of his preliminary analysis, the writer now has a list of topics, such as the one given below. It is for an article on *The Scribblers Club*.

1. Meetings.
2. Membership.
3. History.
4. Purpose.
5. Organization.
6. Accomplishments of the club.

7. Officers and committees.
8. Greater sociability.
9. Encouragement of members to write.

This list furnishes an inventory of the topics which are to be discussed in the article. It is not, however, a systematic working plan. To make this plan, the writer must organize his material:

(a) by assembling related material into groups,
(b) by arranging the groups in logical order.

Assembling the Material into Groups

A4. **All material which is logically a part of one topic should be assembled under one heading.**

Two principles are to be remembered here: First, there should be as few main divisions in the discussion as are consistent with the logical divisions of the thought. Second, all phases of the same main topic should be discussed in a group, not in different places in the article.

Topics 5 and 7 in the preceding list belong together under the general heading *Organization;* 8 and 9 are parts of *4. Purpose.*

The list of topics now appears as follows:

1. Meetings.
2. Membership.
3. History.
4. Purpose.
5. Organization.
6. Accomplishments of the club.

Arranging the Topics in Logical Order

A5. **The groups should be arranged in logical order so that there will be an orderly sequence of thought from one topic to the next, and from the beginning of the article to the end.**

When this is done, the reader is able to follow the discussion with the least possible confusion and wasted effort. Some of the more common principles of arrangement are as follows:

a. Proceed from General Discussion to Details. Ordinarily, any general discussion of the subject precedes the discussion of specific details. Thus, in a description of a house the natural procedure is to tell about its location, size, style of architecture, and other general features before taking up the details of interior arrangement and finish.

> According to this principle, 3. *History* and 4. *Purpose* —in the list under **A 4**—should be placed before the headings which cover the more detailed discussion of the club; and of these two, *History* naturally precedes *Purpose*.

b. Keep Related Topics Together. Those topics which are most closely related in thought should be grouped together.

> Topics 2. *Membership* and 5. *Organization* have to do with the personnel of the club, and should be placed as consecutive headings. They will be discussed in consecutive paragraphs when the article is written.

c. Prepare the Reader for Each Topic. Any topic which the reader needs to have explained in order to understand another one should be discussed first.

> Ordinarily, a reader would want to know what kind of club is being described, what its aims are, before he would be interested in reading an article about it. For this reason, *Purpose* is placed early in the outline (as well as because it is a general topic).

The list of topics, logically grouped and arranged, now forms a simple working outline.

THE SCRIBBLERS CLUB

1. History.
2. Purpose.
3. Membership.
4. Organization.
5. Meetings.
6. Accomplishments.

MAKING THE FINISHED OUTLINE

The spadework in the preparation of the outline has already been done in the analysis and organization of material. Some matters of form, however, remain to be considered.

Types of Outlines

A6. **The kind of outline that should be used for a particular article is determined by the length and nature of the discussion.**

a. Outline of Paragraph Topics. For short articles, the simple type of outline shown in the preceding section is usually sufficient. It consists of a series of main headings, each of which is to be discussed in a separate paragraph in the finished theme. If a paragraph becomes so long that it has to be divided (see Sec. **B 9**), the outline should be revised to show a main heading for each new group.

b. Detailed Outline with Subheadings. For a longer article a more detailed outline with subheadings is often required. These sometimes run into two or three degrees of subordination. The main headings indicate the main groups of thought in the discussion, and the subheadings show the different steps in the larger groups. Ordinarily, in the finished article a paragraph is given to each of the subheadings that represent the final subdivision of a topic. Thus, in the outline below, A and B under I would each be discussed in a separate paragraph; and 1, 2, and 3 would indicate the paragraph division in III A.

NEWTOWN ESTABLISHES A COMMUNITY FAIR

I. Preliminary campaign.
   A. Newspaper publicity.
   B. House-to-house canvass.
II. Community mass meeting.
   A. Subscription to a guarantee fund.
   B. Appointment of committees.
III. Detailed work of organization.
   A. Committee on arrangements.
      1. Securing a site for the fair.
      2. Arranging for the erection of booths.
      3. Supplying the necessary materials.
   B. Committee on publicity.
      1. Arranging for the sale of tickets.
      2. Advertising by the press and posters.
      3. Compiling the official program.
   C. Committee on exhibits.
      1. Securing demonstrators.
      2. Assigning the booths.
      3. Placarding the booths.
      4. Arranging for the sale of exhibits.
IV. Efficiency of the plan.
   A. Co-operation among the workers.
   B. Success of the fair.

All headings of the same rank, it will be noted, have the same indention.

c. Sentence Outline. A sentence outline is one in which each main heading, in combination with its subheadings, makes a complete sentence. It is a variant form of the outline described in **b** above.

NEWTOWN ESTABLISHES A COMMUNITY FAIR

I. The preliminary campaign consisted of
   A. newspaper publicity
   B. a house-to-house canvass

   II. The community mass meeting resulted in
      A. a subscription to a guarantee fund
      B. the appointment of committees
  III. The detailed work of organization was handled by
      A. the committee on arrangements, which attended to
         1. securing a site for the fair
         2. arranging for the erection of booths
         3. supplying the necessary materials
      B. the committee on publicity, which attended to
         1. arranging for the sale of tickets. Etc.

Correct Form for the Outline

A7. **The outline should be correct in form.**

a. Unnecessary Division into Introduction, Body, and Conclusion. In an outline for a short article it is better to avoid making a threefold division into Introduction, Body, and Conclusion.

A short article does not usually require a formal Introduction or Conclusion (see pages 34 and 40). If they are necessary, they are represented in the outline by main headings of the same rank as those for the other main divisions.

THE LIFE OF ABRAHAM LINCOLN

Not Good:
    I. Introduction.
      A. An example for American boys.
   II. Body.
      A. Early life.
      B. Education.
      C. Early political career.
      D. Career as President.
      E. Assassination.
  III. Conclusion.
      A. His influence.

Better:
    1. Introduction: an example for American boys.
    2. Early life.
    3. Education.
    4. Early political career.
    5. Career as President.
    6. Assassination.
    7. Conclusion: his influence.

b. False Introductions and Conclusions. Do not label as Introduction or Conclusion any material that is an integral part of the discussion.

Wrong:

1. Introduction: early life.
2. Education.
3. Early political career.
4. Career as President.
5. Conclusion: assassination.

Correct:

1. Early life.
2. Education.
3. Early political career.
4. Career as President.
5. Assassination.

c. Faulty Co-ordination and Subordination. Do not make a heading co-ordinate if it is logically subordinate, or subordinate if it is logically co-ordinate.

ENFORCING PROHIBITION

Wrong (illogical co-ordination):

I. Obstacles encountered.
  A. Lack of appropriations.
  B. Corruption of officials.
II. Adverse public opinion.

Right:

I. Obstacles encountered.
  A. Lack of appropriations.
  B. Corruption of officials.
  C. Adverse public opinion.

("Adverse public opinion" is one of the "Obstacles encountered," and should be a subheading.)

WORK IN A PRINTING OFFICE

Wrong (illogical subordination):

I. Preparing the copy.
II. Setting the type.
  A. Machine composition.
  B. Hand composition.
  C. Proofreading.

Right:

I. Preparing the copy.
II. Setting the type.
  A. Machine composition.
  B. Hand composition.
III. Reading the proof.

("Proofreading" is not a part of "Setting the type.")

d. Unimportant Subheadings. Do not make subheadings for unimportant details.

Not Good:	Improved:
I. Appearance.	I. Appearance.
A. Black.	
B. Square.	

Not Good:	Improved:
I. Binding.	I. Binding: leather.
A. Leather.	

e. Parallel Form for Headings. Headings of the same rank should be made as nearly as possible parallel in form.

MAKING A SMALL TABLE

Not Good:	Improved:
1. Drawing the plans.	1. Drawing the plans.
2. Select the material.	2. Selecting the material.
3. How the separate parts are made.	3. Making the separate parts.
4. Assemble the parts.	4. Assembling the parts.
5. The finishing.	5. Finishing the table.

Exercises

A. Point out faults in logic or form in the following outlines. Reconstruct the outlines so that they will present a clear, logical framework for an adequate discussion of the subject. Make any changes—additions or omissions—that you think are needed.

1. A DRIVER'S LICENSE

  I. Nature of a driver's license
    A. How to apply for the license
    B. Taking the test
  II. The purpose of a driver's license
    A. Prove physical fitness
    B. Prove mental ability
    C. Prove driving ability

III. Results of a driver's license
  A. Make people more careful
  B. Reduce accidents
  C. Means of identification

2. HOW TO TAKE A SNAPSHOT

I. Types of cameras
  A. Many types available
    1. Box type
    2. Photographer's camera
    3. Movie cameras
    4. Candid camera
  B. Use the best quality of film
II. Taking the snapshot
  A. Watch the angle of shooting
  B. Check exposure
  C. Correct lighting
  D. Have subject assume interesting pose
  E. Select background carefully
    1. Poor background spoils picture
  F. Hold camera steady
    1. Tripod is useful
    2. Unsteady camera blurs picture
III. Conclusion
  A. Practice makes perfect
  B. Development of the film

B. Make a preliminary analysis of one of the following subjects, and then arrange your points in a logical topic outline (see **A 6a**). Also select a suitable title for the article. Assume that the article is to be about 500 words in length. Narrow the subject, if it seems too broad.

Preparing for an examination.
Selecting elective courses.
Responsibilities of citizenship.
Marketing of cattle (grain, fruit).
Proper care of a horse (dog, tropical fish).
Selecting a camp site (home, clothes).
A hobby.
Working on the school paper.

Class elections.

Work of a counselor in a boys' (girls') camp.

Work of a secretary (clerk, junior accountant, etc.) in a business concern.

Applying for a job.

C. Assume that an article of 1200 words is to be written on one of the subjects under B above. Make a preliminary analysis, and arrange your points in a detailed outline with subheads, as in Sec. **A 6b.**

D. Make a detailed outline (as in Sec. **A 6b**) of a class lecture in one of your courses.

BEGINNING THE ARTICLE

After the outline is completed, the writer is ready for the actual writing of the article. This process consists in filling in the outline by means of details, the different headings serving as nuclei around which the paragraphs in the article are developed.[1]

The first problem is to make a suitable beginning. Since this is the place where the reader obtains his initial impression of the article, it is important that the opening sentence and paragraph shall be so framed that this impression will be a favorable one.

A8. The beginning of an article should be direct and interesting.

Direct Beginnings

As a general rule, especially in a short article where space is limited, the first paragraph should lead the reader directly into the subject by making a worth-while statement about it.

---

[1] The process of writing involves the structure of paragraphs and sentences, the choice of the right words, and punctuation. These matters are taken up in detail in succeeding chapters. The present discussion is devoted to some general problems connected with the article as a whole.

Various forms of direct beginnings may be used:

a. Repetition of the Title. The first sentence may repeat the title.

THE NEW SPIRIT IN BUSINESS

The new spirit in business is the spirit of co-operation —co-operation between employer and employee, between manufacturer and jobber, etc.

b. Paraphrase of the Title. The first sentence may be a paraphrase or an informal statement of the title.

POLITICAL DUTIES OF THE CITIZEN

In the early days of the republic it was expected that every citizen would devote part of his time to political life. To the man who was desirous of amusement, politics supplied an attractive game. To him who was anxious to do public service, it furnished the best, and often the only available, channel, etc.[2]

c. Pertinent Setting for the Subject. The opening statement may give a concise, pertinent setting for the discussion.

LIBERTY AND DISCIPLINE

We are living in the midst of a terrific war in which each side casts upon the other the blame for causing the struggle; but in which each gives the same reason for continuing it to the bitter end—that reason being the preservation from destruction of the essential principles of its own civilization. One side claims to be fighting for the liberty of man; the other for a social system based on efficiency and maintained by discipline, etc.[3]

d. Outline Paragraph. An article may begin with an outline paragraph, which enumerates the points that are to be discussed.

[2] A. T. Hadley, *Standards of Public Morality*, The Macmillan Company.

[3] A. L. Lowell, "Liberty and Discipline," *Yale Review.*

COHERENCE IN WRITING

The principle of coherence, as applied to writing, requires that the material shall be combined into logical groups, that the groups shall be arranged in an orderly sequence, and that the relation between the different groups shall be indicated by the proper connectives.

The remainder of the article would be an elaboration of these three topics, one paragraph or more being devoted to each. The discussion of the points should follow the order in which they are enumerated in the outline paragraph.

e. Caution: Avoid a Rambling Approach. Since a good beginning is direct and definite, it follows logically that a rambling, generalized approach should be avoided. In this type of opening the writer starts at a distance from the subject, and creeps upon it cautiously as if he were afraid to make a direct attack.

CITY COMFORTS FOR COUNTRY TEACHERS

Nowadays, when we enjoy without question the benefits of free education, we little realize how great is this gift, nor what a struggle our ancestors had a few hundred years ago to obtain even a meager education. While education improved in the cities as time went on, it remained a big problem to the country folk. One of the chief factors in this problem was that the poor housing facilities and the custom of boarding out the teacher made the work unpleasant, with the result that there was always a dearth of teachers in the country and scattered rural districts.

f. Caution: Avoid an Abrupt, Incomplete Beginning. The beginning should be direct; but, on the other hand, it should not be abrupt or incomplete. It must not leave the reader even momentarily in doubt as to the meaning.

NORTHWEST PASSAGE

Abrupt—Not Good: Born in Kennebunk, Maine, in 1885, Kenneth Roberts vividly describes the frontier days of his native state and its struggles with the French and Indians.

Improved: In his novel, *Northwest Passage*, Kenneth Roberts vividly describes the frontier days of his native state, and its struggles with the French and Indians.

A common form of incomplete beginning is one in which the first sentence refers to the title by means of a pronoun like *this, he,* or *it.* In cases of this sort, the subjects should be stated.

RAISING SILVER FOXES

Not Good: This is a comparatively new business, but it gives promise of rapid development.

Improved: Raising silver foxes is a comparatively new business, but it gives promise of rapid development.

Special Interest Devices

At the beginning of informal and popular articles, special devices for securing interest are often used.

a. **Narrative Beginning.** A story has an almost universal human appeal.

An article on Juvenile Courts, for example, might begin with a brief story of the handling of a specific case —showing the court in action. Or one might start a discussion of how to drive an automobile on icy roads by relating an instance of faulty driving which resulted in an accident; then, with this as a text, he could proceed to the explanation of the principles of correct driving.

The following narrative passage introduces an expository theme on the technique of fishing for muskellunge:

MUSKIE WILES

Our Indian guide made three disgusted stabs with his paddle. "Got to hit 'em," he grunted. Joe, my companion, had hooked a fighting tiger muskie—a king of the muskellunge tribe. The fish bored straight for the bottom; then, reversing, he made a rush to the surface and leaped clear of the water, shaking his head viciously. Joe's line went slack, and the bucktail boomeranged almost into our laps. The hook had not been set securely.

b. "You" Beginning. A reference to the reader brings him personally into the discussion.

FAMILIAR SUPERSTITIONS

What would you do if you unexpectedly found yourself to be one of thirteen people sitting at a formal banquet?

c. Reference to a Well-known Person. People are interested in what famous persons do and think and say.

"WHAT'S THE USE?"

Woodrow Wilson once deplored the fact that many persons—when a worthy course of action is suggested to them—evade the issue by saying, "Oh, what's the use?" He was alarmed that this state of mind was so prevalent.

d. Concrete Beginning. Specific, concrete statements are more effective than general, abstract statements in stimulating interest.

FIRST AID FOR FACTORY WORKERS

General: When a workman is injured in a factory, it is important that there shall be available some means for giving prompt attention to the injury.

Concrete and Specific: In a lumber mill, the loud drone of steel teeth biting into wood is suddenly punctured by a sharp cry of pain. Not realizing that one of the circular blades is in motion, a workman has cut his hand badly. The foreman rushes forward, and with kindly, efficient authority takes the injured man to a cabinet at the side of the room. Here, in a white wall box, are all the materials necessary to bandage the wound in clean white gauze and strong tape. On this box is painted a large red cross, and over the cross are the words, "First Aid."

Formal Introduction

Much of the difficulty that the inexperienced writer has in beginning an article is due to the mistaken idea that there must be a formal introduction. An introduction, as the name implies, is not an integral part of the subject: it paves the way for the real discussion—leads into the subject—by supplying any preliminary information that the reader should have in order to obtain a clear understanding of the problem. Most short articles deal with comparatively simple subjects, and consequently do not need this preliminary explanation. For these articles, the writer should generally discard the traditional threefold division—Introduction, Body, and Conclusion. He should concentrate on the Body. In the language of the athletic field, the discussion should be a *standing* jump, not a *running* jump.

If a formal introduction seems necessary, the material in it should be a direct preparation for the discussion that is to follow. For example, if the subject is *The Present Crisis in India,* the introduction might give a brief account of the conditions which led to this crisis.

Exercises

A. Discuss the following titles and beginnings for themes. Are they clear? Are they interesting? Suggest improvements for any that are ineffective.

1. LEARN HOW TO DRIVE IN SLIPPERY WEATHER

You should do this if you do not want to have an accident. Driving on a slippery pavement is very dangerous. Accidents caused by skidding greatly increase when the weather is slippery. It is important, therefore, that every driver should know how to control his car.

2. MUSKRAT AT PLAY

My interest in muskrats began quite suddenly. Although I had seen the animals many times on my fishing trips to

Salt Creek, I had never stopped casting to watch them. Early one morning last summer, however, as I waded cautiously around a bend, a muskrat at play made me forget about black bass.

3. COLLEGE

What will college mean to you?

The greatest contribution that college can make will be to teach you how to think. Up through high school much of your thinking was done by other agencies—by your parents, your teachers, and your community customs. Now it will be different. You will find college dynamic and suggestive.

4. CRIME

One of the most serious problems that confront the people of America today is the great prevalence of crime. There have always been a great number of criminal cases in the United States, but in the last ten years crime has been on the increase. At present more than sixty thousand Americans are sent to prison annually, for terms varying from one to ninety-nine years.

5. WHAT IS PROGRESS?

In my attempt to define progress, I shall confine my discussion to three points. First, I shall argue that progress means the attainment of a high level of material comfort; second, I shall show that progress requires greater emphasis on intellectual and spiritual values; third, I shall prove that progress depends upon solidarity in the social organization.

6. THE PROBLEM OF CLEAN SIDEWALKS

Winter always brings hardships, suffering, and inconvenience. Most people are fortunate in that they do not have to endure anything worse than inconvenience. To some, one of the inconveniences is the task of shoveling snow off the sidewalks and paths about their home.

B. Choose five articles in good magazines or essays in a book of selections. Comment on the effectiveness of the titles and the beginning paragraphs.

DEVELOPING THE ARTICLE

With his outline before him and a good beginning made, the writer is now ready to develop the series of topics into a complete article.

In this process he is confronted not only with new problems but also with the necessity of checking and verifying the conclusions that he reached in making the outline. Presumably that work was done carefully, and, in general, he will follow the original plan. As he gets into the actual task of writing, however, and looks at the subject more closely, he must be on the alert to recognize any changes that may be required. In the first place, he should check his procedure by the three major principles which were discussed earlier in the chapter:

1. All important points should be included in the discussion (see Sec. **A 3a**).

2. Any point which, on second sight, is not important should be excluded (see Sec. **A 3b**). Some topics may prove to be of less importance than they seemed to be in the original analysis; they may need to be combined with other material.

3. The topics should be arranged in logical order (see Sec. **A 5**).

In addition to these, two other principles are to be observed.

Tying the Topic to the Subject

A9. The discussion of each topic should be definitely tied to the subject of the article so that the relation will be immediately evident to the reader.

In the following article, the writer is discussing the different classes of immigrants who should be denied admittance. Three classes are described in successive paragraphs, as indicated in the outline:

TO WHOM SHOULD IMMIGRATION BE DENIED?

1. Introduction: general conditions.
2. The foreigner who does not intend to become a citizen.
3. The criminal class.
4. The feeble-minded and imbecile.

The fifth paragraph begins:

Rigid educational tests should be given to all those who seek admittance. They should be required to pass tests equivalent at least to those given in the sixth grade of our public schools. . . .

The relation of this paragraph to the general subject of the article is not clear. The material in it is not presented definitely as a discussion of another class of undesirable immigrants, though this was what the writer intended. The relation would have been clearer if he had begun:

The next class to whom admittance should be denied are those who are unable to pass a simple educational test. This test should be equivalent at least to the ones given in the sixth grade of our public schools. . . . (Or)

Another objectionable class consists of those foreigners who are unable to pass a simple educational test.

Apportioning the Space to Different Topics

A10. **In general, the space in an article is apportioned among the different topics according to their relative importance.**

The most important topic is given the most space, the least important occupies the least space, and the other points receive their corresponding share of attention.

Thus, William Howard Taft, in an article on *The Present Relations of the Learned Professions to Political Government*, devotes about 1100 words to the legal profession, 800 to the ministry, 375 to the profession of teaching, and 350 to that of writing. This proportion, it may be assumed, shows approximately his idea of the relative importance of each in his discussion.

In determining which topics are the more important and are therefore to be discussed at greater length, the writer will be guided by the purpose of the article and the class of readers for whom it is intended.

For instance, in an article intended to attract the attention of prospective settlers to a new country as an agricultural El Dorado, more space will be given to the fertility of the soil and the abundance of crops than to the beautiful scenery. On the other hand, if the purpose is to create interest in the country as a winter resort for people of wealth and leisure, the proportion will be reversed.

An exception to the general principle laid down above should be noted. An important topic may be so well known that a detailed discussion of it is unnecessary; whereas a point which is less important may need to be treated at greater length because the readers are not familiar with it.

Suppose, for example, that the makers of a standard fountain pen put on the market a new pen, like the old one except for a different and improved self-filling device. Naturally, the sales literature will give more attention to the new feature than to such matters as durability of construction and easy writing qualities. The latter are just as important—probably more important—but the public is already acquainted with them.

ENDING THE ARTICLE

A11. The end of the article should give the impression of completeness.

It should round out the discussion and convince the reader that he has arrived at a definite, predetermined goal.

a. Ending with a Detail—Incomplete. As a general rule, the closing statement should not deal with some detail of the discussion; it should leave with the reader the main thought of the article.

Incomplete Ending:

PROBLEMS OF THE DISARMAMENT CONFERENCE

1. Purpose of the Conference.
2. Attitude of the United States.
3. Japanese problems.
4. British problems.
5. French problems.

(The article closes with the following paragraph:)

France also wanted a guarantee from the United States and Great Britain that they would come to her assistance in the event of another invasion by Germany. The French had not forgotten the Franco-Prussian War, and memories of Germany's attack at the beginning of the World War were vivid and terrifying. . . . It was not surprising, therefore, that France deemed it necessary to maintain a large standing army.

Instead of ending with a detail concerning the attitude of France, the writer should have returned to the main thought—the problems of the Conference (see **b**, below).

b. Effective Endings. A simple, and usually effective, means of giving the impression of completeness and bringing the reader back to the main thought is to re-state the title or refer definitely to some part of it in the last sentence of the final paragraph.

For instance, in the preceding illustration the writer might have added another sentence to the paragraph, such as,

This was a serious situation—and it was only one of the many problems that the Disarmament Conference attempted to solve.

Another example, from an article on *The Survival of Civil Liberty*, by F. H. Giddings:

> If you and those others who, like you, have enjoyed the privileges of a liberal training, as educated men and women, as citizens of our republic, shall do your whole duty rationally, conscientiously, fearlessly, there can be no failure of our experiment in self-government, *no diminution of the blessings of civil liberty.*[4]

Not all articles, of course, end with a definite restatement of the subject or a direct reference to it. Any other statement—a sentence or a phrase, or, in a long article, a separate paragraph—that gives the impression of finality, of completeness, may be used for ending the theme. But if the writer is not sure that he has succeeded in making this impression by other means, he will usually find that restatement or direct reference offers a simple and ready way out of the difficulty.

c. Formal Conclusion. A formal conclusion carries the discussion beyond the limits of the subject proper by bringing in material that is related to it but is not an integral part of it. In a short article this formal conclusion is not often necessary, and takes up space that might more profitably be used in the discussion of the subject itself. In a longer article there is more room for a leisurely close. Thus a fairly long paper on the life of Abraham Lincoln might end with a paragraph or paragraphs dealing with his influence on American life and thought; this would be a formal conclusion carrying the discussion beyond the actual facts of his life. On the other hand, the article might close with his death. In a short theme the latter method would probably be preferable.

SUBJECTS FOR THEMES

The subjects in the following lists are offered as suggestions to show the student the possibilities for theme

[4] F. H. Giddings, *Democracy and Empire*, The Macmillan Company.

material in the life about him. They should suggest other subjects which will perhaps appeal to him more directly. Many of those in the list are too broad to be handled in a short theme, and should be narrowed to a particular phase. A suitable title should be given for the theme that is written on any of the subjects.

LIFE ON THE CAMPUS

Freshman week
Registration day
Fraternity (sorority) rushing
Trying out for the band
Band practice
The cheering section
Cheer leaders
College drum majors
The glee club
College dramatics
A college formal
A specific extracurricular activity—value of
My first week in college
Getting adjusted to college
College YWCA (YMCA)
Chapel
A college publication (yearbook, daily or weekly, humor magazine, etc.)

Work of the editor (business manager) on a college publication
Student government
Student-faculty relations
A college student's religion
Extracurricular activities versus studies
Cheating in examinations
Are grades significant?
Working one's way through college
My physical education class
The ROTC
English (or chemistry) in high school
Keeping within my budget
Making an eight-o'clock class
Campus politics
Inspection trips
Field trips

LIFE OFF THE CAMPUS

A boys' (girls') camp
Girl (Boy) Scouts at work
Girl (Boy) Scouts at play
A camp counselor
An overnight automobile camp
A trailer camp
Life in a trailer
Driving licenses
Youth hostels

My scrapbook
My diary
After the fire (flood, tornado, dust storm)
Dude ranches
Movies for children
Radio programs for children
The Salvation Army
The Red Cross
The Community Chest

LIFE OFF THE CAMPUS (*Continued*)

Planning an automobile trip
A beauty parlor
Palm reading
Tea reading
Astrology—the modern way
Newspaper columnists
Newspaper comics
Swing bands
Accident prevention
Traffic rules
Delivering the morning
   papers
The milkman
In a broadcasting station
Bill boards
Streetcar advertising
Radio advertising
Television
Frozen foods
Family history in our attic

Growth of the suburbs
Reforesting
Return of the bicycle
Soil erosion
Tenant farming
Strikes
Restriction of immigration
Settlement work (in Hull
   House, etc.)
Christmas in the country
Fascism
Nazism
My work as a clerk (ac-
   countant, secretary, etc.)
My first (or present) job
New Year's resolutions
Vitamins
Were the "good old days"
   good?

SPORTS AND HOBBIES

College football
Professional football
Night football (or baseball)
Football (or baseball, etc.)
   practice
Duties of a fullback (center,
   etc.) in football
Duties of a forward (guard,
   etc.) in basketball
College boxing
College wrestling
Fencing
Figure skating
Effective strokes in tennis
   (golf, etc.)
Bowling
Intramural sports

Six-man football
Canoeing
Camping out
Bait-casting
Fly-casting
Fishing for bass (muskies,
   trout, etc.)
Deep-sea fishing
Archery
Badminton
Candid photography
Hunting with a camera
Model airplanes
Stamp collecting
Rare-book collecting
My first time in the air

PLACES AND LOCALITIES

My home town

My college town

An art gallery

A museum

The Capitol at Washington

Rockefeller Center (or any other well-known building)

Children's playroom (in a department store)

A dentist's (physician's) office

Central Park (Lincoln Park, etc.)

The ghetto

Chinatown

An Amish settlement

A summer resort

A historic spot

PEOPLE

An egotist

A local politician

A campus politician

A country doctor

A city specialist (physician)

My dentist (physician, barber, etc.)

The janitor (waitress) looks at college students

An eccentric instructor (student, artist, etc.)

A football (basketball, etc.) coach

A snob

A Phi Beta Kappa

Panhandlers that I have met

DIRECTIONS AND PROCESSES

How to treat a certain injury (fracture, burn, etc.)

How to mount butterflies (flowers, etc.)

How to fire a furnace

How to make a campfire

How to prepare for a final examination

How to keep a notebook

How to train a bird dog (or other pet)

How to draw a cartoon

How to take a picture

How to remove stains

How to form a good habit

How to break a bad habit

How to make a lemon pie (or a cake, bread, etc.)

How to do a certain laboratory experiment

How glass is made

How leather is tanned

How steel is hardened

How starch is made

How pulp paper is made

How invisible ink is made

How a certain cereal is made

How tobacco is cured

How a certain plastic is made

How sugar is refined

How rubber is vulcanized

STUDIES

Make a list of subjects suggested in your various courses—subjects which interest you and which you would like to investigate further. Keep your list up to date.

CURRENT AFFAIRS

Make a list of suitable subjects from your reading of the daily paper and current news magazines. Check through the periodicals with this purpose in mind.

Chapter Three

THE PARAGRAPH

A typical paragraph, considered as part of a longer article, is a group of sentences dealing with one unit of thought which forms a definite stage in the development of the subject of the theme.

Two important points, it will be noticed, are involved in this definition:

1. The paragraph should deal with only one topic.
2. This topic should be a significant and important part of the subject as a whole. It must be remembered that in writing we are concerned with different units of thought which vary in degree of importance and in size. The theme itself is a unit, dealing with one subject. The theme is made up of paragraphs, each of which is a unit covering one of the main divisions of the subject. Finally, each paragraph consists of sentences, each of which is also a unit presenting a still smaller division of thought. The paragraph, therefore, differs in content from the sentence in that it covers a larger topic, one that carries the discussion forward through a definite stage.

Mechanically, the paragraph is set off by indenting the first line.

UNITY OF THOUGHT

B1. Each paragraph should deal with a single topic.

Every sentence in a paragraph must bear on the topic and contribute something worth while to its development. In this way the thought is presented as a unit which can be readily understood by the reader.

The following paragraph is lacking in unity of thought:

Walt Spencer is an interesting character. Fat and jolly, he is a living example of Scattergood Baines, Clarence Budington Kelland's famous small-town character. He wears a mail-order suit bought five years ago, but the stock on the shelves of his store is never allowed to grow stale. He drives one of the first Fords; yet the machinery in his two mills is up to the minute. He owns several farms and residences; still his home is one of the smallest on the street. *The house is a tiny, unpretentious bunga-low, with only the shadow of a porch—for it stands in a bare yard devoid of trees. Its paint, which was originally white trimmed with green, has faded into a nondescript gray of two indistinguishable shades. The window cur-tains, however, are always white and starched.* No one is too far down in life to receive Walt's cheery "hello"; no one who comes to his door for help is turned away. He is mayor, judge, commissioner, and everything else that a doting public can wish upon him. He is truly a character.

The purpose of this paragraph, according to the topic announced in the opening sentence, is to show that Walt Spencer is an interesting character. As the discussion proceeds, it becomes evident that he is interesting be-cause he is inconsistent. The writer keeps to the topic until mention of the house leads him off into details which are not relevant to the topic. Paragraph unity requires that the superfluous details in the italicized sentences be eliminated, only enough being retained to show the inconsistency of the character. A single sen-tence might then read:

The house is an unpretentious bungalow, bleak and weather-beaten; but the window curtains are always white and starched.

In the following paragraph the writer selected as his topic one specific qualification of the engineer—*accuracy;* then he drifted into a discussion of other qualifications:

The engineer must be accurate. He must be careful in drawing specifications and plans, and in carrying out the plans of others. Even a slight error in specifications or in construction may mean the falling of a bridge or the collapse of a building. An engineer must not allow himself to be influenced by political favors or friendship. He should be fearless and above temptation. He has to be able to assume responsibility for an undertaking, and carry it to completion on scheduled time. And to do this he must know how to handle men and keep the workmen satisfied—not antagonize them but get their cooperation.

What has been said concerning unity of thought applies particularly to paragraphs in exposition and argumentation, and, to a considerable extent, to those in scientific description also (such as the description of apparatus, machinery, and the like). In what may be called artistic description and in narration, the structure of the paragraphs is usually less formal and the units of thought are not so strictly defined. Even here, however, a certain unity is necessary, each paragraph dealing with objects closely related in space, for example (as in the description of a landscape), or with one incident or a series of closely connected incidents (as in a narrative covering a day's outing in the country).

Note. Sometimes it is permissible to enumerate a number of minor points, with little or no discussion of each, in a single paragraph. In this case, both the paragraph itself and the heading for it in the outline should clearly indicate to the reader the miscellaneous character of the group.

STATEMENT OF THE TOPIC

The Topic Sentence

B2. **The topic of the paragraph is often stated in a brief sentence, called the topic sentence, which sums up the entire contents of the paragraph.**

This practice is particularly common in exposition and argumentation.

The topic sentence is generally the first sentence of the paragraph, but is sometimes placed near the middle or at the end. One advantage of placing it at the beginning is that this procedure forces the writer to state his topic definitely before starting to develop it, and he is therefore less likely to wander from the subject. Moreover, this method allows the reader to see just what he may expect to find in the paragraph. Until the writer has mastered the principles of unified structure, it will be well for him to construct the majority of his paragraphs according to this plan. (For illustrations of the use of the topic sentence, see Sec. **B 10,** where it is indicated by the word "Topic.")

For special emphasis the topic sentence is sometimes placed at the beginning, and restated or paraphrased at the end (see example in Sec. **B 10d**). This type, however, is too formal for constant use.

Exact Statement of the Topic. The topic sentence should give an exact statement of the material covered in the paragraph; and conversely, the paragraph must contain an adequate discussion of the subject stated in the topic sentence. In the following example, the two are not in agreement. The topic sentence declares that tennis is *more strenuous than any other sport;* whereas the paragraph shows only that tennis is *strenuous*—the comparison with other games is not supported by any evidence.

> Tennis is more strenuous than any other sport. A tennis player cannot relax one moment. He must be alert, agile, and tireless. The game is strenuous because it requires continual strain in following the ball. In one of his championship matches Tilden lost thirteen pounds in one afternoon. There is no such exertion required so continuously in any other sport. Tennis is highly exciting, and therefore a strain on the nervous system. It requires so much endurance that it cannot be played strenuously for more than two hours. If you do not believe that this is the most strenuous sport, play tennis for two or three

hours straight—when you become forty years of age—
and decide for yourself.

Informal Statement of the Topic

B3. Sometimes, especially in scientific description,
the topic is mentioned in the opening sentence, but the
latter is not a formal topic sentence.

In this case, the first sentence contains some of the
details concerning the topic, but does not sum up the
contents of the entire paragraph. The difference between
the two types of beginnings may be shown by the following example, taken from a description of a steamboat:

> Throughout the *superstructure* of the boat the con-
> struction is entirely fireproof—steel, asbestos, and other
> non-combustible materials being used exclusively. The
> strength and rigidity of the structure are secured by
> means of a system of stanchions between the decks.
> These are of steel placed in four rows extending prac-
> tically the whole length of the vessel. By means of con-
> nections to the longitudinal girders and deck beams, the
> entire structure is thoroughly braced to withstand the
> hogging and sagging stresses set up by the rapid shifting
> of the load on the boat. . . . (*International Marine
> Engineering.*)

If the first sentence of this paragraph were a topic
sentence, the entire paragraph would deal with the
fireproof construction of the superstructure; whereas
in the present instance that particular feature is only
one detail and is not referred to after the introductory
statement. The topic is the superstructure as a whole.
This is brought to the attention of the reader by means of
the single word in the opening sentence.

The hull, the propelling system, and other features
of the boat are discussed in separate paragraphs.

Note. Sometimes the topic is not definitely stated, but
must be gathered by the reader as he proceeds through the

paragraph. This form is most common in description and narration, but is also found in exposition and argumentation. It may be used when the topic can be easily inferred from the discussion.

ENDING THE PARAGRAPH

B4. The end of the paragraph, like the end of the whole article, should give the impression of completeness.

The impression of completeness is sometimes secured by a restatement or paraphrase of the topic (see Sec. **B 10d** and **b**), or by a reference to a significant word in the topic sentence (see Sec. **B 10g**: *city* repeated; **B 10e**: *tolerance* and *intolerance*). These methods, however, are not always necessary; some other statement—a sentence or a phrase that rounds out the discussion—frequently makes an effective ending.

Incomplete Ending:

   Modern inventions have brought the people of the world closer together. The ocean liner of today makes the trip to England in five days, as contrasted with the seventy-two-day voyage of the *Mayflower*. In this way letters, magazines, and papers, carrying the ideas and opinions of various nations, are quickly and constantly interchanged. Inventions in the field of electricity have made possible the electric train, the automobile, the airplane, the telephone, the telegraph and cable systems, and also wireless communication. Improved methods of transportation have been of great aid in populating various parts of the globe with new settlers. Each of these brings with him the customs, traditions, ideals, and ideas of his own country.

This paragraph should have been completed by adding an appropriate sentence: such as,

By all these means, the nations have been brought closer together not only in time and space, but also in sympathy and understanding.

ARRANGEMENT OF MATERIAL

B5. In the paragraph, as in the article as a whole, there must be an orderly sequence of thought.

There must be no shuttling back and forth between ideas—from one idea to another and then back to the first. Related parts should be kept together. One phase of the thought should be completed; and then the discussion should proceed to another phase which logically follows.

Illogical Arrangement:

Improvement in the moving-picture field came rapidly. *The first step was made when imaginary ranch life was dropped, and pictures with stories more true to life were portrayed.* The picture theaters were improved until a better class of patrons was attracted. The music was brought into closer harmony with the setting and atmosphere of the picture. With these changes there came an increase in the price of admission, which in turn was an important factor in the production of still better films. *Where formerly the picture represented the adventures of cowboys riding vicious bronchos or engaging in desperate fights with the Indians, dramas were now shown dealing with more realistic subjects. They came closer to the real problems of life—its pleasure and pathos, its success and failure.* The industry was making rapid progress.

Here one phase of the topic—covered by the sentences in italics—is discussed in two places, separated by other material. The two parts should be combined at the beginning of the paragraph, and this phase of the subject finished before other improvements are introduced.

Likewise, in the following paragraph on the art of the salesman, the writer has not chosen the best arrangement:

Haphazard Arrangement:

Knowing *when* to act is of the utmost importance, more important even than knowing exactly *how*. You may be lacking in some of the technique of a strategic approach, but you will always receive encouragement at least if you strike at the correct time. There is such a thing as knowing when to make yourself heard so as to make the best impression. Your style of attack may not be the best, your arguments may even be faulty, and there may be many things which are not according to the approved standards of salesmanship; yet if you can locate the psychological moment when the prospect is in the best mood to receive your ideas, you have nearly accomplished your object.

Here the thought shifts back and forth between *how* and *when*. If, after the topic sentence had been announced, all the discussion of *how* had been put together, and then the *when* element introduced, the paragraph would have been more compact and logical:

Logical Arrangement:

Knowing *when* to act is of the utmost importance, more important even than knowing exactly *how*. You may be lacking in some of the technique of a strategic approach, your style of attack may not be the best, part of your arguments may even be faulty, and there may be other features which are not according to the approved standards of salesmanship. Yet if you strike at the correct time, you will always receive at least some encouragement; if you can locate the psychological moment when the prospect is in the best mood, you have nearly accomplished your object.

Exercises in Sections B 1–B 5

Do the following paragraphs deal with only one topic; or are unrelated, or remotely related, ideas introduced?

Does the discussion adequately prove or support the assertion made in the topic sentence? Do the paragraphs give the impression of being complete, or do they seem merely to stop, without rounding out the discussion? Are they logically arranged? Point out any faults that you find, and make whatever improvements are needed.

1. Today the person who wants to succeed in a profession must attend college. In pursuing his studies, he must resign himself to hard work. He must not go to college with the idea of enjoying himself exclusively. He will soon discover that colleges were designed for workers. If he does not have the necessary qualities, he will not pass his courses. Advanced courses require long hours of study. If the student cannot apply himself he will never complete college and consequently will not be able to enter his chosen profession.

2. Trains of today have abandoned the elaborate gaudiness of earlier days for the simplicity of subdued modernism. The designers have incorporated straight lines, wide windows, and indirect lighting. Throughout the train one finds chromium trim and natural wood paneling. The number of private compartments, bedrooms, and drawing rooms has increased, but in the opposite direction there are more comfortable coaches with reclining chairs. These trains serve modestly priced meals, and some of them run special coaches for women and children so that the passengers can get into house coats at night. Their service to passengers includes a free courier-nurse. We are no longer amazed at glassed-in observation cars, air-conditioning, maid and valet service, barbers, and bath attendants. Diners often serve regional delicacies. In the Colorado Rockies several roads make a specialty of wiring ahead the individual orders of diners for mountain trout which are served to the gourmets fresh from stream to skillet.

3. Science has played an important part in the increase of modern entertainment. Radio, movies, and automobiles are examples of the important part science has played in this field. The movies are among the most popular forms of entertainment, because of the price, their availability at so many hours of the day and evening, their variety, and their spec-

tacular features. We also have stage plays in the legitimate theater, but they are more expensive. Dancing is a popular form of entertainment which appeals especially to young people. Sports also play an important part in entertainment. We are interested spectators of football, basketball, baseball, and hockey games. We have skating rinks, bowling alleys, and swimming pools. Nearly everyone owns a car and a radio. If we prefer to stay at home, we tune in on our favorite programs on the radio, or read a good book. Travel also plays an important part in our amusement program—we can travel to many places of interest at little cost. These are a few ways in which people amuse themselves, and people of the next century will probably think them as dull as we do those of the nineteenth century.

4. Everyone should keep an account of his expenditures. If he does not, the results are unsatisfactory. Money is not so valueless that it can be thrown away; nor does it grow on trees. When one works hard to earn a living, he should work just as hard to see that his money is well spent. The contention is not made that failure to keep accounts means that money will be wasted, but it does mean that more money will be spent.

5. The outstanding object of interest in the city is the old Mission. It is built of rough, gray stone, retaining most of the original walls. All its interesting history is told on tablets placed throughout the rooms and halls of the building. The courtyard with its shrubbery and flower beds is a novel sight to a person from the North. The walls are covered with climbing ivy, and the historic aspect of the Mission is truly preserved. The mission is situated in the heart of the city, directly across from the Post Office and Federal Building. Because of civic pride, large offers have been refused for the purchase of the ground for commercial use. All the historic relics illustrating the life of the Southwest during the old days of Spanish rule are preserved in the mission, each of them accompanied by an explanatory card, as in a museum. There is no charge for admission, but one may leave a free-will offering for the maintenance of the building.

6. There are two types of freight tunnels: the trunk lines and the lateral branches. The former are placed under the main business sections of the city, and the latter run to the

outlying districts. The cars and engines are of special design, the cars being four feet wide and ten feet long, with a height of five feet. They are made of steel, double-trucked, and have a capacity of fifteen tons each. These cars are capable of handling freight of every description. The tunnels are built on a foundation of concrete, and the walls and roofs are of the same material. The tunnel is double-tracked and is twelve and a half feet high by eleven feet wide. Imbedded in the sides of the tunnels are the conduits for telephone and telegraph cables.

7. Not everything that a daily newspaper prints is intended to be read for its educational value. Many persons turn to the newspaper for pleasure and relaxation. They are perhaps interested in the sports news. In season they turn first to the accounts of football, basketball, and baseball games. The comics also have a large following who wait daily for the fresh adventures of Dick Tracy and Skeezix. Then there are other interesting features in the newspaper. Following the daily comments of a favorite columnist is important in keeping acquainted with expert opinions on matters of national and world-wide interest. Their interpretation of the news, sometimes actually written on the scene of an important event, adds greatly to our appreciation of what is happening. Therefore the habit of reading a daily newspaper is a pleasant pastime as well as an obligation.

8. The seven hundred orphan boys live in thirty-one separate houses scattered over the countryside. The houses are modern, and are equipped to furnish all the comforts and conveniences of a well-appointed home. They are, in fact, real homes, with none of the bleakness that one so often finds in other institutions. There are ten large brick cottages, each having thirty smaller boys cared for by three house mothers. The other twenty-one are farmhouses with some two hundred acres of land surrounding each one. The boys over twelve years of age live here, and for ten months of the year they go to school, the remaining two months during the summer being devoted to working the land. Before entering high school each boy must decide whether he wants to take a commercial, industrial, or academic course. Most choose a trade. The school has well-equipped shops and offers detailed courses in bricklaying, carpentry, machine-shop prac-

tice, printing, and other trades. At the age of eighteen each boy is sent out into the world with $100 in his pocket. The school always finds a starting job for each of its graduates.

9. Besides being near the mountains, Rockland has the advantage of being near Denver. Denver is just close enough for the people of Rockland to visit frequently. They enjoy the theaters in the winter and the mountain resorts in the hot weather. Hunting for arrowheads is a popular sport in the mountains. Several of my friends have interesting collections which they have made in their spare time. In cold weather winter sports are greatly enjoyed. During the summer everyone lives in his cabin in the mountains and enjoys the freedom of life there.

TRANSITION BETWEEN SENTENCES

B6. A transition device should be used between sentences if it is needed to make the relation in thought clear to the reader.

Connectives Omitted—Relations Not Clear:

For years there was a serious misunderstanding between the two countries over a question of boundaries. Recent reports indicated that the difficulty had been settled, at least for a time. It was a surprise to read in the papers this morning that war had been declared and that actual fighting had begun.

Connectives Inserted—Relations Made Clear:

For years there was a serious misunderstanding between the two countries over a question of boundaries. Recent reports, *however*, indicated that the difficulty had been settled, at least for a time. It was *therefore* a surprise to read in the papers this morning that war had been declared, and that actual fighting had begun.

A connective is not needed if the relationship in thought between two sentences is clear and unmistakable.

Classes of Transition Devices. Transition devices fall into three general classes:

1. Conjunctions and conjunctive phrases. Care must be taken to choose the connective that accurately represents the logical relation between the sentences. A list of some of the more frequently used connectives, classified according to their meaning, follows:

> Continuation of the same line of thought: *and, moreover, too, likewise, furthermore, again, also, in like manner, similarly.*
>
> Contrast, or change in the line of thought: *but, however, nevertheless, yet, on the contrary, on the other hand.*
>
> Result or consequence: *therefore, hence, consequently, thus, accordingly, as a result, as a consequence.*
>
> Miscellaneous relations: *for example, for instance, of course, then, here, fortunately, in fact.*

2. Direct reference to the preceding sentence by means of pronouns or the repetition of significant words (see the italicized words in the following paragraph):

> But while heat and moisture decide where the different kinds of trees can grow, their influence has comparatively little to do with the struggles of individuals and species against each other for the actual possession of the ground. The outcome of *these struggles* depends less on heat and moisture than on the possession of certain qualities, among which is the ability to bear shade. With regard to *this* power, trees are roughly divided into two classes, often called shade-bearing and light-demanding, following the German, but better named tolerant and intolerant of shade. *Tolerant* trees are those which flourish under more or less heavy shade in early youth; *intolerant* trees are those which demand a comparatively slight cover, or even unrestricted light.[1]

3. Placing at the beginning of a sentence the part that is most closely related to the thought of the preceding sentence.

Unless this significant part is the subject, which nat-

---

[1] Gifford Pinchot, *A Primer of Forestry*, U.S. Department of Agriculture.

urally stands at the beginning, it may be necessary to invert the order or change the construction so that the word or phrase which makes a better transition will be in this position.

> Loose Transition: We were conducted down a long corridor until we came to the reception room. Our guide turned us over to one of the governor's secretaries *here,* and we were ushered into the private office.
>
> Improved: We were conducted down a long corridor until we came to the reception room. *Here* our guide turned us over to one of the governor's secretaries, who ushered us into the private office.

Exercises in Section B 6

A. Supply any transitional devices that are needed to make clear the logical relation between sentences.

1. Sunbathing is recommended by physicians as an excellent way to improve one's physical condition. When wisely engaged in, it builds up resistance to infections and tones up the whole system. Too much exposure may be injurious to health. Calcium in the bone structure may be depleted. A painful overdose of sunburn may develop into something really serious. Other dangers lurk in the blazing rays of the midsummer sun. Caution should be exercised when one is taking a sunbath, especially if he is not accustomed to it.

2. Latin and English were difficult subjects for me in high school. Botany, sociology, and bookkeeping had little attraction for me. I made good grades in mathematics, chemistry, and physics. The subject matter in these courses appealed to me and I was especially interested in handling the equipment in the laboratories. When I went to college it was natural that I should take the engineering course.

3. In our complex economic structure, collective bargaining is said to be indispensable. This, both groups agree, is the best plan that we have been able to develop. It has benefited labor in many ways. Capital has gained some advantages. For the nation as a whole the results are not so encouraging. Strikes seriously delayed production of ma-

chines for national defence. For many months our armed forces were not adequately equipped. . . .

B. Select a page from a standard book or magazine— not a novel or a story. Note the transitional devices used between sentences.

TRANSITION BETWEEN PARAGRAPHS

B7. A transition device should be used between paragraphs whenever it is needed to show the logical sequence of thought.

For instance, if a paragraph presents a contrast to the thought of the preceding one, the writer shows this relation by some connective like *however, yet,* or *nevertheless.* If a paragraph indicates a result following from the discussion in the preceding group, he uses *therefore, consequently, accordingly,* or some similar connective. These devices serve as guideposts to show the reader the course which the thought of the theme is taking. Connection may also be made by means of pronouns, the repetition of words, or the repetition of a statement.

The following illustration gives the first lines of a number of successive paragraphs in an article; the transition devices are italicized:

> The average western American of Lincoln's generation was fundamentally a man who subordinated his intelligence to certain dominant practical interests and purposes. . . .
>
> Lincoln, *on the contrary,* much as he was a man of his own time and people, was precisely an example of high and disinterested intellectual culture. . . .
>
> In addition, *however,* to *these* private gymnastics Lincoln shared with his neighbors a public and popular source of intellectual and human insight. . . .
>
> *Of course,* it was just *because he shared so completely the amusements and the occupations of his neighbors*

that his private personal culture had no embarrassing effects. . . . [The paragraph ends:] and his actions were instinct with sympathy and understanding.

Just because *his actions were instinct with sympathy and understanding,* Lincoln was certainly the most humane statesman who ever guided a nation through a great crisis. . . .[2]

Transition devices are not always necessary between paragraphs, but they should be used when they are needed to make the relation clearer.

(For a more complete discussion of transition devices, see Sec. **B 6.** Practically all that was said there about transitions between sentences applies also to paragraphs.)

LENGTH OF PARAGRAPHS

Short Paragraphs

B8. As a general rule, the writer should avoid the frequent use of short paragraphs, each consisting of only a few lines.

The presence of a number of short paragraphs in an article generally indicates one of two faults:

1. A significant topic, which normally would be treated in one paragraph, has been divided into two or more groups, each of which deals with a comparatively unimportant detail. When this is done, the points of division between the main topics of the article are not clearly indicated, and consequently it is difficult for the reader to see the larger steps in the development of the subject. The article then appears to be a series of notes rather than a well-organized discussion of significant topics.

The remedy, of course, is to combine into one paragraph those groups which logically belong together.

[2] Herbert Croly, *The Promise of American Life,* The Macmillan Company.

Note. It is the policy of some newspapers in their editorials and news articles to break up the discussion into small units, the idea being that the reader will grasp the thought in these small groups more readily than he would in larger ones. This practice is open to the objection mentioned above, and should not be carried to excess.

2. Topics which in themselves are of sufficient importance to be treated in separate paragraphs have not been properly developed. The remedy is to amplify them by methods like those illustrated in Sec. **B 10**.

Special Cases. 1. In a passage containing conversation or dialogue, the alternate remarks of the various speakers are put into separate paragraphs, although they may consist of only a few words.

"Why are you going now?" she asked. "Do you have to leave so early?"

He nodded his head.

"But why not wait until they telegraph?" She spoke with scarcely concealed impatience.

"They won't telegraph—they expect me to come."

"You told me you would be here until Saturday," she wailed. "And I've invited the Shaws for dinner on Friday."

2. Sometimes an especially important statement contained in a single brief sentence is set off as a separate paragraph in order to give it extra prominence. Thus Woodrow Wilson, in *The New Freedom,* introduces one phase of the discussion by means of a paragraph of three words: "What is liberty?" This device, it is hardly necessary to add, is to be used only occasionally.

3. In certain instances where the writer is enumerating a number of separate points without discussing them in detail, a series of short paragraphs is desirable. The different points are thus presented to the reader clearly and forcibly as distinct units.

This is what I have got out of college—not counting the classroom and books.

I have evolved a simple philosophy in which such standards as truth and loyalty are fundamental.

I have learned that my daily life is based on order, and that I must be systematic.

I have learned that a college degree does not make me superior to anyone—that it only gives an advantage which must be supplemented by honest labor.

It will be noted that a series of short paragraphs of this sort is very different from the kind described in **B 8 (1)**. In the latter case the discussion of a single topic is divided into a number of fragmentary groups; in the present case each small paragraph presents a small but complete unit of thought.

Paragraphs Unduly Long

B9. If the discussion of a topic requires much space—for instance, a page or more of typewritten or printed matter—it should usually be divided.

A long paragraph looks heavy and difficult to read; and although occasional groups of this size may be used without serious results, a succession of them will almost invariably create an unfavorable impression on the reader.

The division should be made at a point where there is a fairly definite turn in thought. This procedure does not destroy the unity of the paragraph; it merely divides the discussion into two smaller units or phases of the larger topic.

DEVELOPING TOPICS INTO ADEQUATE PARAGRAPHS

B10. An important topic should be adequately developed.

The method by which a topic may be developed into a paragraph varies according to the nature of the topic, its purpose, and other conditions. An experienced writer, knowing the purpose of each paragraph and its place in the development of the whole subject, almost unconsciously follows the method which will make the most effective presentation. Less experienced writers, however, frequently have difficulty in this matter. After stating the topic, they do not readily see how it can best be amplified and supported. For these, it may be helpful to suggest some common methods of development.

It must be understood that these are given as suggestions, not as arbitrary rules which must be followed for every paragraph. They merely represent various types of development which are naturally suited for certain cases. For instance, if the topic is "The American man of wealth is generally philanthropic," the natural way of supporting this statement is to cite specific examples of wealthy men—Mr. Carnegie, Mr. Rockefeller, and others—who have given freely to philanthropic causes. Or if the topic is "Life on the modern farm is comfortable," an obvious way to develop it is to contrast the old and the modern manner of living. These methods are inherent in the nature of the subject.

Some of the more common and effective devices employed in the development of paragraphs are:

Specific details	Cause and effect
Specific instances and examples	Definition and explanation of terms
Comparison and contrast	Repetition
Proof	A combination of methods

a. Specific Details. A topic may be amplified by giving specific details illustrating the general statement.

[TOPIC:] In contrast with our old attitude of tolerance for social assassination, however, we are now beginning an energetic campaign of human conservation. [SPECIFIC DETAILS:] We are instituting excellent and, in many places, free hospital and dispensary service. We are making nurse and doctor public servants, and are introducing them into the public schools. We are fighting typhoid fever with uncontaminated water supplies, and tuberculosis not only by direct attack but with improved housing and factory conditions. We are improving city and state Boards of Health, and are striving for a National Board of Health, which shall supervise the general health conditions of the nation. In our cities we are providing public recreation centers, public baths. Our city and state authorities are doubling the protection of the milk, meat, and other foods of the people. Our factory legislation and our laws regulating dangerous occupations have resulted in a considerable saving of life, while our laws against child labor have had an enormously beneficial effect. All of these changes, together with a rapid advance in sanitary science and a vast improvement in the standards of living of the people, have resulted in a rapid decline in the death rate, especially in the city.[3]

[TOPIC:] And the rain now seemed to have made the heat more intense. [SPECIFIC DETAILS:] Before the rain the air had at least been dry and the perspiration evaporated and brought some relief, but now with the brassy sun striking full on the wet rocks and the bare muddy fields, the steam rose up, enveloping houses, cattle, laborers, even the moving train itself, until the whole of the vast Deccan plateau was like one gigantic Russian bath. In the train, windows were closed again because the air which entered was more suffocating than the air inside. In the ditches along the tracks the flood water flowed blood red, diminishing almost as you watched it into a fine trickle, swallowed up altogether presently by the heat of the sun and the greedy thirst of the hot, red earth.[4]

b. Specific Instances and Examples. A topic may be amplified by giving one or more instances or examples showing specific applications of the general statement.

[TOPIC:] In medical research this country has done noble work. [SPECIFIC EXAMPLES:] An American, Wil-

---

[3] W. E. Weyl, *The New Democracy,* The Macmillan Company. Reprinted by permission of the author and the publisher.

[4] Louis Bromfield, *Night in Bombay,* Harper & Brothers. Reprinted by permission of the author and the publisher.

liam T. G. Morton, gave suffering humanity the boon of anaesthesia. His priority in this great discovery has been disputed, it is true, but all the other claimants were also natives of the United States. Theobold Smith is the founder of one of the most important branches of bacteriology—for it was he who first discovered the part played by insects in conveying infectious diseases. It was Doctor Smith, also, who conquered that scourge of childhood—diphtheria—by his discovery of toxin-antitoxin. Equally important was the work of the American Federal Commission, under Doctor Walter Reed, in demonstrating that a certain species of mosquito is the agent for spreading yellow fever. But it is only within the past few decades that the United States has taken its place as the undisputed leader in medical research. The founding of the Rockefeller Institute has not only brought to this country some of the world's greatest investigators but it has organized and financed preventive work in almost every part of the world. The headquarters of the scientific army which is warring against disease is now in the United States.[5]

c. Comparison and Contrast. A topic may be developed by comparing one thing with another that is similar, or contrasting it with something dissimilar.

[TOPIC:] The same causes have greatly reduced the independence of personal and family life. [CONTRAST:] In the eighteenth century life was simple. The producer and consumer were near together and could find each other. Everyone who had an equivalent to give in property or service could readily secure the support of himself and family without asking anything from government except the preservation of order. Today almost all Americans are dependent upon the action of a great number of other persons, mostly unknown. About half of our people are crowded into the cities and large towns. Their food, clothes, fuel, light, water—all come from distant sources, of which they are in the main ignorant, through a vast,

[5] Thomas J. Wertenbaker, "What's Wrong with the United States," *Scribner's Magazine*. Reprinted by permission of the author and the publisher.

complicated machinery of production and distribution with which they have little direct relation. If anything occurs to interfere with the working of the machinery, the consumer is individually helpless. To be certain that he and his family may continue to live, he must seek the power of combination with others, and in the end he inevitably calls upon that great combination of all citizens which we call government to do something more than merely keep the peace—to regulate the machinery of production and distribution and safeguard it from interference so that it shall continue to work.[6]

[TOPIC:] Peru is also a miniature of South America in its social and economic problems. [COMPARISON:] It has an aristocracy relatively as powerful as that of Argentina and much older. It resembles Bolivia and Ecuador in that two-thirds of its population is Indian and as yet unassimilated. Like Chile and Venezuela, it is dominated by foreign capital and foreign industry, which it has not yet been able to supplant. Like Bolivia and Paraguay, it is embroiled in a dispute (with Ecuador) over a huge chunk of land in the interior. Like Brazil and Chile, it is the battleground for the fierce trade rivalry between Germany and the receding Japanese, at the expense of other competing powers. And like almost all of South America, it is a theoretical republic controlled by a practical dictator around whom there seethes the potential warfare of fascism, communism, and indigenous ideologies.[7]

d. Proof. A topic may be supported by logical proof, or reasons showing that it is true.

[TOPIC:] The surface [of the moon] differs from that of the earth in the fact that it lacks the envelopes of air and water. [PROOF:] That there is no air is indicated by the feature above noted—that there is no diffusion of the sunlight, the shadows being absolutely black and having perfectly clean-cut edges. It is also shown by

[6] Elihu Root, *Experiments in Government*, Princeton University Press. Reprinted by permission of the author and the publisher.
[7] "South America II: Peru." Copyright Time, Inc. (*Fortune*, January, 1938.) Reprinted by permission.

the fact that when a star is occulted or shut out by the disc of the moon it disappears suddenly without its light being displaced, as it would be by refraction if there were any sensible amount of air in the line of its rays. This evidence affords proof that if there is any air at all on the moon's surface it is probably less in amount than remains in the nearest approach to a vacuum that we can produce by means of an air pump. Like proof of the airless nature of the moon is afforded by the spectroscope applied to the study of the light of an occulting star or that of the sun as it is becoming eclipsed by the moon. [TOPIC RESTATED:] In fact, a great body of evidence goes to show that there is no air whatever on the lunar surface. [The next paragraph takes up the subject of lack of water.] [8]

e. Cause and Effect. A topic may be developed by the method of cause and effect. The paragraph may show (1) the cause of the phenomenon or condition stated in the topic sentence; (2) the effect of it; or (3) both the cause and the effect.

[TOPIC:] A corollary of American optimism was tolerance. [TOPIC REPEATED WITH SPECIFIC DETAILS:] This tolerance, which was half-part indifference, extended to slavery, slums, piratical business, and political corruption. [CAUSE:] The presence on the continent of a great community of unlike, free, and nominally equal men stimulated this toleration, as did also the fluidity of American life, the facile escape from local evil conditions, the easy association in business and society of diverse elements, and the free exchange of goods and ideas between different sections. Prosperity, too, made for tolerance. To a well-fed, well-housed, suitably mated man, few beliefs, opinions, or prejudices are intolerable; and the ready humor of America, tinged with the joy of mere well-being, was both an antidote and an alternative to intolerance. [9]

[8] N. S. Shaler, article in *Smithsonian Contributions to Knowledge*. Reprinted by permission of the author and the publisher.
[9] W. E. Weyl, *The New Democracy*, The Macmillan Company. Reprinted by permission.

[TOPIC:] Every system of society carries within itself the seeds of life and its own potential death. [SPECIFIC EXAMPLE AND CAUSE AND EFFECT:] Democracy in the United States had a favored childhood. The continent was there to conquer, and opportunity beckoned to all who had the strength to reach out for it. The land was stored with riches which were recklessly and lavishly spent and, though the wealth was not distributed equally, it did provide for the majority of Americans the highest standard of life to be found in the world. Under such circumstances democracy could thrive, and the potentialities of its death be kept down. But the economic system has changed to the disadvantage of the individual. Industrialism and concentrated finance shifted power to the relatively few, and political power has not been able to restore to the individual his full economic initiative. Indeed it may never achieve this restoration. The old birthright may already be lost in its original form. And this may be the potentiality of death within our own democracy, a postulation which deserves the most searching thought.[10]

f. Definition and Explanation of Terms. One or more of the terms used in the statement of the topic may need to be defined or explained. This process sometimes includes negative definition—telling what a thing is not, as well as what it is.

[TOPIC:] What is civilization? [DEFINITION:] It is a set of rules by which most men abide, of promises to which most men adhere. It is a set of institutions, of homely customs, which express the experience of centuries. It has its roots in cultural disciplines, religious and humanistic, which give life its meaning. Man creates these disciplines and supports them, to foster what is good in his nature and control what is bad. When he begins to break his own rules and ignore his customs (instead of making them ever more subtle and humane with the passing decades) civilization sickens at the roots.[11]

[10] Raymond Gram Swing, "Over Here," *Survey Graphic*. Reprinted by permission of the author and the publisher.
[11] Herbert Agar, "The Truth Is Good News," *Harper's Magazine*. Reprinted by permission of the author and the publisher.

[TOPIC:] Religion apart, they [Americans] are an un-reverential people. [NEGATIVE DEFINITION:] I do not mean irreverent—far from it; nor do I mean that they have not a great capacity for hero-worship, as they have many a time shown. [POSITIVE DEFINITION:] I mean that they are little disposed, especially in public questions—political, economical, or social—to defer to the opinions of those who are wiser or better instructed than themselves. [CAUSE:] Everything tends to make the individual independent and self-reliant. He goes early into the world; he is left to make his way alone; he tries one occupation after another, if the first or second venture does not prosper; he gets to think that each man is his own best helper and adviser. Thus he is led, I will not say to form his own opinions, for even in America few are those who do that, but to fancy that he has formed them, and to feel little need of aid from others toward correcting them.[12]

g. Repetition. The topic may be repeated in different words to make the thought more emphatic or to give the reader more than one view of it. Sometimes the repetition includes a broadening of the statement, or makes it more concrete by adding specific details.

[TOPIC:] While the pioneer was felling the forest, the city had been growing apace. [TOPIC REPEATED:] The city, which all over the world was becoming the new home of civilization, had developed in America more rapidly than elsewhere. It grew with the progress of the pioneers; it grew even faster after the pioneer period ended. [CAUSE:] As the supply of free western farms ceased, as the settlers, with no further place to go, began to exploit what they had, the alternative which the frontier once offered to the city disappeared. The progress of agriculture enabled one farmer to perform what two had performed before, and the surplus rural population moved to the up-growing cities. The immigrants, finding the new lands pre-empted, remained at the ports of entry. The new opportunities, the chances

[12] James Bryce, *American Commonwealth*, Macmillan. Reprinted by permission.

which the pioneer had sought among the trees, on the plains, or in the sands of California's rivers, were now sought in the mysterious, congested, surcharged life of the city.[13]

h. A Combination of Methods. Many paragraphs are developed, not by any single method, but by a combination of two or more. For examples see **f** and **g** above.

Moreover, it is to be noted that all these methods may be used in developing or supporting any statement in a paragraph as well as the topic sentence. For instance, a statement in the middle of the paragraph may be amplified by means of specific details, a specific example, repetition, and so on.

i. Other Methods. The list given above includes the most common and most definitely classified methods of developing a topic, but it does not cover all the possible methods. No formula or set of formulas can fit every case. Each topic presents a new problem of procedure. Hence the writer must not attempt to force every paragraph into one of the suggested forms. If a better way suggests itself, that is to be chosen.

Exercises in Section B 10

A. Select one of the following topic sentences and develop a fair-sized paragraph from it by using specific details.

1. In the spring the campus is beautiful.

2. Life in a small town (or in the country) is pleasant (or is unpleasant).

3. The furniture in the room was aggressively modern (or mid-Victorian).

4. A large city offers the student many extracurricular opportunities for education.

B. Develop by the use of specific instances and examples.

[13] W. E. Weyl, *The New Democracy*, The Macmillan Company. Reprinted by permission.

1. Our colleges owe much to wealthy philanthropists.
2. The reading of novels may enlarge one's knowledge of history (or social conditions, life in different localities, etc.).
3. Most people are superstitious.
4. The airplane has made the world a small place.

C. Develop by the use of comparison or contrast.

1. Campus politics are similar to city politics.
2. It is cheaper to rent than to own a house (or vice versa).
3. I prefer a small college to a large university (or vice versa).
4. Formerly children amused themselves; now their amusements are arranged for them.

D. Develop by the use of cause and effect.

1. Installment buying does not encourage thrift.
2. More and more people are moving from the cities to outlying districts.
3. In February he had a nervous breakdown.
4. An unbalanced diet seriously affects health.

E. Develop by the use of proof.

1. Lincoln was truly a "man of the common people."
2. Life in an apartment is easy for the man of the family (or housewife).
3. Final examinations do not always give a true picture of a student's knowledge of a subject.

F. Develop by the use of definition and explanation of terms, and specific examples.

1. An agnostic is not the same as an atheist.
2. Blank verse is ———.
3. A squeeze play in baseball is ———.
4. A mouse trap in football is ———.
5. A man-to-man defense in basketball is ———.

G. Develop by the use of any one or more than one of the methods given in the text. Indicate the methods that you employ.

1. A basketball player requires more stamina than a football player.

2. A knowledge of chemistry is valuable in the kitchen.

3. Electricity has lightened the housewife's work.

4. Freedom of speech does not mean license to say whatever we please.

5. —— is a real gentleman.

6. The constant use of slang impoverishes one's vocabulary.

7. We are all collectors by nature.

8. Temperance in all things is a virtue.

9. What is meant by the "American way of life"?

10. —— is very meticulous.

Exercises in Words

A. The following words are often confused because of their similarity in form. Look them up in the dictionary and use them in sentences.

healthy, healthful	ingenious, ingenuous
allusion, illusion	human, humane
balance, remainder	feminine, effeminate

B. Do you know these words and use them in your writing? Look them up in the dictionary, form a sentence containing each of them, and then make yourself use them in your writing.

exotic	pungent	frugal	dearth
tawdry	poignant	fragile	excerpt
garish	impeccable	immaculate	bigotry

C. Learn the first five pairs of synonyms on page 288 and use them in sentences.

Chapter Four

GRAMMATICAL CORRECTNESS

OUTLINE OF GRAMMAR

A sentence is a group of words which makes a statement.

The two essential parts of a sentence are the *subject* and the *predicate:* something to talk about and something to say about it.

The *subject* is a word or group of words that names the person or thing about whom or which the statement is made. In its simplest form it consists of a noun or a pronoun.

The *predicate* is a word or group of words that makes a statement about the subject. In its simplest form it consists of a verb alone, and it always contains a verb.

Trees | grow.

Simple Subject   Simple Predicate

Both the Simple Subject and the Simple Predicate may have modifiers and other adjuncts.

The pine trees of the North | grow to a great height.

In the sentence above, the noun *trees* is the Simple Subject, and *the pine trees of the North* is the Complete Subject. Likewise, the verb *grow* is the Simple Predicate, and *grow to a great height* is the Complete Predicate.

A clause or a phrase may be used as a substitute for a noun to form the subject (see page 144).

That he will go | is certain.
Taking a walk | makes me tired.
To do the work well | requires time.

73

The order in a sentence may be inverted, the verb being placed before the subject.

Never *was* the *sea* so calm.

Parts of Speech

A sentence is made up of words, each of which has a particular function to perform. Words are classified according to these functions into eight Parts of Speech:

Nouns	Verbs	Prepositions
Pronouns	Adverbs	Conjunctions
Adjectives		Interjections

NOUNS

A Noun is the name of something: as, *tree, boy, health, happiness.*

Classification of Nouns

Nouns are classified as follows:

A **Common Noun** is the name belonging to all the members of a class of persons or things: as, *city, country, man, church, store.*

A **Proper Noun** is a name belonging to an individual member of a class: as, *Chicago, England, Henry Adams, St. Paul's Cathedral, Bartlett and Company.*

A **Collective Noun** names a group of persons or things: as, *army, committee, jury, family.*

Uses of Nouns

A noun may be used as follows:
Subject of a Verb. See page 73.

The *soldiers* fought bravely.

Direct Object of a Verb. A Direct Object regularly follows a transitive verb, and names the person or thing that receives the action expressed by the verb.

He wrote the *letter*.
We saw *John*.

A direct object answers the question *what?* or *whom?* Thus, "He wrote *what?*" (answer, the *letter*). "We saw *whom?*" (answer, *John*).

Indirect Object of a Verb. An Indirect Object names the person or thing toward whom or toward which the action of the verb is directed.

He gave the *city* a library.
We bought the *boy* a coat.

An indirect object answers the question *to whom?* or *to what?—for whom?* or *for what?* Thus, "He gave a library to *what?*" (answer, to the *city*). "We bought a coat for *whom?*" (answer, for the *boy*).

An indirect object is never used without a direct object, and always precedes it in a sentence.

Object of a Preposition. The Object of a Preposition completes the relation indicated by the preposition (see page 91).

He went to *town*.
She came from *Washington*.

Predicate Noun. A Predicate Noun is placed in the predicate, usually after the verb, and names the same thing or person as the subject.

Jenny was a *waitress*.
His house is a *palace*.

Appositive. An Appositive, or Noun in Apposition, is a noun that follows another noun and names the same person or thing.

James Abbot, the *mayor*, will speak.
I met the principal, *Mr. Hughes*.
His first book, a *novel*, was written in 1912.

Direct Address. A noun in Direct Address specifies the person or persons to whom a remark is directed.

John, we must go at once.
This, *gentlemen,* is my answer.
Harry, give me your knife. (The subject of the verb is an "understood" *you.*)

Objective Complement. An Objective Complement occurs after verbs of *making, choosing, electing,* etc. It follows a direct object.

They made his father a *colonel.*

The Objective Complement shows the result of the action of the verb upon the direct object. Thus, "They made his father *what?*"—answer, "They made his father a *colonel.*"

Subject of an Infinitive. A noun may be used as the Subject of an Infinitive (see page 87).

We believe the *man* to be honest.

In this sentence the whole infinitive phrase, *the man to be honest,* is the object of the verb *believe:* it tells *what* we believe. The phrase is the equivalent of a noun clause: *that the man is honest.* Compare, "We believe *that the man is honest*" and "We believe *the man to be honest.*" In the phrase, *man* is called the subject of the infinitive *to be,* just as in the clause *man* is the subject of the verb *is.*

Object of an Infinitive. A noun may be used as the object of an infinitive, participle, or gerund (see page 88).

He likes to play *chess.*
I saw a man cutting *wheat.*
Writing *letters* was his hobby.

Nominative Absolute. The Nominative Absolute construction consists of a noun (or a pronoun) and a participle, together with any modifiers that may be present.

Night having come, we hurried to the camp.
We drove slowly, *the roads being icy.*

NOUNS

It will be noticed that the subject and the verb of the first sentence, for example, are *we hurried,* not *night having come.* The latter construction is an adverbial modifier telling why we hurried. The nominative absolute may also express time and other adverbial relations.

Other Characteristics of Nouns

Number. Number indicates how many persons or things are designated by a noun.

The *Singular Number* designates one person or thing: *boy, man, mouse.*

The *Plural Number* designates two or more persons or things: *boys, men, mice.*

Gender. Gender indicates the sex of an object.

The *Masculine Gender* indicates a being of the male sex: *boy, man, buck, rooster.*

The *Feminine Gender* indicates a being of the female sex: *girl, woman, doe, hen.*

The *Neuter Gender* indicates an object without sex: *house, city, patriotism.*

The *Common Gender* designates a person of either male or female sex, without specifying which one: *child, parent, cattle, deer.*

Person. See under Pronouns, page 80.

Case. According to their use in a sentence, nouns have three cases: the Nominative, the Objective, and the Possessive.

The *Nominative* and the *Objective* Cases have the same form and offer no practical difficulties.

The *Possessive Case* indicates possession. Its sign is an apostrophe: *man's, people's, families'.*

Exercises

A. Point out the nouns and tell how they are used.

1. A sailor then threw the box over the rail.

2. Quincy, the county seat, is a prosperous city on the Mississippi River.

3. The instructor gave the class a long reading assignment.

4. This book, gentlemen, was a gift to my mother from Mrs. Lincoln, the wife of President Lincoln.

5. The train having left, the crowd dispersed.

6. Never again would the sound of the bugle call this company together.

7. Happiness is an attitude of mind which should be cultivated.

8. The missionary told his audience the story of the suffering among his people in India.

9. At the head of the procession rode General Miles, the commander-in-chief of the army.

10. John, please send Mr. Graham a copy of the report.

11. Here, in a dilapidated one-story house, lived Mrs. Hagen, the daughter of a former governor of the state.

12. The club elected Mr. Mayer president for a fourth term.

13. Mr. Mayer has been president for three terms.

14. Whistling loudly, the boy hurried past the cemetery.

15. The arbiter granted the carpenters an increase in pay.

16. The arbiter granted an increase in pay to the carpenters.

17. The case was dismissed, the principal witness having disappeared.

18. The case was dismissed, for the principal witness had disappeared.

19. During the winter, all the families were on relief.

20. The captain ordered the crew to man the lifeboats.

B. Point out common nouns, proper nouns, and collective nouns in the sentences in A above.

C. Give the gender of each noun in A.

PRONOUNS

A Pronoun is a word used for a noun.

The noun to which a pronoun refers is called its Antecedent.

Classification of Pronouns

Pronouns are classified as follows:

Personal Pronouns: as, *I, you, he, she, it,* together with their various forms to indicate number and case (see Sec. **C 2**). Words like *myself, herself,* and *themselves* are called Compound Personal Pronouns.

Relative Pronouns: as, *who, which, that, what, whoever, whosoever, whatever, whatsoever, whichever, whichsoever,* together with their various case forms (see Sec. **C 2**). These pronouns introduce relative clauses, and are used as nouns in these clauses: that is, as subject or object of a verb, and so forth (see Sec. **C 3**).

> This is the man *who* wrote the book.
> You must do *whatever* he requires.

Interrogative Pronouns: as, *who, which, what.* They are used in asking questions.

> *Who* made this cake?
> *What* did he say?

Demonstrative Pronouns: as, *this, that, these, those.* They are used to point out the person or thing to which a reference is made.

> *This* is the best book.
> *Those* are the ripest grapes.
> Give me some of *that.*

Indefinite Pronouns: as, *some, somebody, each, everyone, any, anyone, one.* They refer to some indefinite person or thing, not to a specific one. Compare "*Someone* will do it" (indefinite) with "*He* will do it" (definite).

Uses of Pronouns

Pronouns have the same uses as nouns (see page 74).

Subject of verb: *We* studied the lesson.
                    This is the boy *who* was hurt.

Direct object of verb:	John saw *them.*
	I know the man *whom* you mentioned.
Indirect object of verb:	They gave *him* a book.
Object of preposition:	You must go with *them.*
	He is the man to *whom* I wrote.
Predicate pronoun:	This boy is *he.*
	We know *who* you are.
Appositive:	Only two students, *you* and *I,* were invited.
Direct address:	Here, *you,* what is your name?
Subject of infinitive:	They asked *him* to stop.
Object of infinitive, participle, or gerund:	John told Harry to see *them.*
	This is the man *whom* we came to see.
	I heard the man calling *me.*
	We enjoyed meeting *them.*

Other Characteristics of Pronouns

Person. Pronouns are classified in three grammatical Persons.

The *First Person* indicates the speaker: *I, me, my, mine;* or in the plural, it indicates the speaker and others associated with him: *we, us, our, ours.*

The *Second Person* indicates the person who is addressed: *you, your, yours.*

The *Third Person* indicates the person or thing about whom or which a statement is made: *he, his, him; she, her hers; it, its; they, their, theirs, them.*

Gender. The pronouns *he, his, him* are definitely of the masculine gender; *she, her, hers* are feminine; and *it, its* are neuter. The other pronouns do not have specific forms to indicate their gender. They are masculine, feminine, or neuter according to whether they are used to refer to a male, a female, or an object without sex.

Case. For the forms and uses of the different cases, see Sec. **C 2.**

Number. For the forms indicating the singular and plural numbers of pronouns, see Sec. **C 2.**

Exercise

Point out the pronouns, give their classification (personal, relative, etc.), and tell how they are used.

1. I saw them before they sent you the telegram.
2. This is he whom you chose as a delegate.
3. This being Sunday, we shall not find anyone at the office.
4. Will you bring me the names of those who have contributed to the fund?
5. Which is the book that was assigned for reading?
6. That is the letter that she wrote.
7. Each of the girls whom the judges selected will receive a scholarship.
8. Who brought the letter, and what did he do with it?
9. It was I whom they saw.
10. He ordered them to arrest the driver.
11. Either you or I can finish the work which they began.
12. Never had we seen anyone who made more mistakes.
13. One of you must go if the principal calls you.
14. Whom did they want to help?
15. I had never heard of the man whom she mentioned.
16. Someone had told them the story of the quarrel between her and me.
17. The officers voted themselves an increase in salary.
18. You may have whatever you find in the purse.
19. The only members present were Jack and I.
20. She must have seen Mary and him at the party.

ADJECTIVES

An Adjective modifies a noun or a pronoun.

The *first* speaker had a *pleasant* voice.
The players, *weary* and *discouraged,* forfeited the game.

Predicate Adjective. A Predicate Adjective is one that is placed in the predicate, but modifies the subject of the verb.

The traveler was *hungry*.
She seemed *happy*.

Comparison of Adjectives. Adjectives have three degrees of comparison.

The *Positive Degree* is the form of the adjective used in describing an object without comparing it with another object.

This is a *large* house.

The *Comparative Degree* is used in comparing two objects.

His house is *larger* than mine.

The *Superlative Degree* is used in comparing more than two objects.

He has the *largest* house in town.

Typical forms for the three degrees are:

POSITIVE	COMPARATIVE	SUPERLATIVE
strong	stronger	strongest
good	better	best
intelligent	more intelligent	most intelligent

Articles. *A, an,* and *the* are called Articles. They are used as adjectives.

The is a Definite Article; *a* and *an* are Indefinite Articles. "Bring me *the* book" specifies a definite, particular book. "Bring me *a* book" refers indefinitely to any book.

Other Parts of Speech Used as Adjectives. Nouns and pronouns may be used as adjectives to modify other nouns.

They came on *Monday* morning.
College football is thrilling.
Your house is a *brick* building.
Please give me *that* book.
Which car do you like best?

Exercises

A. Point out the adjectives and tell what nouns they modify. Name specifically the predicate adjectives and the articles.

1. These stone houses are new and are being sold at reasonable prices.
2. Most of the assigned problems were easy for the better students.
3. Their latest home is a snug little house on wheels.
4. About us stood the gaunt, stark trunks of trees dead for many years.
5. The man was old and bent, and walked with a slight limp.
6. An earlier attempt would have been unwise and futile.
7. What plan seems most practical to the present officials?
8. Most people have a very real desire to be friendly.
9. His father was a just man, firm but reasonable in all his dealings.
10. It was a cold, bracing September morning, and the Wisconsin farmlands were white with frost.

B. Indicate the degree of comparison for each adjective in A above.

VERBS

A Verb is a word that makes a statement about the subject of a sentence or of a clause.

It expresses action: as, *throw, think, will swim, has given, had been working;* or state of being: as, *is, has been.*

He *threw* his hat into the ring.   I *have* never *seen* him.
She *had driven* to the city.   They *are* at home.

Classification of Verbs

Finite Verb. All forms of a verb—with the exception of infinitives, participles, and gerunds—are Finite Verbs. There must be a finite verb in every predicate.

Transitive Verb. A Transitive Verb is a verb that takes an object to complete its meaning.

We *knew* the *answer*.
She *lost* the *money*.

Intransitive Verb. An Intransitive Verb does not take an object.

We *traveled* across the country.
They *live* quietly.

Linking Verb. A Linking Verb—sometimes called a Copula, or Copulative Verb—is used to connect the subject of a sentence with a predicate noun or a predicate adjective.

His brother *is* a lawyer.
The address *was* brief.
She *seems* happy.

Is, was, has been, and other forms of the ver*b be* are the chief linking verbs. *Seem, appear, look, become,* and a few other similar verbs are also used in this way.

Auxiliary Verb. An Auxiliary Verb helps to make some form of another verb.

He *will* go tomorrow (*will* helps to make a form of the verb *go*).
The papers *have been* lost (*have been* helps to make a form of the verb *lose*).

Some of the chief auxiliary verbs are *is* and other forms of the verb *be; have* and its various forms; *will, shall, can, may, would, should, could, might*.

can talk	*would* stay	*might* lose
may sing	*should* go	*could* fail

Principal Parts of a Verb. The present infinitive, the past tense, and the past participle are called the Principal Parts of a Verb. They are used in making other parts of the verb.

INFINITIVE	PAST TENSE	PAST PARTICIPLE
(to) drink	drank	drunk
(to) see	saw	seen
(to) be	was	been
(to) walk	walked	walked

From the infinitive form are made the present tense (I *drink*), the future tense (*will drink*), and the present participle (*drink*-ing). From the past participle are made the present perfect tense (*have drunk*) and the past perfect tense (*had drunk*).

Properties of Verbs

Voice. The Voice of a verb indicates whether the subject of the verb is acting or receiving the action.

The *Active Voice* represents the subject as acting.

The lightning *struck* the house.

The *Passive Voice* represents the subject as receiving the action.

The house *was struck* by lightning.
He *has been promoted* to a professorship.

Tense. The Tense of a verb indicates the time when the action described by the verb occurred.

The *Present Tense* regularly indicates that the action is taking place in present time.

He *is working*.
He *lives* in Chicago.

The *Past Tense* indicates that the action took place at a definite time in the past. If this definite point of time is not clearly implied in the context, it should be stated in the sentence.

He *was working*.
He *lived* in Chicago a year ago.

The *Future Tense* indicates that the action is to take place in the future.

He *will work* tomorrow.
He *will be living* in Chicago next year.

Will and *shall* are the signs of the future tense.
The *Present Perfect Tense* regularly indicates that the action took place at some indefinite time before the present (see Sec. **C 6**).

He *has worked* in a coal mine.
They *have been living* in Chicago.

Has and *have* are the signs of this tense.
The *Past Perfect Tense* indicates that the action was completed before some point of time in the past.

He *had worked* in a coal mine before going to college.
He *had been living* in Chicago before the war.

Had is the sign of this tense.
The *Future Perfect Tense* indicates that the action is to be completed before some point of time in the future.

By the first of September, he *will have worked* in the mine for two years.

Some Special Uses. The Present Tense is sometimes used to indicate future time if the context shows the future relation.

He *goes* (*is going*) to New York tomorrow.

Action in the future may also be indicated by a present form of the verb *be* combined with an infinitive.

He *is to go* tomorrow.

The Past Tense sometimes indicates a future action that was planned in the past but is now doubtful.

He *was going* next week, but some difficulties have arisen.

Person. The verb *be* has three different forms in the present tense to represent Person.

Other verbs have a different form only in the third person, singular number. This form ends in -*s*.

The verb *Be:*

	SINGULAR	PLURAL
First Person	I am	we are
Second Person	you are	you are
Third Person	he is	they are

Other verbs:

First Person	I know	we know
Second Person	you know	you know
Third Person	he *knows*	they know

Mood. See page 114.

Verbals—Infinitives, Participles, and Gerunds

Infinitives, Participles, and Gerunds are called Verbals. They are formed from verbs, but they are not used as finite verbs: that is, they cannot serve as the predicate of a sentence.

An **Infinitive** is regularly introduced by *to:* as, *to see, to know, to have written, to be sold.*

It may be used as a noun, as an adjective, or as an adverb.

Noun:	*To err* is human (subject of the verb).
	I want *to study* (object of the verb).
Adjective:	There was no time *to lose* (modifies *time*).
Adverb:	He was glad *to come* (modifies the predicate adjective *glad*).

In some instances, *to* is omitted in the infinitive.

They dare not *try* it (instead of *"to try* it").

A **Participle** is a verbal adjective.

The boy *resting* in the shade was tired.
The crew had left the *burning* ship.
They repaired the *broken* lock.

Note. Participles are also combined with auxiliary verbs to form finite verbs.

The moon is *shining*.
He has *seen* the king.

A **Gerund**—sometimes called a "Verbal Noun in -ing" —is used as a noun.

Running is good exercise (subject of the verb).
I enjoy *walking* (object of the verb).
He was tired from *running* (object of the preposition).

Because they are derived from verbs and retain part of their verbal nature, infinitives, participles, and gerunds may have objects and may be modified by adverbs.

Objects: I want to get a *book*.
              The boy leading the *procession* is my brother.
              Reading the *text* was difficult.

Adverbial   He preferred to walk *slowly*.
modifiers: The boy finishing *first* will get a prize.
              Reading *rapidly* is an art.

For forms of Verbals and some further discussion, see Sec. **C 7.**

Infinitives, participles, and gerunds, with their objects and modifiers, form Infinitive Phrases, Participial Phrases, and Gerundive Phrases. These phrases have the same uses as the single verbals (see above, and Sec. **D 7b**).

Exercises

A. Point out the verbs and name their subjects. Indicate whether they are transitive, intransitive, or linking verbs. Point out auxiliary verbs. Remember that there may be more than one clause in a sentence, and, consequently, more than one verb and subject.

1. We saw the moon clearly as it rose slowly over the trees.
2. Soon the commission will make new regulations to govern suburban traffic.

3. He has never been accused of being dishonest.

4. Mr. Johnson had come here immediately after the Civil War and had built a large factory.

5. A theme is always more legible when it is neatly typed.

6. Could you find a duplicate of the machine anywhere in the city?

7. The apples seem almost ripe and ready to be shipped to market.

8. Suddenly the silence was broken by the most terrifying noise that I had ever heard.

9. We have already made him an offer which he should accept.

10. They did not give him the prize then, for he was too young to appreciate it.

11. The little boat was struck and completely overturned by the first big wave.

12. He is visiting his aunt in New York, and later he will go straight to London.

13. We had sent a message urgently requesting an immediate decision.

14. The letter had been sent early, for it was very important.

15. They have already been living in this neighborhood for two years.

16. Will you bring us a full report of the meeting?

17. This house soon became a refuge for the poor and the destitute.

18. If he is not more careful, he will certainly fall on the rocks and perhaps break a leg.

19. Finally, one of the party drove twenty miles to town and sent a telegram.

20. Your father is looking unusually well for a man who works so hard.

B. Name the tense and voice of the verbs in Exercise A.

C. Point out the verbals and tell how they are used.

1. I spoke to a man standing at the door.
2. He expects to come today.
3. His best plan will be to go by train.
4. John prefers fishing to hunting.

5. To fail now would be disastrous.

6. The injured boy made no attempt to walk.

7. His favorite sport was swimming, but he also enjoyed hiking.

8. The crew were swimming away from the burning ship.

9. They were afraid to go into the deserted house.

10. A word spoken in anger may mean the breaking of a valued friendship.

ADVERBS

An Adverb is a word that modifies a verb, an adjective, or another adverb.

He stepped *quickly* to the door (modifies the verb).

This is an *unusually* stupid book (modifies the adjective *stupid*).

They came *very* late (modifies the adverb *late*, which in turn modifies the verb *came*).

A word used as an adverb generally answers one of the following questions: *when? where? why? how?* or *how much?* (See also pages 145–146.)

He will go *now* (will go when?—answer, *now*).

They ran *rapidly* (ran how?—answer, *rapidly*).

Many adverbs end in -*ly:* as, *slowly, clearly;* but some have other forms: as, *now, then, once.*

Not all words that end in -*ly* are adverbs. They may be adjectives: as, a *lovely* day, a *ghastly* sight.

Comparison of Adverbs. Adverbs have the same Degrees of Comparison as adjectives (see page 82).

POSITIVE	COMPARATIVE	SUPERLATIVE
soon	sooner	soonest
cordially	more cordially	most cordially

Exercise

Point out the adverbs in Exercise A under Verbs, and tell what they modify.

PREPOSITIONS

A Preposition is a connecting word used to show the relation of a noun or a pronoun to some other word in the sentence: as, *to, from, for, below, against.*

He went *to* the house *with* us.

A preposition is followed by an object—a noun, a pronoun, or a substitute construction. Thus, in the example above, *house* is the object of the preposition *to,* and *us* is the object of *with.*

A preposition and its object form a prepositional phrase: as *to the house, with us.*

CONJUNCTIONS

A Conjunction is a connecting word used to join words or groups of words in a sentence: as, *and, or, while, if, as.*

A **Co-ordinate Conjunction** connects words or groups of words that are equal in rank: as, *and, but, or, nor.*

John *and* Henry are brothers.
You can buy the car, *or* you can rent it.

A **Subordinate Conjunction** connects a subordinate clause with a main clause or with a word that it modifies: as, *since, when, if, although.*

I have not seen him *since* he came home.
He will go *if* he can.

When a subordinate clause precedes the main clause, the subordinate conjunction stands at the beginning of the sentence instead of between the two clauses.

Although he was hungry, he refused the food.

Logically, the conjunction connects the clauses just as it does when the sentence is rearranged: "He refused the food, *although* he was hungry."

Correlative Conjunctions are conjunctions used in pairs: as, *either—or, neither—nor, both—and, not only— but also.*

Either the boy *or* the father will be there.
They invited *not only* the seniors *but also* the juniors.

INTERJECTIONS

An Interjection is an exclamatory word which has little or no grammatical relation with the rest of the sentence.

Oh, did you call?
This story, *alas,* is true.

Exercises

A. Point out the prepositions and conjunctions. Name the objects of the prepositions and tell what words or groups of words the conjunctions connect.

1. We cannot write and type the article before Saturday.

2. He will wait until Monday or Tuesday before he files the complaint.

3. The people in both the city and the suburbs will be affected by the change.

4. They were here yesterday, but they did not have time to see you.

5. If the roads are icy, he will come by train, and you can meet him at the station.

6. Either you or I will have to finish the work.

7. They told us that the bill would be passed, although the governor was opposed to it.

8. He said that he had not received the letter that you wrote.

9. The mercury had fallen ten degrees and the wind had shifted to the north.

10. We called a taxi, for we were already late for dinner.

11. The explorer told us about his adventures in Africa, and his latest expedition through the Sahara.

12. Neither the wheat nor the corn was injured by the hail.

13. He has no one to blame except himself for his failure to pass the examination.

14. They will meet us in Boston or in Philadelphia.

15. We walked until we were tired and then rested under a big pine tree.

16. The instructor gave us three hours to finish the examination because he knew that it was long and difficult.

17. You cannot do this work without plenty of help.

18. After the corn is harvested, the winter supply of wood must be cut.

19. The book is not only interesting but also instructive.

20. The country people came to the circus in Fords and on horseback.

B. Name the co-ordinate, subordinate, and correlative conjunctions in A above.

WORDS AS DIFFERENT PARTS OF SPEECH

The part of speech to which a word belongs is determined by its use in a particular sentence. The same word may serve in different capacities.

Thus we ordinarily think of *Sunday* as a noun, but it also has other uses.

Sunday is a day of rest (noun—subject of the verb).

Then we ate our *Sunday* dinner (adjective—modifies the noun *dinner*).

He came last *Sunday* (adverb—modifies the verb *came*).

Again, a word may be either a preposition—when it is followed by a noun or pronoun used as its object; or a conjunction—when it introduces a clause (a group of words having a subject and a verb).

He went *after* dinner (preposition).

He went *after* he finished dinner (conjunction).

But is a conjunction when it connects words, phrases, or clauses of co-ordinate rank. It is a preposition—equivalent to *except*—when it introduces a phrase.

He found the purse *but* the money was gone (conjunction).
The day was cloudy *but* warm (conjunction).
Everybody works *but* father (preposition. Compare "Everybody works *except* father").

Words like *up, on, under,* and the like, which are prepositions when followed by an object, may function as adverbs when they do not have an object.

He walked *up* the hill (preposition).
He looked *up* as I entered (adverb).

Note. Phrases and subordinate clauses may serve as single parts of speech—as nouns, adjectives, or adverbs. (See Sec. **D 7b.**)

Exercise

Tell the parts of speech to which the italicized words belong.

1. *Those* are *my* gloves.
2. I do not like *those* people.
3. *Which* book do you want?
4. *Which* is the better book?
5. We stayed *until* midnight.
6. We stayed *until* the clock struck four.
7. I will tell you *tomorrow.*
8. *Tomorrow* will be another day.
9. I must see you before *tomorrow* morning.
10. He came *on* and saw us standing *on* the corner.
11. *Some* books are good and *others* are bad.
12. *Frank's* mother was *their* aunt.
13. I got *up* early and walked *up* the hill for exercise.
14. The *January* thaw began yesterday.
15. *January* is the coldest month of the year.
16. *That* is the house *that* Jack built.
17. *What* did he say, and *what* answer did you give?

18. His hat blew *down* the street when he fell *down*.
19. I saw *her* and *her* brother.
20. There will be a *late* harvest, for we planted the corn *late*.

AGREEMENT OF SUBJECT AND VERB

C1. Be sure that a verb and its subject agree in number—singular verb with singular subject; plural verb with plural subject.

Errors in agreement are frequently made because the writer mistakes the wrong word for the subject, or because the subject is of a form which he does not analyze correctly. Especial care should be taken in the following constructions:

a. Intervening Words Between the Subject and the Verb. When there are words intervening between the subject and the verb, the careless writer sometimes makes the verb agree with the nearest noun instead of with the real subject.

Wrong: A *study* of his last two novels *show* a remarkable change in his attitude toward the small town.
Right: A *study* of his last two novels *shows* a remarkable change in his attitude toward the small town.

b. The Subject Following the Verb. When the subject follows the verb, instead of preceding it, be sure that the two are in agreement.

Wrong: Before us to the south *lies Harper's Ferry and the Shenandoah Valley.*
Right: Before us to the south *lie Harper's Ferry and the Shenandoah Valley.*

Wrong: The monument is a marble shaft on which *is engraved* the *names* of those who fell in the battle.
Right: The monument is a marble shaft on which *are engraved* the *names* of those who fell in the battle.

After the introductory word *there,* the verb is singular if the subject—which follows the verb—is singular; plural, if the subject is plural.

Right: There *is* one *objection* to this plan.
Right: There *are* several *objections* to this plan.

c. Expressions like *One of the Best.* In a relative clause following expressions such as *one of the best, the first of many,* and the like, the verb is plural when the relative clause refers to the class as a whole, not to the one member of the class.

Wrong: This is one of the richest *gold fields* that *has* been discovered since the Klondike rush.
Right: This is one of the richest *gold fields* that *have* been discovered since the Klondike rush.

d. Expressions Introduced by *Together With, As Well As, In Addition To.* Connectives like *together with, as well as,* and *in addition to* do not affect the number of the subject. The verb agrees with the word or words to which the expression introduced by these connectives is affixed.

Wrong: The *cheapness* of the article, together with its durability, *make* it very desirable.
Right: The *cheapness* of the article, together with its durability, *makes* it very desirable.

Wrong: A *report* of the meeting, as well as a list of the new officers, *are* printed on the third page.
Right: A *report* of the meeting, as well as a list of the new officers, *is* printed on the third page.

Note. These expressions form a subject which, from one point of view, is plural in meaning. Thus in the first sentence above, there are two features which make the article desirable; but the fact that the writer chose the form *together with* shows that he wanted to emphasize the *cheapness.* He did this by using that word as the subject and putting the other idea into a modifying phrase. To carry out the emphasis, the verb is made singular to agree with this single word. He might have said, "The cheapness of the article *and* its durability *make* it very desirable," in which case the plural verb would have been correct; but he would have sacrificed the emphasis on *cheapness*.

e. *None*. After *none* used as a subject, the verb is plural if the *none* refers to a number of units; singular if it refers to a word expressing mass, in which the idea of separate units is not present.

Right: *None* of the *members* were absent.
Right: *None* of the *sugar* was spilled.

Some writers always use a singular verb after *none*. This is the older practice and is still correct, but it is being supplanted by the one given above.

f. *Either—Or, Neither—Nor*. With a compound subject whose members are connected by *either—or, neither—nor*, a singular verb is used if the separate units are singular; a plural verb if the units are plural.

Right: Either the *pen* or the *paper is* (not *are*) defective.
Right: Neither the *officers* nor the *men were* responsible.

When one member of the subject is singular and the other is plural, the verb is usually made to agree with the nearer noun.

Right: Neither the *car* nor the *occupants* were injured.

However, it is generally better to avoid this construction by a recasting of the sentence: "*Both* the car *and* the occupants were uninjured."

g. Compound Subject Connected by *And*. A compound subject whose members are connected by *and* takes a plural verb.

Right: *Rapidity* and *accuracy* in using this machine *are* acquired only by constant practice.

h. *Each, Every, Everybody, Anybody* When one of the pronouns *everybody, anybody, everyone, anyone,* and the like, or a word or series of words introduced by *each* or *every*, is used as the subject, the verb is singular (compare Sec. **E 10a**).

Right: *Everybody* in the audience *was* (not *were*) cheering wildly.

Right: *Every* man, woman, and child *is* (not *are*) invited to be present.

Right: *Each* of the ten men *has* (not *have*) been ordered to report to the superintendent.

Right: *Any one* of you *has* (not *have*) the right to file an objection to this decision.

i. Collective Nouns. In a sentence having a collective noun as the subject, the general rule is that a singular verb is used when the group is regarded as a unit; a plural verb when the action involves the individual members of the group.

Right: The jury *is* in session.

Right: The jury *are* unable to agree on a verdict.

Right: The committee *has refused* to consider the amendment.

Right: The committee *are requested* to invite their friends.

This rule, however, is not strictly observed. The tendency is to use the singular verb except in cases where it is obviously illogical. Thus, in the second sentence above, the singular verb *is* would be permissible; but in the fourth, *is requested* would not express the exact idea.

j. Singular Subject and Plural Predicate Noun (or Vice Versa). When the subject is singular and the predicate noun is plural, or vice versa, the verb agrees with the subject, not with the predicate noun.

Right: The best time for sleep *is* (not *are*) the three hours before midnight.

Right: Our many successful graduates *are* (not *is*) the best evidence of the quality of the work offered by this school.

Exercises in Section C *1*

A. Point out the faults and make the corrections.

1. Neither the size nor the color of the gloves were right.

2. He was one of those men that believes everyone to be honest.

3. The rhythmic beating of the drums were heard far off in the jungle.

4. His hat as well as his overcoat were found on the end of the dock.

5. Either the name or the address were obviously incorrect.

6. In this book is recorded the name and the address of every voter.

7. Every one of the survivors have told the same story about the accident.

8. Have either of these suggestions been considered by the president?

9. The first two chapters in this very interesting book was written by John Burroughs.

10. From this nation has come not only great composers and singers, but also great conductors.

11. The president with the members of his cabinet are to be present at the dedication.

12. As neither of us have had dinner, why not stop in the next town?

13. Only the income from these funds are used for current expenses.

14. The prisoner, together with his two guards, were taken to the station in an armored car.

15. From each city has come disturbing reports about the damage done by the flood.

16. This year there has been a great many changes in personnel.

17. This is one of the most inspiring songs that has ever been written.

18. Each of these trays are then filled with the bleaching solution.

19. Does the president and the treasurer get a bonus this year?

20. Why is there so many errors in your theme?

B. Supply the correct form of the verb.

1. Here .... the mayor and his secretary to attend the council meeting (come, comes).

2. .... either the boy or his father know of these conditions (do, does)?

3. Every one of these articles .... been written to stir up class hatred (have, has).

4. Naval protection is one of the safeguards which .... necessary for national safety (are, is).

5. None of the stolen jewels .... been recovered (have, has).

6. None of the stolen money .... been recovered (have, has).

7. Each of the witnesses .... summoned to appear in court on Monday (were, was).

8. Neither the house nor the barn .... been painted for many years (have, has).

9. At the far end of the street .... the village school and the chapel where Parker used to preach (stand, stands).

10. The index as well as the table of contents .... to be made more complete (need, needs).

11. Every man, woman, and child .... been asked to contribute to the Community Chest (have, has).

12. The class in geology .... asked to serve as ushers at the meeting (were, was).

13. The army .... on the march long before sunrise (were, was).

14. Lying on the table .... a hat and a notebook (was, were).

15. It is one of the most interesting plays that .... been produced in Chicago this year (have, has).

16. .... there four or five rooms in this cottage (is, are)?

17. One of the worst floods that .... occurred in years is now sweeping the Ohio valley (have, has).

18. This is the only one of all his novels that .... worth reading (seem, seems).

19. Some parts of the venison .... too tough to eat (was, were).

20. He is one of the boys that .... the trombone in the band (play, plays).

CASE OF PRONOUNS

C2. **Be sure that the case of a pronoun is the one called for by the use of the pronoun in the sentence.**

The forms for the different cases of the most commonly used pronouns are:

NOMINATIVE CASE	POSSESSIVE CASE	OBJECTIVE CASE
I	my, mine	me
we	our, ours	us
you	your, yours	you
he	his	him
she	her, hers	her
it	its	it
they	their, theirs	them
who	whose	whom
which	(whose)	which
that	. . . .	that
what	. . . .	what

The **Nominative Case** is used when the pronoun is the subject of a finite verb or a predicate pronoun after a finite verb (see pages 79–80).

We are going tomorrow (subject).
There is the boy *who* won the prize.

This man is *he* (predicate pronoun).
They did not know *who* the man was.

The Objective Case is used when the pronoun is the direct object or the indirect object of a verb, the object of a preposition, the *subject* of an infinitive, or a predicate pronoun after an infinitive (see **e** and **f** below).

John saw *them* at school (direct object of verb).
I know the boy *whom* you sent.

The messenger brought *him* a telegram (indirect object).

The book was intended for *her* (object of preposition).
These are the people with *whom* he lives.

We expect *them* to be here (subject of infinitive).

A pronoun in **Apposition** has the same case as the noun to which it refers.

Two boys—John and *I*—were there.
He chose two boys—John and *me*.

Some Common Errors

Special care should be taken with the following constructions, in which mistakes are frequent:

a. Double Object of a Preposition. The object of a preposition is in the objective case. When a single pronoun is the object, there is small likelihood of a mistake. One would hardly write, "This party was given for *I*." But when there is a compound or double object, the writer may become confused and use the wrong case.

Wrong: This party was given for you and *I*.
Right: This party was given for you and *me*.

Right: This question must be settled between John and *me* (not John and *I*).

b. Appositives. Errors occur also when a pronoun is used in apposition with a noun.

Wrong: An easier assignment was given to *we* younger *students*.
Right: An easier assignment was given to *us* younger *students*.

Wrong: *Us* students were not invited.
Right: *We* students were not invited.

c. Pronouns After *Than* and *As*. A pronoun following *than* or *as* is in the nominative or the objective case, according to the meaning of the sentence.

Right: My brother is older than *I* (subject of the "understood" verb *am:* "older than *I am*").
Right: He likes you better than *me* (object of the "understood" verb *likes:* "better than he *likes me*").
Right: You must obey your father as well as *me* ("as well as *obey me*").

These constructions are elliptical; the test for determining the correct case of the pronoun is to fill in the "understood" part, as shown in the examples above.

d. Predicate Pronoun After a Finite Verb. A predicate pronoun following a finite form of the verb *be* (such as *is, are, were, has been*) is in the nominative case. Predicate pronouns have the same case as the subject of the verb.

Right: It is *I* (not *me*).
Right: That man is *he* (not *him*).
Right: It was *they* who made the mistake.

e. Subject of an Infinitive. The subject of an infinitive is in the *objective* case. Especial care should be taken to use the right case when the subject is compound.

Wrong: They expect *he* and *I* to do the work.
Right: They expect *him* and *me* to do the work.

Wrong: It was necessary for Mary and *I* to be at the office.
Right: It was necessary for Mary and *me* to be at the office.
(*Mary* and *me* are the subjects of the infinitive *to be*; they are not the objects of the preposition *for*. The entire infinitive phrase, *Mary and me to be at the office*, is the object of the preposition.)

Wrong: Let's you and *I* wash the dishes.
Right: Let's you and *me* wash the dishes.
(*Let's* is a contraction of *Let us*, and *you* and *me* are in apposition with *us*, which is the subject of the infinitive (*to*) *wash*. In expanded form the sentence would read "Let us—you and me—wash the dishes." An infinitive is regularly introduced by *to*, but here, as in a number of similar cases, the *to* is omitted (see page 87).

f. Predicate Pronoun After the Infinitive *To Be*. A predicate pronoun following the infinitive *to be* is in the objective case if the *infinitive has a subject*. This subject is in the objective case (see **e** above), and the predicate pronoun agrees with it in case.

Right: I took this man to be *him* (not *he*).

If the infinitive *does not have a subject,* the predicate pronoun is regularly in the nominative case.

Right: This man appears to be *he* whom the voters prefer.

Here *he* refers to *man,* the subject of the finite verb *appears.* They are both in the nominative case. The writer should keep in mind the general principle, that a predicate pronoun agrees in case with the subject to which it refers.

g. Interrogative Pronouns. An interrogative pronoun should be given the case form required by its use in the sentence.

Right: *Whom* (not *who*) do you want? (Object of the verb *do want.*)

Right: *Whom* (not *who*) did you wish to see? (Object of the infinitive *to see.*)

Right: *Whom* (not *who*) did you ask for? (Object of the preposition *for.*)

Right: *Who* (not *whom*) do you think will be there? (Subject of the verb *will be.*)

Right: *Whom* (not *who*) does he consider to be the most efficient? (Objective case, subject of the infinitive *to be.*)

An interrogative pronoun—no matter what its grammatical use may be—regularly stands at the beginning of the sentence. A convenient way to determine its use is to rearrange the sentence tentatively, putting the subject first and letting the other parts fall logically into place. Thus, "*Whom* do you want?" becomes "You want *whom?*" in which *whom* is clearly the object of *want.* "*Whom* did you ask for?" becomes "You asked for *whom?*" in which *whom* is the object of the preposition *for.*

Relative Pronouns

C3. **Be sure to use the correct case form for relative pronouns.**

The case of a relative pronoun depends upon the use of the pronoun in the clause which it introduces—not upon the case of its antecedent.

Compare the two following sentences, in which the antecedent is in the nominative case but the pronouns are in the nominative and objective cases, respectively, because of their use in their own clauses.

Right: This is *he who* came yesterday (nominative—subject of the verb *came*).

Right: This is *he whom* you saw (objective—object of *saw*).

Study also the sentences below. In determining the use of the relative pronoun in a clause, it may be convenient to rearrange the clause tentatively, as described in Sec. C 2g above.

Right: The student *who* is selected must be reliable (subject of the verb *is selected*).

Right: The student *whom* you select must be reliable (object of the verb *select*).

Right: The student *whom* you vote for must be reliable (object of the preposition *for*).

Right: Give the package to *whoever* comes (subject of the verb *comes*, not the object of the preposition *to;* the whole relative clause is the object of *to*).

Right: Give the package to *whomever* you see (object of the verb *see*, not the object of the preposition *to*).

Parenthetical expressions like *I believe, we thought, they said,* and the like, should be carefully watched, for they frequently lead to confusion in the use of pronouns.

Right: He was a man *who* we thought was honest (subject of the verb *was*).

Right: He was a man *whom* we thought to be honest (objective case—subject of the infinitive *to be*—see Sec. C 2e).

Special Uses of the Possessive Case

C4. Two special uses of the possessive case should be observed.

a. Possessive Case of Nouns Referring to Inanimate Objects. As a general rule, the possessive case should not be used with nouns referring to inanimate objects. A phrase introduced by *of* is preferable.

Not Good: The *building's* windows were protected by iron bars.
Right: The windows *of the building* were protected by iron bars.

Not Good: The *tree's* branches were broken.
Right: The branches *of the tree* were broken.

Exceptions. In certain expressions the use of the possessive case of nouns indicating inanimate objects is permissible:

1. In expressions denoting measure or extent (time, cost, and the like): *a penny's worth, an hour's time, two weeks' wages, a boat's length.*

2. In certain other idiomatic expressions of various sorts: *the sun's heat, the water's edge, for pity's sake, the earth's surface, at his wit's end, the cannon's mouth.*

There is also a growing tendency to use the possessive case of words such as *city* and *country*, and the names of particular cities, countries, and the like: *the city's shame, his country's call, England's navy, Russia's vast resources, Cook County's quota.*

b. Possessive Case Before a Gerund. A noun or pronoun preceding a gerund used as the object of a preposition should preferably be in the possessive case.

Not Good: We had not heard of *him* being in town.
Improved: We had not heard of *his* being in town.

Not Good: He objected to the *janitor* having a key to the office. (This might mean that he objected to the particular janitor who had a key to the office.)

Improved: He objected to the *janitor's* having a key to the office.

Questionable: There is a law against a *man* carrying a concealed weapon.
Improved: There is a law against a *man's* carrying a concealed weapon.

Note. Even good writers do not always follow this rule to the letter. If the objective case does not cause an awkward or ambiguous construction, they sometimes use that form instead of the possessive.

If the noun names an inanimate object and should therefore not be used in the possessive case (see **a** above), it is generally advisable to change the construction.

Questionable: He had not heard of the *work's* being finished.
Improved: He had not heard that the work was finished.

Exercises in Sections C 2–C 4

A. Supply the proper case form of the pronouns. Tell why the form that you use is correct.

1. They found only two persons in the office: the secretary and .... (I, me).
2. The only persons in the office were the Secretary and .... (I, me).
3. He suggested to Harry and .... that we should enter the contest (I, me).
4. He expected Harry and .... to enter the contest (I, me).
5. John is two years older than .... (I, me).
6. .... girls are going to the concert tonight (we, us).
7. They told .... girls to be ready at eight o'clock (we, us).
8. Let's you and .... go first (I, me).

9. His father did not approve of .... working on the farm (him, his).

10. He asked you and .... to stay after the meeting (I, me).

11. I had not heard of .... being in town (their, them).

12. There will be no one in the house except you and .... (I, me).

13. It was .... whom they wanted to see, not .... (she, her; I, me).

14. You can do the work better than either .... or .... (she, her; I, me).

15. We believed his brother to be .... (he, him).

16. May I speak with Mr. Shannon? Yes, that is .... at the first desk (he, him).

17. Lucy is not as good a student as .... (he, him).

18. He was a man .... everybody admired (who, whom).

19. We will find a place for .... comes (whoever, whomever).

20. We will find a place for .... you send (whoever, whomever).

B. Follow the instructions given for Exercise A.

1. I should like to know .... you were waiting to see this morning (who, whom).

2. They should select the candidate .... they think will best represent them in Washington (who, whom).

3. There was only one officer .... they considered worthy of the honor (who, whom).

4. It was George .... the teacher believed made the disturbance (who, whom).

5. It was George .... the teacher believed to be responsible for the disturbance (who, whom).

6. .... did you think would be there? (who, whom).

7. .... did you expect it to be? (who, whom).

8. .... are you working for now? (who, whom).

9. .... do you think is the most logical candidate? (who, whom).

10. .... would you choose as the most logical candidate? (who, whom).

TENSE

Tense indicates the time of the action represented by a verb.

The more common tense forms of a finite verb in the active voice, indicative mood, are as follows (only the first person is given):

Present: I think (am thinking).
Past: I thought (was thinking).
Future: I shall think (shall be thinking).
Present Perfect: I have thought (have been thinking).
Past Perfect: I had thought (had been thinking).
Future Perfect: I shall have thought (shall have been thinking).

Sequence of Tenses

C5. The sequence of tenses should indicate the logical time relation between the parts of the sentence.

Wrong: If he *cannot* come, he *would* let you know.
Right: If he *cannot* come, he *will* let you know.
Right: If he *could* not come, he *would* let you know.

Wrong: The work *was* easy, as the factory *is* equipped with modern labor-saving machinery.
Right: The work *was* easy, as the factory *was* equipped with modern labor-saving machinery.

a. Indirect Discourse and Clauses of Purpose. In indirect discourse and in clauses expressing purpose, a past tense in the main clause usually requires a past tense in the subordinate clause.

Right: They said that they *would* be here next week (not *will*).
Right: We thought that they *were* coming tomorrow (not *are*).
Right: He bought the house so that he *might* have a home in his old age (not *may*).
(Compare "He *is buying* the house so that he *may have* a home in his old age.")

The basis for this use of the past tense is that the statement in the subordinate clause holds true logically only at the time when it was made or when the purpose was formed. Conditions may change later, and the intended result may not come to pass. This uncertainty is implied in the past tense.

Exception. In indirect discourse, when the subordinate clause expresses a universal truth, the verb is in the present tense.

Right: He said that air *is* lighter than water.

b. Past Perfect Tense. The past perfect tense should be used when it is needed to place one past action definitely before another past action.

Not Clear: I heard that John *was* in town. (Is he still in town?)
Clear: I heard that John *had been* in town.

Not Clear: He felt tired, for he *walked* twenty miles that day.
Clear: He felt tired, for he *had walked* twenty miles that day.

When no ambiguity results, the past tense is frequently substituted for the past perfect.

Right: The troops *surrendered* before the reinforcements arrived (instead of *had surrendered*).

Present Perfect Tense

C6. The present perfect tense should not be used to refer to a definite point of time in the past.

For this definite reference, the past tense is the correct form.

Wrong: He *has finished* the work last week.
Right: He *finished* the work last week.

Wrong: Until two months ago, the business of the company *has been* flourishing.

Right: Until two months ago, the business of the company *was* flourishing.

Wrong: After the war there *have been* many minor quarrels between these countries.

Right: After the war there *were* many minor quarrels between these countries.

The present perfect tense always places an action somewhere in a period which has the present as one of its limits—which extends up to *now*. Notice, therefore, that if in the last example *after* is changed to *since,* the present perfect is the correct tense.

Right: Since the war, there *have been* many minor quarrels between these countries (that is, from the time of the war up to *now*).

Tenses of Participles and Infinitives

C7. **Be sure that the tense form of a participle or an infinitive expresses the correct time relation.**

The most frequently used forms of the participle and the infinitive are:

Present Participle: seeing, being seen
Past Participle: seen
Perfect Participle: having seen, having been seen

Present Infinitive: to see, to be seen
Perfect Infinitive: to have seen, to have been seen

a. Present Participles. A Present Participle should not be used to indicate an action which occurred before the action expressed by the main verb. In this case, a perfect or a past participle is the correct form.

Wrong: He has been with the company for twenty years, *entering* its employ in 1922.

Right: He has been with the company for twenty years, *having entered* its employ in 1922.

Wrong: He is now penniless, his fortune *being lost* in the recent stock crash.

Right: He is now penniless, his fortune *having been lost* in the recent stock crash.

b. Perfect Infinitives. A Perfect Infinitive should be used only when the action expressed by the infinitive occurred before the action indicated by the main verb.

Right: I am sorry *to have troubled* you. (This means, I am sorry *now* to have troubled you *previously*.)

Wrong: I meant *to have called* your attention to this matter later.

Right: I meant *to call* your attention to this matter later.

Wrong: He fully intended *to have been* in the office to-day.

Right: He fully intended *to be* in the office today.

Exercises in Sections C 5–C 7

A. Explain the mistakes, and correct them.

1. If you spend more time in revising your themes, I am sure they would be better.

2. He still lives in the old house which was the home of the family for three generations.

3. I have taken several long trips with my mother when I was a small girl.

4. When it came time to pay for the dinner, I found that I left my pocketbook at home.

5. He told us that he will be here next week.

6. Since the first of the year over two hundred automobile accidents occurred in the city.

7. He is one of the oldest inhabitants of Hanover, coming to the city shortly after the Civil War.

8. That would have been too early for us to have met you at the station.

9. This man, he discovered, was a former friend who was supposed to be killed in the last war.

10. She had known Mr. Williams previously, meeting him some months before moving to Chicago.

11. The price of clothing has greatly increased last summer because of increased wages for the garment workers.

12. She said that they are sailing for Europe next week.

13. They decided to make the case of steel so that it will not break.

14. They always stayed at the most expensive hotels in London, for they have plenty of money.

15. She said that she is living in Brooklyn.

16. He explained to the children that frogs could live either on land or in the water.

17. The meat was too moldy for us to have eaten it.

18. He has not had any trouble with the car when he was driving to California.

19. John was working for the company forty-two years when he retired.

20. I would not have spoken if I had thought that she would have been so angry.

B. Supply the correct tense forms, and explain why they are correct.

1. He .... writing steadily since eight o'clock this morning (was, has been).

2. I .... busy until late last evening (was, have been).

3. He said that he .... leaving for Boston tomorrow (was, is).

4. In the morning the room was cold, for the fire .... out during the night (went, had gone).

5. He believed that blood .... thicker than water (was, is).

6. Last week I .... three letters to the home office (wrote, have written).

7. That night he brought a book that he .... to let me read (promised, had promised).

8. After the accident he .... in the hospital for a month (was, has been).

9. Since the accident he .... in the hospital for a month (was, has been).

10. His coat was threadbare because he .... it for five years (wore, has worn, had worn).

11. His coat is threadbare because he .... it for five years (wore, has worn, had worn).

12. We hoped .... present at the meeting (to be, to have been).

13. It would have been easy for her .... the report (to deny, to have denied).

14. He is supposed .... a leader in the Jersey riots last fall (to be, to have been).

15. I should like .... on the early American frontier (to live, to have lived).

16. He arrived early this morning, ... the distance in four hours (covering, having covered).

17. .... afraid of the dark, Harry ran all the way home (having been, being).

18. At the close of the war it .... estimated that over a million men .... killed (was, has been; were, had been).

19. .... warned beforehand, we knew just what would happen (being, having been).

20. Before taking his present position, he .... the secretary of an insurance company (was, has been).

MOOD

Mood, in a verb, indicates the manner in which a statement is made. There are three grammatical moods.

The **Indicative Mood** is used in making a positive statement of fact or in asking a question.

> He *has made* an excellent record in school.
> Where *will* he *leave* the book?

The **Subjunctive Mood** is used primarily to make a statement contrary to fact or to express a wish. (See also **C 8b** and **c.**)

> If the house *were* larger, we could entertain our friends more often.
> I wish that the work *were* more interesting.

The **Imperative Mood** is used in expressing a command.

> *Come* here.   *Bring* me the book.

The following table shows the important differences in form between the subjunctive and the indicative moods in the verb *be,* the verb in which the greatest variation in form exists:

Present Tense		*Past Tense*	
SUBJUNCTIVE	INDICATIVE	SUBJUNCTIVE	INDICATIVE
(If) I be	I am	(If) I were	I was
(If) you be	You are	(If) you were	You were
(If) he be	He is	(If) he were	He was
(If) we be	We are	(If) we were	We were
(If) you be	You are	(If) you were	You were
(If) they be	They are	(If) they were	They were

In the other tenses the forms are, for all practical purposes, identical.

In all verbs except *be,* the only significant difference in form occurs in the third person, singular number, present tense. Here the verb *have* takes the form *have* in the subjunctive, *has* in the indicative; and every other verb drops the *-s* in the subjunctive.

SUBJUNCTIVE	INDICATIVE
(If) I have	I have
(If) you have	You have
(If) he *have*	He has
(If) I think	I think
(If) you think	You think
(If) he *think*	He thinks

Subjunctive Mood

C8. **The subjunctive mood is regularly used:**

> In conditions contrary to fact
> In wishes
> After *as if* or *as though*

a. In Conditions Contrary to Fact. 1. In a *present* condition contrary to fact the past tense of the subjunctive is required.

Here the only mistake that is likely to be made is the use of *was* for *were*. In all other verbs, the subjunctive and the indicative moods have the same forms in the past tense, and there is no chance for error.

The important point to remember, therefore, is this: "In a present condition contrary to fact, do not use *was* for *were*."

> Wrong: If I *was* you, I would go at once.
> Right: If I *were* you, I would go at once.

> Wrong: If the director *was* in his office, you could see him.
> Right: If the director *were* in his office, you could see him.

In these sentences the conditions are obviously *contrary to fact*: in the first, I am *not* you; in the second, the director is *not* in his office.

Notice that although *were* is called the subjunctive past tense of the verb *be*, it refers to a condition in present time.

2. In a condition contrary to fact in *past* time, the past perfect tense is used.

> If he *had been* there, the accident would not have occurred.
> If he *had come*, I could have seen him.

In Conditions Not Contrary to Fact. 1. In a *present* condition not contrary to fact, either the indicative or the subjunctive mood may be used. The indicative is the more common form.

> Right: If that *is* (or *be*) the case, he will come.
> Right: If the train *is* (or *be*) late, he will not be at the meeting.

2. In a *past* condition not contrary to fact, the indicative mood is used.

> Right: If he *was* tardy, he must take the consequences (perhaps he was tardy—perhaps not).

b. In Wishes and After *As If* (*As Though*). 1. In wishes and after *as if* or *as though*, the past subjunctive is used when the time indicated in the subordinate clause is the same as, or later than, that expressed by the main verb.

> Right: I wish (now) that he *were* here (now)—(not *was*).
>
> Right: I wished (yesterday) that he *were* here (yesterday).
>
> Right: He acts as if he *were* ill (now)—(not *is* or *was*).
>
> Right: He acts (now) as if he *were* going to be ill (tomorrow)—(not *is* or *was*).
>
> Right: He acted (yesterday) as if he *were* ill (yesterday)—(not *was*).

Here, as in a above, *were* and *was* are the only verbs that cause trouble.

2. The past perfect subjunctive is used when the time indicated in the subordinate clause is earlier than that expressed by the main verb.

> Right: I wish (now) that he *had been* here (yesterday).
>
> Right: I wished (yesterday) that he *had been* here (before yesterday).
>
> Right: He acts (now) as if he *had been* ill (yesterday).
>
> Right: He acted (yesterday) as if he *had been* ill (before yesterday).

c. With Words Expressing Command, Necessity, etc. With words expressing command, necessity, and the like, either the subjunctive form is used, or a verb-phrase containing the auxiliary *shall* or *should* is substituted for it. The indicative mood should not be used.

> Right: It is necessary that the work *be* (or *shall be*) finished before we leave (not *is*).
>
> Right: The judge commanded that the prisoner *be* (or *should be*) brought into court.
>
> Right: It is essential that the operator *make* (or *shall make*) the connections quickly and accurately (not *makes*).

Exercises in Section C 8

A. Supply the proper form of the verb, and tell why that form is correct.

1. He spoke as if he .... in a daze (was, were).

2. If the story .... shorter, the editor might publish it (was, were).

3. If he .... uncertain about the time of the meeting, he should have asked me (was, were).

4. The instructor asked that all papers .... handed in on time (be, are).

5. I wish that your writing .... more legible (was, were).

6. I wish that I .... in Washington when Lincoln was President (was, were, had been).

7. When I read your letter, I wished that it .... longer (was, were, had been).

8. If it .... not so late, you could meet them at the station (was, were, had been).

9. If the book .... published last year, it would have had a larger sale (was, were, had been).

10. If she .... at home, why did she refuse to see you? (was, were).

11. He demanded that his name .... stricken from the record (be, was, should be).

12. If I .... the President, I would ask Congress to repeal this undemocratic law (was, were).

13. He watched the prisoners carefully, as if he .... expecting them to try to escape (was, were, had been).

14. He watched them carefully, as if he .... warned that they would try to escape (was, were, had been).

15. He talks as if he .... angry (is, was, were).

16. She looks as if she .... studying too hard (was, were, had been).

17. She spoke as if she .... meeting him for the first time (were, was, had been).

B. Explain the difference in meaning in the following pairs of correct sentences:

18. If he is in trouble, he will write.
If he were in trouble, he would write.

19. If he was in trouble, he should have written.
    If he had been in trouble, he would have written.
20. I wished that the sermon were shorter.
    I wish that the sermon were shorter.

SHALL, WILL, SHOULD, WOULD

C9. **Distinguish between** *shall* **and** *will*, *should* **and** *would*.

In colloquial English the tendency is to discard *shall* and *should* and to use *will* and *would* instead of them, regardless of distinctions in meaning. Some of the distinctions, however, are worth preserving.

a. Simple Futurity. To express simple futurity—the idea that something is expected to occur—*shall* or *should* is used with the first person: *I* and *we; will* or *would* is used with the second and third persons: *he, she, it, you, they, man,* etc.

I shall (should)	We shall (should)
You will (would)	You will (would)
He will (would)	They will (would)

Right: I *shall* be late.
Right: You *will* be late.
Right: We *should* like to see you.
Right: They *would* like to see you.
Right: I *shall* drown; he *will* not help me.

b. Determination. To express determination, a promise, a command, etc., on the part of the speaker, *will* is used with the first person; *shall* is used with the second and third persons.

Right: We *will* go in spite of that.
Right: I *will* not speak to her.
Right: He *shall* go with me.
Right: You *shall* not speak to her.
Right: I *will* drown; he *shall* not help me.

To express strong determination on the part of the doer of the action, *will* or *would* is used with all persons.

Right: I (you, she) *will* persist in talking, in spite of the warning.

Right: I (you, she) *would* go, although the danger was obvious.

Exercise

Supply the proper form of the verb. Tell why it is correct. If both forms might be used, explain the difference in meaning.

1. I .... be surprised if he wins (shall, will).
2. I .... not take "No" for an answer.
3. We hope that we .... hear more by noon.
4. We promise that we .... repay the money.
5. All right, I .... do it, since you insist.
6. We .... be expecting you tomorrow.
7. She .... be expecting you tomorrow.
8. You .... not pay for my dinner.
9. They .... not play in my yard if I can prevent them.
10. We .... not be sorry when school is out.
11. I .... never do anything so silly as that again.
12. I .... be glad to see you again.
13. I .... not consent to do that.
14. They .... not consent to do that.
15. I .... think that they .... want to go (would, should).
16. We .... go today if we could.
17. I .... like to have a copy of the book.
18. He .... like to have a copy of the book.
19. You surely don't think that I .... deceive you.
20. I .... say that he is not more than twenty years old.

c. Questions. In a question, the form that is expected in the answer is used.

Right: *Shall* I come? (You *shall* come.)
Right: *Will* I see him? (You *will* see him.)

Right: *Will* you do that? (I *will* do it.)
Right: *Shall* he get the book? (He *shall* get it.)
Right: *Will* he get the book? (He *will* get it.)
Right: *Should* he bring it? (He *should* bring it.)
Right: *Would* he bring it? (He *would* bring it.)

d. Habitual Action. For expressing habitual or customary action, *would* is used in all persons.

Right: Every morning I (you, she) *would* walk two miles to work.

e. Obligation or Duty. For expressing obligation or duty, *should* is used in all persons.

Right: I (you, she) *should* go to class more regularly.

Exercise

What is the difference in meaning in the following pairs of sentences?

1. Shall he write the letter?
   Will he write the letter?
2. Shall I find his name in the directory?
   Will I find his name in the directory?
3. Shall they go by train or by bus?
   Will they go by train or by bus?
4. Would you pay so much for a coat?
   Should you pay so much for a coat?
5. Would he go even if he could?
   Should he go even if he could?
6. Before each class I would review the previous lesson.
   Before each class I should review the previous lesson.
7. We would not give him the money.
   We should not give him the money.
8. I shall see him next week.
   I will see him next week.
9. He will not sell the book.
   He shall not sell the book.
10. I shall not take any more of your time.
    He shall not take any more of your time.

ADJECTIVES AND ADVERBS

C10. Do not confuse adjectives and adverbs.

a. An Adjective for an Adverb. An adjective should not be used for an adverb.

Wrong: This machine for bending wood works very *satisfactory*.

Right: This machine for bending wood works very *satisfactorily*.

Wrong: A heavy gas diffuses *slower* than a light gas.

Right: A heavy gas diffuses *more slowly* than a light gas.

Frequent mistakes are made in the use of the following words:

ADJECTIVE	ADVERB
good	well
bad	badly
real	really, very
previous to	(previously to), before
some	somewhat, a little
sure	surely

Right: He can write as *well* as you can (not *good*).

Right: The boys behaved very *badly* at the meeting (not *bad*).

Right: I feel *very* happy over the election (not *real* happy—see page 273).

Right: The injured man is *somewhat* better today (not *some*. *Some* used as an adverb is a colloquialism—see page 274).

Right: He walks a *little* every day (not *some*).

Right: *Before* the election, the candidate made some promises (not *previous to* the election—see page 273).

Note. *Well* is in correct use as an adjective in sentences like "The sick boy is almost *well*."

In certain brief commands the short form of the adverb may be correctly used instead of the form ending in *-ly*.

Right: Drive *slow*. Come *quick*.

Slow and *quick* are legitimate adverbial forms (see the dictionary), and are not to be regarded as adjectives in sentences of this sort. When the comparatively weak syllable *-ly* is omitted, the command has a stronger ending and is thus more emphatic. Notice that when an emphatic command is not expressed, the regular form is used.

Right: They drove *slowly* down the street (not *slow*).
Right: He came *quickly* when he heard the outcry (not *quick*).

b. Adverb or Predicate Adjective. After certain verbs such as *smell, look, taste, feel, sound, stand, sit,* and the like, an adjective is used if the modifier describes the subject; an adverb, if it shows the manner in which the action indicated by the verb is performed.

Right: The prisoner looked *sullen* (describes the subject).
Right: The prisoner looked *sullenly* at the floor (shows the manner in which he looked at the floor).
Right: The troops stood *firm* as the enemy approached (describes the condition or attitude of the troops).
Right: In addressing the ball, the golfer should stand *firmly* on both feet (shows the manner of standing).

Notice the correct use of the adjective in the following examples:

Right: The rose smells *sweet* (not *sweetly*).
Right: His voice sounded *shrill* (not *shrilly*).
Right: This peach tastes *bitter* (not *bitterly*).
Right: The cake looks *good*.
Right: The audience sat *silent* for a moment.

Note. In some instances either an adjective or an adverb may be used, with little difference in meaning: for example, "The moon is shining *bright*," or "The moon is shining *brightly*." The former emphasizes the appearance of the moon; the latter, the manner of its shining.

Exercise in Section C 10

Use the correct form—adjective or adverb; explain why that form is correct.

1. The price of the stock remained .... during the week (steady, steadily).

2. He is rather slow, but he keeps at his work .... all day long (steady, steadily).

3. The machine is as .... perfect as human hands can make it (near, nearly).

4. The artificial grapes looked .... enough to eat (good, well).

5. He didn't feel so .... after the accident (good, well).

6. The radio never sounds so .... during a storm (good, well).

7. The house will look .... after it is painted (different, differently).

8. I could do the work .... in half the time (easy, easily).

9. His voice sounded .... when he spoke to her (harsh, harshly).

10. The patient is .... better (somewhat, some).

11. The senator emerged .... from his conference with the governor (smiling, smilingly).

12. He is dressed .... enough, but his clothes are threadbare (neat, neatly).

13. Farmers can get to town .... than they could in the horse and buggy days (quicker, more quickly).

14. She goes to church .... every Sunday (regular, regularly).

15. Time passes .... when we are busy (swifter, more swiftly).

16. Time passes .... when we are busy (faster, more fastly).

17. She felt .... proud of what she had done (very, real, really).

18. The patient has improved .... during the past week (considerable, considerably).

19. They will .... be here in time for dinner (sure, surely).

20. This change made the trip .... for the tourists (easier, more easily).

Exercises in Chapter Four

A. Explain the mistakes, and restate the sentences in correct form.

1. Over the tomb hangs the shield and helmet of the Black Prince.

2. In this instance, who would you recommend for the position?

3. The novel is interesting, but I wish that it was shorter.

4. He would have liked to have finished the book before he returned it.

5. There were only two applicants for the position— Frank Tate and me.

6. If the membership was larger, there would be more diversity of interests.

7. John with two of his friends have gone on a fishing trip to Canada.

8. The urn will look differently after it is cleaned and polished.

9. She could see no reason for her husband being at the office so late.

10. Neither of the contestants were in the proper physical condition to do their best work.

11. He is now out of debt, the final note being paid last April.

12. She has completed the work more than a week ago.

13. The prize will be given to whomever makes the best speech.

14. They believed John and I to be brothers.

15. During their visit to Washington last summer, they have been the guests of Senator Graham.

16. Whom did you think made the best talk last night?

17. There was only a slight difference in age between Frances and I.

18. In the South an almost unlimited supply of natural gas and fuel oil are available.

19. John feels some better today, but not as good as he did last week.

20. If I really tried, I could write as good as him.

B. Follow the instructions given for Exercise A.

1. If he was in your position, he would do as you did.

2. Which one of you boys think you can swim better than her?

3. He is one of the few men in the neighborhood that has kept his land free from mortgage.

4. He promised that he will pay the debt by the first of next month.

5. The book's title was suggested by an incident in the author's own childhood.

6. Every railroad, bus line, and steamship company in the western states are affected by this ruling.

7. All of we seniors are invited to the dean's reception.

8. There was no place for he and his family to live during the summer.

9. I have not heard from him after he left home in June.

10. I would like to see the play once more, and then I will be satisfied.

11. Mary is not as tall as her brother though she is a year older than him.

12. The family was destitute, the father being without work for a year.

13. Sometimes in the winter I wish that our house was not so near the ocean.

14. Where is the hat and coat that you wore yesterday?

15. Do either of the boys want to go to the theater with me tonight?

16. After dinner he said, "Mary, let's you and I go for a ride in the launch."

17. The man whom we thought was a stranger proved to be an artist whom I met in Paris.

18. He is a prolific writer, and he has published two novels last year.

19. Some of we older members should be present at the meeting.

20. The cloud came up very sudden in the west.

Exercises in Words

A. The following words are often confused because of their similarity in form. Look them up in the dictionary, and use them in sentences.

artisan, artist	amend, emend	principal, principle
dual, duel	hung, hanged	stationary, stationery
rhyme, rhythm	overlook, look over	persecute, prosecute

B. Look up these words in the dictionary; use them in sentences; make yourself use them in your writing.

temerity	fallacious	innovation	adept
decrepit	fortitude	virulent	demur
disparage	ominous	vociferous	devious

C. Learn the second five pairs of synonyms on page 288, and use them in sentences.

Chapter Five

THE SENTENCE – ITS THOUGHT CONTENT

A sentence is a group of words which express a single, complete thought.

The larger units—not single words—which make up a sentence are Main (or Co-ordinate) Clauses, Subordinate Clauses, and Phrases.

Clauses and Phrases

A **Main Clause,** as the name implies, is the clause which makes the main statement in a sentence.

He will come when the work is finished.

In the simplest form of a sentence, the main clause is the complete sentence.

His father is a lawyer.

Two or more main clauses in the same sentence are called Co-ordinate Clauses: that is, clauses of equal rank.

The lightning flashed and *the thunder roared.*

A **Subordinate Clause** is a group of words which has a subject and a verb, but which is dependent upon a main clause: that is, it cannot stand by itself and "make sense."

If you will go with me.
That the plan was successful.
Which shaded the house.

To make a complete statement, a subordinate clause must be combined with a main clause.

If you will go with me, we will drive to town.
We thought *that the plan was successful.*
The tree *which shaded the house* was blown down.

A **Phrase** is a group of words which does not have a subject and a verb, and which, like a subordinate clause, is dependent on a main clause.

After the game.
Seeing the danger.
To find a substitute.

To make a complete statement, a phrase must be combined with a main clause.

After the game, our team disbanded.
Seeing the danger, the driver stopped.
He was trying *to find a substitute.*

A phrase consists of an introductory word—a preposition, a participle, a gerund, or an infinitive—plus an object and whatever modifiers may be present. Phrases are called Prepositional Phrases, Participial Phrases, Gerundive Phrases, or Infinitive Phrases—according to the nature of the introductory word.

For a further discussion of clauses and phrases, see Sec. **D 7.**

Classification of Sentences

According to the way in which clauses are combined, sentences are classified as Simple Sentences, Complex Sentences, and Compound Sentences.

A **Simple Sentence** contains only one clause, which is, of course, a main clause.

The clock was striking nine.

A simple sentence may have a compound subject or a compound predicate, or both.

They *came* before noon and *stayed* until midnight.
John and *Harry came* and *brought* the paper.

A **Complex Sentence** contains one main clause and one or more subordinate clauses.

The clock was striking nine | as we entered the station.

A **Compound Sentence** contains two or more main clauses (these are called co-ordinate clauses).

The clock was striking nine | and the train had already left.

A compound sentence may also contain any number of subordinate clauses. It may then be called a **Compound-Complex Sentence.**

The clock was striking nine | as we entered the station, | and the train had already left.

Exercise

Point out the main clauses, subordinate clauses, and phrases in the following sentences. Classify each sentence as simple, complex, or compound.

1. This is a vital question which concerns every American citizen.
2. The town was crowded with refugees who wanted to get passage on the first steamer to America.
3. The gray lines of cadets marched up the street, keeping perfect time to the music.
4. The windows were broken, and the door was hanging by one hinge.
5. For two hours we listened to the lecture and took copious notes.
6. The building, when it is completed, will cover a solid block.

7. It was still raining, but the clouds were breaking in the west.

8. If the rain continues much longer, the fields will be flooded.

9. Wherever we went, we found crowds of people, but they seemed sullen and depressed.

10. We thought that they would go to Florida before the cold weather began.

11. We thought that they would go to Florida before the beginning of winter.

12. The artist painting the picture studied with Du Bois in Paris.

13. The artist who is painting the picture studied with Du Bois in Paris.

14. A desire to see his old home once more was responsible for his unexpected trip to Ireland.

15. We drove to Detroit, and there we took passage on a lake boat to Buffalo.

16. We drove to Detroit and then took passage on a lake boat to Buffalo.

17. We drove to Detroit, where we took passage on a lake boat to Buffalo.

18. Women and children were running and screaming in the street.

19. Women were running and children were screaming in the street.

20. At our next class meeting, we shall have an examination on the first three chapters in our textbook.

COMPLETENESS OF THOUGHT AND GRAMMATICAL CONSTRUCTION

By definition, as we have seen, a sentence should express a complete thought. Completeness of thought also implies completeness of grammatical construction. As a general rule, the two are inseparable.

The requirements of a complete sentence, therefore, are:

1. It should contain a statement that will stand by itself and "make sense."

2. It should have a subject and a verb.

Note. The subject and the verb are regularly omitted in certain elliptical constructions—like "Yes," "Of course," and similar expressions—when the missing elements can be readily supplied from the context. These elliptical constructions are especially common in conversation.

Will you go? *Yes.*
When did you come? *Last Saturday.*

A Subordinate Clause or a Phrase Punctuated as a Sentence

D1. A subordinate clause or a phrase should not be punctuated as a sentence.

A subordinate clause has a subject and a verb, but it does not make a complete statement: it is dependent upon a main clause. It therefore lacks one of the requirements of a complete sentence (see (1) and (2) above).

A phrase does not have a subject or a verb, and it does not express a complete thought. It lacks both requirements of a sentence.

Instead of being punctuated as a separate sentence, the dependent group should ordinarily be combined with the preceding one. A small letter and a comma or other appropriate mark of punctuation are used instead of a capital letter and a period. Sometimes it is preferable to recast the fragment into a separate, complete sentence.

Subordinate Clauses Misused as Sentences:

Not Good: He was the author of a number of books on folk customs. Each of which represented years of research among the native tribes in Africa.

Improved: He was the author of a number of books on folk customs, each of which represented years of research among the native tribes in Africa. (Or)

Improved: He was the author of a number of books on folk customs. Each of *these* represented years of research among the native tribes in Africa.

Not Good: Our report was handed to the president last evening. Although it was not due until noon today.
Improved: Our report was handed to the president last evening, although it was not due until noon today.

Not Good: The coat was priced at eighty dollars. Which was more than I wanted to pay.
Improved: The coat was priced at eighty dollars, which was more than I wanted to pay.

Not Good: We were told that there had been a wreck on the main line. And that the train would be four hours late.
Improved: We were told that there had been a wreck on the main line, and that the train would be four hours late.

Phrases Misused as Sentences:

Not Good: During the past month employment has been increasing. Especially in the textile mills of New England.
Improved: During the past month employment has been increasing, especially in the textile mills of New England.

Not Good: The mayor lives in the first house on the right. The one with the stone gateway in front.
Improved: The mayor lives in the first house on the right—the one with the stone gateway in front.

Not Good: We set out at four o'clock in the morning. Our destination being Augusta, six hundred miles to the south.
Improved: We set out at four o'clock in the morning, our destination being Augusta, six hundred miles to the south.

Not Good: In the afternoon we caught five bass. The largest one weighing four pounds.
Improved: In the afternoon we caught five bass, the largest one weighing four pounds.

A participial phrase is especially likely to be misused as a sentence (as in the last two examples above). Since the participle is a form of a verb, the careless writer assumes that the phrase is a complete sentence. A participle, however, is never used as a finite verb to make a predicate (see pages 87, 166).

Note. An incomplete sentence is sometimes employed by good writers to secure certain effects. No one should attempt to use this construction, however, until he has mastered the conception of a sentence as a complete unit. Then it is safe for him to deviate from the standard form occasionally, if he has a good reason for doing so.

A Co-ordinate Clause Punctuated as a Sentence

D2. **As a general rule, a co-ordinate clause beginning with *and*, *but*, or *or* should not be punctuated as a separate sentence.**

Questionable: The story that the man told seemed plausible. But there was something in his manner that made us hesitate.

Improved: The story that the man told seemed plausible, but there was something in his manner that made us hesitate.

Questionable: He had a definite purpose in view. And all our efforts to change his opinion were futile.

Improved: He had a definite purpose in view, and all our efforts to change his opinion were futile.

This construction is not always objectionable. The best of writers sometimes begin a sentence with a co-ordinating conjunction in order to make a smooth, informal transition or to give a touch of colloquial ease. It should be remembered, however, that *and, but,* and *or* are primarily to be used for connecting like elements within a sentence. They are not to be employed to excess—or without good reason—between separate sentences.

Short, Choppy Sentences

D3. A thought which logically belongs in one sentence should not be put into two or more short, choppy sentences.

To remedy this fault, it is usually not sufficient to combine the fragments into a single sentence by connecting them with *and* or *but*. In most cases one or more of them will need to be subordinated.

Choppy: The tinder must be some soft, inflammable material. This may be dry grass, leaves, or wood shavings.

Improved: The tinder must be some soft, inflammable material, such as dry grass, leaves, or wood shavings.

Choppy: This mill is merely a steel tube, five feet in diameter and twenty feet long. It contains many thousand flint stones.

Improved: This mill is merely a steel tube, five feet in diameter and twenty feet long, which contains many thousand flint stones.

Choppy: Our ship was at the mercy of the waves. She was being pounded to pieces on the rocky reef.

Improved: Our ship was at the mercy of the waves, which were pounding her to pieces on the rocky reef.

A Series of Choppy Sentences. Especially to be avoided are a number of short, choppy sentences in a series.

When these are combined, care should be taken that each of the longer sentences thus formed contains only ideas which are related in thought. There will be as many sentences as there are distinct groups of thought in the series. For example, in the following "improved" passage the two divisions of the process—bringing the logs to the carriage and moving them to the saw—are described in two separate sentences:

Choppy: The logs are fastened to a chain running up an incline. When they reach the floor of the mill they are rolled onto the carriage. The carriage is about forty feet long by fifteen feet wide. It moves the logs toward the saw after each cut, by means of an automatic feeding device.

Improved: The logs are fastened to a chain and hauled up an incline to the floor of the mill, where they are rolled onto the carriage. The latter is about forty feet long by fifteen feet wide, and is provided with an automatic feeding device by means of which the logs are moved toward the saw after each cut.

Choppy: In those days the motorist wore a linen duster. A pair of huge goggles were also a part of his equipment. Both of these articles were needed as a protection from the dust of the unpaved roads.

Improved: In those days the motorist wore a linen duster and a pair of huge goggles as a protection from the dust of the unpaved roads.

Exercise in Sections D 1–D 3

See that each sentence makes a complete statement, and that a thought is not unnecessarily split into two or more short sentences. Be sure that each group of words punctuated as a sentence has a subject and a verb. State the fault definitely, and then make the correction.

1. They sailed on Monday for a week's visit in Naples. After which they will make an extended trip through Greece.

2. He was almost eighty years old. But he still did his share of work on the farm.

3. It was cold on the lake that afternoon. The wind being in the north and blowing a stiff gale.

4. *David Copperfield* was written by Charles Dickens. It is one of his earlier works. This story is autobiographical in many of its details. From it the reader gets a graphic picture of the author's struggles as a boy in London.

5. You will enjoy a week or two spent at this camp. Especially if you enjoy hiking and fishing.

6. In the final game of the season we defeated Rayburn College. The score being 7 to 6, which, however, did not indicate our real superiority.

7. Near the village park is a historic inn. It was built in 1700. In revolutionary times it was the headquarters of General Gage.

8. During the night the river had overflowed its banks. And by noon of the next day the first floors of houses in the lower part of town were under water.

9. Last evening we were at Music Hall. Here we listened to a concert by Alma Sabin. She is a local girl who has just returned from Europe. There she had made a great reputation for herself as a singer.

10. He has written two books on the Spanish revolution. Each of them describing his experiences as a war correspondent with the loyalist troops.

11. We were not allowed to write to our parents in America. Or even to cable them that we were safe.

12. Latin was difficult for me. But my father wanted me to take four years of it. He thought that it would help me in my English.

13. We went by boat from St. Louis to New Orleans. A trip we had often thought of taking.

14. Our camp site was picturesque and fairly pleasant. Although at night the mosquitoes were too numerous for real comfort.

15. He was a man without principle or honor. A man who would betray his own father.

16. He had failed in most of his business ventures. Not because he lacked ability but because his judgment was faulty.

17. The best time for swimming is in the morning. Preferably before breakfast if the water is not too cold.

18. A strong wind was blowing from the north. And the waves were beating against the pier in front of the cabin.

19. The shopkeeper receives half of the proceeds from the slot machine. The remainder being the "take" which goes to the syndicate owning the machine.

20. The next year taxes were doubled and orders dwindled to almost nothing. As a result of which he closed the factory and began looking for a job.

SINGLENESS OF THOUGHT

In preceding sections we have considered the sentence as a unit which expresses a *complete* thought. The converse of that principle is that a sentence should contain only a *single* thought, and each part should contribute to the development of that thought.

Unrelated Thoughts in a Sentence

D4. Thoughts which are not logically related to each other should not be put in the same sentence.

Not Good: The Mississippi River was discovered by DeSoto in 1541, and its source is in Minnesota.

Not Good: The first speaker wore a gray coat, and he delighted in flights of oratory.

The obvious remedy for this fault is to make a separate sentence for each thought. In some cases it may be necessary to add other relevant material to one group or to both, in order to avoid short, choppy sentences.

Improved: The Mississippi River was discovered by DeSoto in 1541. Its source is in Minnesota (followed by additional facts about the source).

Improved: The first speaker wore a gray coat (additional details of his appearance). He delighted in flights of oratory (other facts about his manner of speaking).

Sometimes two statements which are not closely related in thought may be retained in the same sentence if one of them is made subordinate: that is, made into a subordinate clause or a phrase instead of a main clause.

This combination is permissible only when the subordinated element is so unobtrusive that it does not arouse a feeling of incongruity.

> Questionable: The book was published in New York, and it gives a brief account of our early political institutions.

> Improved: The book, which was published in New York, gives a brief account of our early political institutions.

An idea which is conspicuously foreign to the main thought should not be included in a sentence, even in a subordinate relation.

> Wrong: After a hard fight, the murderer was arrested by Sheriff Adams, who is a prominent member of the First Baptist Church at Harrisburg.

Long, Rambling Sentences

D5. Especially to be avoided are long, loose sentences which ramble from one thought to another.

> Rambling: At the beginning of the first semester, each member of the club receives a printed schedule of the events, usually one every two weeks, that are to take place during the year, and held, with the exception of the banquet and dance, in the club room, located on the fourth floor, which is well furnished with a piano, magazines, games, and other conveniences.

> Improved (Divided, and Amplified to Avoid Choppy Sentences): At the beginning of the first semester, each member of the club receives a printed schedule of the events that are to take place during the year. These include smokers, ladies' nights, and other social affairs, which occur on an average once in two weeks, as well as a banquet and dance which concludes the program of the year. Most of these affairs are held in the club room, since this is centrally located and is furnished with a piano, games, and other conveniences needed for an evening's entertainment. The annual banquet and dinner is given in one of the large hotels of the city, etc.

Improper Division and Combination of Thoughts

D6. A thought should not be so divided that it is partly in one sentence and partly in another sentence which also contains a different thought. The related ideas should be kept together.

Not Good: The book is handsomely bound in blue leather, with a modernistic design stamped in gold, and it contains over a hundred illustrations. Some of these are reproductions of original etchings by Donaldson.

Improved: The book is handsomely bound in blue leather, with a modernistic design stamped in gold. It contains over a hundred illustrations, some of which are reproductions of original etchings by Donaldson. (Original division: 1. Binding and illustrations. 2. Illustrations. Improved division: 1. Binding. 2. Illustrations.)

Exercises in Sections D 4–D 6

A. Do these sentences contain unrelated or remotely connected thoughts? Are they loose and rambling? Are any thoughts illogically separated and combined? Point out the faults; then restate the sentences correctly.

1. He was a staunch Republican, and he has many friends throughout the city.

2. There are two boys in the family, one of whom is a freshman in Columbia. The other is working in his father's law office.

3. He is said to be somewhat eccentric, and he lives with his wife in Chicago.

4. The city, which is in the center of what was once a rich mining district, is built on a high bluff overlooking the Mississippi River, which is half a mile wide at this point, and the streets are very steep and difficult to drive on, especially when they are covered with ice as they are likely to be in this

part of the country where the thermometer often registers twenty degrees below zero.

5. The instructor had assigned two books for us to read, one of which was in German. The other was written in Spanish, and as I could not read either language I was in a quandary.

6. Mark Twain was a humorist, and he wrote a life of Joan of Arc.

7. It was a typical dude ranch, owned by a jolly Englishman by the name of Barclay, whose father, the son of an English nobleman, had come to America when a young man to make his fortune and after a series of misadventures in the East had drifted to western Canada.

8. This little lake is full of rare aquatic plants and it is located in a swamp or bog. It is a favorite spot for botanists and other people interested in nature study.

9. Prentice, the county seat located on the Red River, is a city of about ten thousand inhabitants, which is in the center of a farming community whose chief product is the soy bean which in recent years has become important commercially and industrially and promises to be an economical substitute for some of the rare products formerly imported from the Orient.

10. He was born in Springfield, where he obtained his education in the public schools, after which he entered Harvard. He was graduated from that school with a B.A. degree after taking the pre-medical course and then enrolled in Johns Hopkins where he specialized in surgery which was his major interest in his later practice until he became the dean of the medical school in a western university, a position which necessitated his giving up active work in that field.

B. In each of the following pairs of sentences, which is the better one from the standpoint of unity? Why?

1. The road was lined with poplar trees and we could make seventy miles an hour on it.
   The road was straight and well paved, and we could make seventy miles an hour on it.

2. Kipling, the English author, married an American, and for a time they lived on a farm in Vermont.

Kipling, the English author, married an American, and he wrote the *Jungle Book*.
3. The wind is in the south, and we should go home.
   The wind is in the south, and we should have warmer weather.
4. The letter was typewritten and he looked at it curiously.
   The letter was written in a scrawling feminine hand, and he looked at it curiously.
5. Two of the workmen were injured, but the third, who was more agile, escaped unharmed.
   Two of the workmen were injured, but the third, who was Irish, escaped unharmed.

CO–ORDINATION AND SUBOR–DINATION: MAKING THE MAIN IDEA PROMINENT

We have seen that a sentence should express a complete thought and contain only a single thought. A third requirement is that this thought shall stand out in the proper perspective—with the most important idea featured most prominently and the less important details placed in the background. This result is secured primarily by the correct co-ordination and subordination of the different elements.

The elements with which we are chiefly concerned in the present discussion are main or co-ordinate clauses, subordinate clauses, and phrases.

Co-ordinate and Subordinate Elements

D7. **A careful distinction must be made between co-ordinate and subordinate elements.**

a. Co-ordinate Clauses. The chief kinds of relation existing between co-ordinate clauses are:

1. **Harmony**—a continuation of the same line of thought.

> The work was interesting, *and* the results should be valuable for future reference.
>
> Everyone must be at his desk by 8:55 A.M.; *moreover,* he must be ready to start work promptly at nine o'clock.
>
> Every bolt is in place; the last nail has been driven.

The principal connectives for this group are *and, likewise, moreover, furthermore, in like manner, besides, also,* etc. The connective is sometimes omitted.

Specific Examples and Explanations. The *harmony* group includes a subclass consisting of sentences in which a general statement is followed by a specific example or a specific explanation.

> The employees are well paid: *for example,* an unskilled laborer receives four dollars a day.
>
> This is a rare phenomenon: only two other instances of a similar occurrence are on record.

Sometimes the clauses are connected by *for example, for instance, thus,* or similar expressions. In other cases, a connective is not used. The punctuation is a colon.

2. **Contrast**—a change in the line of thought.

> The summers are pleasant, *but* the winters are bleak and monotonous.
>
> He promised to be here at four o'clock; *however,* it was midnight when he arrived.
>
> John likes to study; Harry despises books.

The principal conjunctions are *but, nevertheless, however, yet, on the contrary, on the other hand,* etc. The conjunction is sometimes omitted.

3. **Alternation or choice.**

> The entire amount must be paid by Saturday, *or* the payments previously made will be forfeited.
>
> *Either* the money was misplaced, *or* it has been stolen.

The principal connectives are *or, nor* (negative), *either—or, neither—nor,* and *otherwise.*

4. Consequence or inference.

> The sun has been shining all day; *consequently* the streets are dry.
> Our neighbors have not been at home for a week; *therefore* they are probably out of town.

The principal connectives are *therefore, consequently, hence, so, accordingly, thus, as a result,* and *for this reason.*

Exercise

Complete the following parts of sentences by adding co-ordinate clauses which show the type of relation indicated:

1. The wind was blowing a gale .... (consequence).
2. The house was burned to the ground .... (contrast).
3. Our football team must improve in blocking and tackling .... (alternation).
4. He had not prepared for the examination .... (consequence).
5. A few of the houses are in the middle price range .... (*a.* specific example; *b.* contrast; *c.* same line of thought—a separate sentence for each).

b. Subordinate Clauses and Phrases. Subordinate clauses and phrases perform the functions of single parts of speech: that is, they are used as (1) nouns, (2) adjectives, or (3) adverbs.

1. Used as a Noun—generally as the subject of a verb, predicate noun, object of a verb, or object of a preposition.

> *What he will do* is uncertain (subject of verb).
> *That he had failed* was not generally known.
> *To do this work well* required concentration.

Reading the book took an hour.
The fact is *that you were late* (predicate noun).
Her ambition was *to become an opera singer*.
His hobby is *collecting butterflies*.
They know *what they want* (object of verb).
He wants *to see you tomorrow*.
She enjoys *writing long letters*.
They object to *whatever we do* (object of preposition).
He was arrested for *stealing a chicken*.

The chief connectives for noun clauses are *that, what, whatever, whether,* etc.

2. **Used as an Adjective**—to modify a noun or a pronoun.

I paid the man *who did the work*.
The farm *which he bought* has doubled in value.
This is the house *where the fire started*.
The man *driving the car* was injured.
He had no desire *to buy a home*.
All members *of the society* are invited.

The majority of adjective clauses are introduced by the relative pronouns *who, which,* and *that;* some by conjunctive adverbs like *where, when, why,* etc. (These conjunctive adverbs may also introduce adverbial clauses.)

3. **Used as Adverbs**—to modify a verb, adjective, or another adverb. The chief adverbial relations expressed by subordinate clauses and phrases are:

a. Time: Adverbs of time answer the question *When?*

He will go *when the meeting is adjourned*.
After his bills were paid, he had a little money left.
You must be there *before midnight*.

b. Place: Adverbs of place answer the question *Where?*

He lives *wherever he can find work*.
You will find the book *where you left it*.
He lives *in Brooklyn*.

c. Manner: Adverbs of manner answer the question *How?*

> She walks *as if she were tired.*
> They did the work *as they were directed.*
> We made the journey *by easy stages.*

d. Degree: Adverbs of degree answer the questions *How much? How far?* (and other similar combinations of *How* not included under Manner).

> I value your help more *than you realize.*
> A man is as old *as he feels.*
> He was too tired *to study his Latin.*

e. Reason or cause: Adverbs of reason or cause answer the question *Why?*

> *As the roads were muddy,* we made slow progress.
> The report was rejected *because it was indefinite.*
> The man was arrested *for treason.*

f. Purpose: Adverbs expressing purpose, like those showing reason, answer the question *Why?* The distinguishing feature between the two classes is that a purpose clause carries the idea that the action was definitely planned beforehand with a particular purpose in view.

> Men work *that they may eat.*
> He came early *so that he might leave early.*
> They have gone to the library *to get a book.*

g. Condition: Adverbial clauses expressing condition are introduced by *if* or some other expression for which *if* can be substituted (*provided that, on condition that,* etc.).

> *If you decide to come,* please write to us at once.
> You may go, *provided it does not rain.*

h. Concession: Adverbial clauses expressing concession are introduced by *although* or some equivalent connective, such as *though, even if,* etc.

Although our first attempt failed, we were not discouraged.

The constitution will be adopted *even if the president disapproves.*

i. Modifiers of certain adjectives: Adverbial clauses and phrases are also used to modify certain adjectives like *sure, sorry, certain, afraid,* etc.

They were sure *that you would come.*
He was certain *that the plan would fail.*
She is afraid *of the dark.*
He was eager *to work.*

Exercises

A. Make sentences in which the following clauses and phrases are used as indicated (a separate sentence for each use):

1. That he will be elected (*a.* subject of a verb; *b.* object of a verb).

2. What you said about the plan (*a.* object of a preposition; *b.* predicate noun).

3. Which you like best (*a.* adjective; *b.* object of a verb).

4. Crossing the bridge (*a.* adjective; *b.* subject of a verb; *c.* object of a verb; *d.* object of a preposition).

5. To find the purse (*a.* subject of a verb; *b.* object of a verb; *c.* predicate noun; *d.* adjective; *e.* adverb).

B. Complete the following parts of sentences by adding subordinate clauses or phrases which show the type of relation indicated:

1. I was late for class .... (reason).

2. .... you may go to the ball game this afternoon (condition).

3. The speaker acted .... (manner).

4. A mammoth office building then stood .... (place).

5. ...., there was a burst of applause (time).

6. The next day, ..., we drove over six hundred miles (concession).

7. He talked slowly .... (purpose).

8. He walked faster .... (*a.* reason; *b.* time—a separate sentence for each).

9. They are living .... (*a.* place; *b.* manner—a separate sentence for each).

10. ...., you can finish the work by noon (*a.* condition; *b.* concession).

c. General Principle Governing Co-ordination and Subordination. The general principle governing co-ordination and subordination of the parts in a sentence is as follows:

Main ideas are to be placed in main clauses; less important ideas in subordinate clauses or in phrases.

By the proper application of this principle, three results are obtained:

1. The important statements are made to stand out prominently.

2. The sentence is made more compact.

3. The monotonous repetition of the co-ordinate connectives *and* and *but* is avoided.

The following sections contain specific applications of the general principle.

Awkward and Unemphatic Co-ordination

D8. Do not make a statement co-ordinate, if subordinating it will make the sentence smoother, more compact, or more emphatic.

Awkward: At the club he met a number of men who greeted him cordially, and he felt that he was among friends.

Improved: At the club he met a number of men whose cordial greetings made him feel that he was among friends.

Awkward: In the evening he came to the house and he wanted to see father.

Improved: In the evening he came to the house to see father.

Awkward: I was walking along the deserted street and a shabbily dressed man spoke to me.

Improved: As I was walking along the deserted street, a shabbily dressed man spoke to me.

Awkward: They lived in a comfortable colonial house and it had once been the home of Governor Talbot.

Improved: They lived in a comfortable colonial house which had once been the home of Governor Talbot.

Unemphatic: This company is the largest importer of diamonds in America, and its headquarters are in New York.

Improved: This company, which is the largest importer of diamonds in America, has its headquarters in New York. (Emphasizes the location of the headquarters.)

Improved: This company, which has its headquarters in New York, is the largest importer of diamonds in America. (Emphasizes the size of the business.)

A Series of Loosely Co-ordinated Statements

D9. **Especially avoid sentences containing a series of loosely co-ordinated statements connected by *and* or *but*.**

The less important ideas should be subordinated.

Not Good: I reached the top of the hill and there I heard a curious throbbing noise, and it sounded like the ringing of a great temple bell in a distant native village.

Improved: When I reached the top of the hill, I heard a curious throbbing noise, which sounded like the ringing of a great temple bell in a distant native village.

Not Good: We finished dinner and then we lounged about the campfire and smoked our pipes, and the guide told us of his adventures as a trapper in the Hudson Bay country.

Improved: After dinner we lounged about the campfire and smoked our pipes, while the guide told us of his adventures as a trapper in the Hudson Bay country.

Not Good: A signal of distress had been sent out and we were waiting for some vessel to answer, and in the meantime the crew lowered the life boats and the passengers got ready to leave the ship if it should begin to sink.

Improved: While we were waiting for some vessel to answer our signal of distress, the crew lowered the life boats, and the passengers got ready to leave the ship if it should begin to sink.

Faulty Subordination of an Important Thought

D10. Do not subordinate the important thought in a sentence, or a statement that is logically co-ordinate with another statement.

This principle is the reverse of the ones discussed in the preceding sections: there the fault consisted in placing a subordinate thought in a main or co-ordinate clause.

The faulty subordination of an important thought occurs frequently in participial phrases and in clauses introduced by *when*.

Not Good: He reached into his pocket, *taking* out a quarter and *tossing* it to the porter.

Improved: Reaching into his pocket, he *took* out a quarter and *tossed* it to the porter.

Not Good: My opponent's ball landed on the green and rolled straight for the flag, *dropping* into the cup with a click which said, "That beats you."

Improved: My opponent's ball *landed* on the green, *rolled* straight for the flag, and *dropped* into the cup with a click which said, "That beats you."

Not Good: We waited for over an hour, *when* we decided to go on without the guide.

Improved: We waited for over an hour, *and then* we decided to go on without the guide. (Or)

Improved: After waiting for over an hour, we decided to go on without the guide.

Exercises in Sections D 8–D 10

A. Is the important idea brought out prominently by proper co-ordination and subordination of the parts of the sentence? Are any statements that might more logically be subordinated expressed in co-ordinate form? Are there too many *and's?* Recast the sentences in the best form possible.

1. These valves are made of iron instead of brass, and they are likely to corrode.

2. A car running through the red light struck a small boy, killing him and speeding away.

3. Cherokee Bill was the leader of the Indians and he was a renegade white.

4. His explanation of the accident was that he was driving down Main Street and another car dashed out from an alley on the right, knocking his car on its side.

5. I got up early the next morning and lifted the flap of the tent, and the air was clear and the sun was bright, and twenty miles away I could see the snow-capped top of Mt. Hood glistening like a huge diamond.

6. He tried to call me three times, when he realized that my telephone was disconnected.

7. A creek ran beside the road and it was filled with ice-cold water.

8. With a supreme effort the two men lifted the crate from the truck, letting it fall to the sidewalk with a crash.

9. The fire was still burning and we decided that the campers had not been gone very long.

10. The chairman was in a hurry to begin the conference and there was a quorum present and so he called the meeting to order.

B. Recast the following sentences. Make one main clause, and subordinate the other parts in clauses, phrases, or perhaps a word or two. Give two or three different versions of the revised sentence.

1. We finished dinner and then we went to the opera.

2. The fog was heavy and the plane could not take off at the scheduled time.

3. Our local agent is Mr. Crosby and he will give you full particulars about our service.

4. *Youth* was written by Joseph Conrad and it is a story of a young man's first visit to the glamorous East.

5. This account was written by a competent observer and it should be authoritative.

6. He must have help or he cannot finish the work on time.

7. It was a cold day and we were almost frozen, but we kept on fishing for we wanted some bass for dinner.

8. The *Mermaid* finished fifth in the race and she was supposed to be the fastest boat on the lake.

9. I was cutting corn in the field, and I saw a black funnel-shaped cloud in the west.

10. He picked up the rock and examined it more closely, and then he saw some glistening particles and these made him think that he had found a gold nugget.

C. Make a single sentence from these fragmentary statements. There is to be one main clause, and the other ideas are to be subordinated in clauses, phrases, or perhaps a word or two.

1. The house has been repainted. It is white. The shutters are green.

2. The president may sign the bill. He may not sign it. It will become a law anyway.

3. Latin was difficult for me. I could not see its value for an engineering student. I decided not to take it.

4. The whole system had broken down. The strain of handling so many passengers was the cause. This was plain.

5. Her husband would start to say something. His wife would interrupt him rudely. This seemed to indicate that she considered his opinions to be of little importance. This happened again and again.

6. The *Claudia* arrived in New York this morning. She is a British freighter. She was two days late. She had been driven from her course by a terrific hurricane.

7. There was a detour from the main highway. This detour was ten miles long. It was over a rough dirt road. We were an hour late for our appointment.

8. The station was crowded with men in uniform. There were soldiers and marines. They were bound for the west coast. There they would be sent to stations in the Far East.

9. She met a young doctor. She met him at the hospital. He was an interne in the hospital. His name was Bancroft.

10. The roads were rough. They were winding. We had to drive at twenty miles an hour or less. We took two hours to make the trip.

The Comma Blunder

D11. A mark of punctuation stronger than a comma is required between co-ordinate clauses that are not connected by *and*, *but*, *or*, or *nor*.

The incorrect use of a comma between co-ordinate clauses not connected by one of these conjunctions is known as a Comma Blunder. This blunder is more serious than an ordinary mistake in punctuation, for it indicates that the writer has failed to recognize the logical relation between the two statements.

In its worst form, the comma blunder consists in the use of a comma between two co-ordinate clauses *which have no connective.*

A comma blunder may be corrected in various ways, the choice depending upon the closeness of relation between the clauses.

1. A semicolon may be substituted for the comma.

2. Two sentences may be made, separated by a period.

3. *And, but, or,* or *nor* may be supplied and the comma retained.

4. One of the statements may be subordinated.

Comma Blunder: The themes are first read by the instructor, they are then returned to the student for revision.

Improved: The themes are first read by the instructor; they are then returned to the student for revision (semicolon). (Or)

Improved: The themes are first read by the instructor. They are then returned to the student for revision (two sentences). (Or)

Improved: The themes are first read by the instructor, and then they are returned to the student for revision (*and,* with a comma). (Or)

Improved: After the themes have been read by the instructor, they are returned to the student for revision (one clause subordinated).

Another form of the comma blunder results from the use of a comma between two main clauses connected by *therefore, however, nevertheless, consequently,* and the like (that is, co-ordinate conjunctions other than *and, but, or,* or *nor*).

Not Good: Our train was late that evening, therefore we were unable to attend the meeting.

Improved: Our train was late that evening; therefore we were unable to attend the meeting. (Or)

Improved: Our train was late that evening, *and* therefore we were unable to attend the meeting. (Or)

Improved: As our train was late that evening, we were unable to attend the meeting.

Not Good: The governor does not approve of the measure, however he will not veto it.

Improved: The governor does not approve of the measure; however, he will not veto it.

Exercise in Section D 11

Give the correct form for the following sentences. Suggest two or three possible forms, and select the one that you think is best.

1. Crowds of country people filled the village streets, they had come to see the parade and do their weekly shopping.

2. We had stayed at the Royal Hotel on a previous visit, therefore we drove to it directly from the station.

3. There was really no need for us to hurry, nevertheless we decided to push on and finish the trip that night.

4. As a boy he liked history and literature, later he became more interested in science and mathematics.

5. A heavy snow had fallen during the night, consequently we could not get to the village for our mail.

6. Most readers know little about the technique of a short story, they are interested only in the emotional reaction they get from it.

7. For three hours he wrote steadily, filling page after page of his examination book, this was his chance to show the instructor that he really knew the subject.

8. They drifted in an open boat two hundred miles to the south, here they found an island inhabited by friendly natives.

9. Colonel Williams had provided three guides for our party, two of these were Indians and the third was a French Canadian.

10. The art of gliding was neglected until 1920, then it was revived in Germany.

Exercises in Chapter Five

A. Point out the faults; then restate the thought correctly.

1. At this rate the lake front could be greatly improved in a few years. The only expense being for dredging and building breakwaters.

2. He will be here Sunday, leaving for New York on Monday.

3. It was only two days before the boat sailed, therefore they had to hurry their preparations.

4. At last five o'clock came and it was time for us to go home, but it was raining and we decided to stay in a downtown hotel for the night.

5. Rip Van Winkle was very lazy and he had a dog named Wolf.

6. The Union Building was finished last spring and it is the favorite gathering place for students.

7. At the far end of the room was a fireplace. Over it was a portrait of Mrs. Adams. It was done in oil by Gilbert Evans. He was one of the early American painters.

8. The Democrats were in power before the election, hence they had a distinct advantage over their opponents.

9. We had walked steadily for three hours and at the end of that time we were very tired and one of the party suggested that we pool our resources and take a taxi to the hotel.

10. The town was crowded with refugees seeking shelter for the night. The flood having driven them from their homes along the river.

11. As the other car got slightly ahead of us, it moved closer, crowding us into the ditch.

12. These associate memberships entitle the holders to all the privileges of the club, including enrollment in the gymnasium classes and free admission to all concerts, four of which will be given this year, beginning in January, by some of the best musical talent in the country.

13. Last summer I spent a week in Washington, this was my first visit to the capital and I enjoyed every minute of my stay.

14. We had visited all the places of historic interest except the Tower. This we had reserved for the last day. It was to be the climax of our stay in London.

15. The book is bound in red leather and it gives an interesting account of the Fascist movement in Italy.

16. During our absence a storm had blown down several large pine trees. One of which had fallen on our cabin, practically demolishing it.

17. Every summer he spent a month on his grandfather's farm, these were the happiest days of the whole year for him.

18. This rod is flexible and yet it is very strong, and that is the reason why I prefer it in fishing for trout.

19. I was all ready to go to class when I remembered that the instructor was ill and would not be there.

20. You should hand in two copies of the outline. Each of them to be in proper form on standard theme paper.

B. Follow the directions under A above.

1. I had just stopped to look at the jeweler's window, when a high-powered car drew up to the curb.

2. He had made two previous attempts to reach the top of the mountain, failing each time by a few hundred feet.

3. At first he refused to sign the petition. For he thought that it was a political scheme devised by the city hall group.

4. The proceeds from the Charity Ball were split two ways. The Red Cross and the Salvation Army each receiving about six hundred dollars.

5. You can make the entire trip by train. Or you can fly to Boston and then drive to your destination in a car.

6. He published a book. It was a novel. It was entitled *Marchmount.* It was published in 1940.

7. We were driving along at seventy miles an hour and came to some loose gravel, and the car skidded and we went into a ditch.

8. The house was too large for our family, therefore we decided to sell it.

9. I had decided to call on him that evening, when I learned that he was not at home.

10. He took the diamond to the bank, putting it in his safe deposit box.

Exercises in Words

A. The following words are often confused because of their similarity in form. Look them up in the dictionary and use them in sentences.

affect, effect (verbs)	loath, loathe	judicial, judicious
compliment, complement	troop, troupe	sensual, sensuous

B. Look up the following words in the dictionary. Use them in sentences, and in your own writing.

pessimist	rancor	premonition	sinister
furtive	tentative	laconic	terse
irascible	tenable	sinecure	whimsical

C. Select any two pages of a good book or magazine. Make two lists of words that you find there:

1. Words which you recognize, but which you yourself do not use.

2. Words which you do not know. Look these up in the dictionary.

Review Exercise in Sentences

The following sentences have faults which were discussed in Chapter Four. Point out the mistakes and correct them.

1. The committee is unwilling to have their names appear on the report.

2. There was never any quarrel between John and I about using the car.

3. If I was a few years younger I would join the marines.

4. I would think that he would be at the office before noon.

5. Each of the witnesses were closely questioned by the lawyers for the defense.

6. You must learn to act quicker in an emergency.

7. The airplane's popularity has increased rapidly during the years before the war.

8. Of course it was him, not me, whom they thought had missed the train.

9. I wish that the school was a little nearer my home.

10. The prices of this article varies considerable in different parts of the country.

Chapter Six

CLEARNESS IN THE SENTENCE

ARRANGEMENT OF THE PARTS OF A SENTENCE

E1. **Related parts of a sentence should not be unnecessarily separated by other elements.**

This principle covers a variety of constructions which are shown in this section and in the succeeding ones.

Not Good: *As the car wound up the narrow road* we found the trees becoming more scattered *as we neared the top of the mountain.* (Two subordinate clauses having the same rank and function are separated.)

Improved: *As the car wound up the narrow road and neared the top of the mountain,* we found the trees becoming more scattered.

Not Good: *The school itself* will be benefited by this change, *as well as the students and the alumni.* (Two parts of the subject are separated.)

Improved: *The school itself, as well as the students and the alumni,* will be benefited by this change.

Not Good: He *discovered,* while rummaging among the papers in an old trunk, *a package of letters* written by his grandfather during the Civil War. (The direct object is unnecessarily separated from the verb.)

Improved: While rummaging among the papers in an old trunk, he *discovered a package of letters* written by his grandfather during the Civil War.

Note. A brief modifier that does not seriously interrupt the thought may be placed between the verb and the direct object.

They *tried* in every way *to effect a settlement.*

Lost Verbs. A verb should not be placed so far from its subject that the relation is not readily seen.

Not Good: In this cabin *an old woman* whom the children of the neighborhood called The Witch, *lived*.

Improved: In this cabin *lived an old woman* whom the children of the neighborhood called The Witch.

Not Good: At the extreme top of the meter, the *dials* which record the amount of electric current that is used, *are placed*.

Improved: At the extreme top of the meter *are placed the dials* which record the amount of electric current that is used.

Position of Modifiers

E2.   A modifier should be placed as near as possible to the word that it modifies.

Difficulty in arrangement is likely to occur in a series of two or more clauses or phrases which modify the same word. Obviously, all of them cannot be placed next to it—the ideal position. The problem is to arrange them so that no one of them cuts off another from a clear reference to the word that it modifies.

In the first "ambiguous" sentence below, for example, the phrase *by the volunteer firemen* seems to refer to the verb *was done*. When the order of the modifiers is reversed, as in the "improved" form, the phrase correctly modifies *was put out,* and it does not obscure the reference between *before any serious damage was done* and *was put out.*

Ambiguous: The fire *was put out* before any serious damage was done *by the volunteer firemen.*

Rearranged and Improved: The fire *was put out by the volunteer firemen* before any serious damage was done.

Ambiguous: The *effect* on a community *of these lawbreakers* is illustrated by the recent disturbances in Chicago.

Improved: The *effect of these lawbreakers* on a community is illustrated by the recent disturbances in Chicago.

Congestion in the body of a sentence can often be removed by placing one or more adverbial modifiers at the beginning of the sentence. This is a recognized and legitimate position for an adverbial element.

Right: *Before any serious damage was done,* the fire was put out by the volunteer firemen.

Ambiguous: They usually *call* us by telephone and ask us whether we are here *before coming.*
Improved. *Before coming,* they usually *call* us by telephone and ask us whether we are here.

Ambiguous: Double *tracks* are found in the main entry to the mine, *similar to the street car tracks in a city.*
Improved: In the main entry to the mine are found double *tracks, similar to the street car tracks in a city.*

a. Relative Clauses. A relative clause should preferably be placed immediately after the noun that it modifies.

Ambiguous: The reporter can occasionally pick up *items* from conversation with friends *that will be of interest to readers of his paper.*
Improved: From conversation with friends, the reporter can occasionally pick up *items that will be of interest to readers of his paper.*

Ambiguous: He carried an oilcloth *satchel* in his left hand *which looked old enough to have belonged to his grandfather.*
Improved: In his left hand he carried an oilcloth *satchel which looked old enough to have belonged to his grandfather.*

Occasionally, a relative clause may be slightly removed from its noun without danger of ambiguity.

Not Bad: Engineers have proved that an *engine* can be built *which will have the required power.*

This construction, however, must always be avoided when there is an intervening noun to which the clause might refer. Even in the example just given, a smoother sentence can be made by putting the clause in its regular position.

> Better: Engineers have proved that it is possible to build an *engine which will have the required power.*

b. *Only, Almost,* Etc. The words *only, almost, nearly,* and others of similar nature belong next to the words that they modify.

> Not Good: We *only* walked a mile.
> Improved: We walked *only* a mile.

> Not Good: He *almost* felt discouraged.
> Improved: He felt *almost* discouraged.

> Not Good: The delay *nearly* drove her frantic.
> Improved: The delay drove her *nearly* frantic.

> Not Good: The train *scarcely* seemed to move.
> Improved: The train seemed *scarcely* to move.

c. Two-way Modifiers. A modifier which might belong to either of two statements should not be placed between them. If it is thus placed, the reader is not certain whether it refers to the statement that precedes or to the one that follows.

> Misleading: A student who does his work conscientiously *at the end of the course* will have a broad and thorough education.
> Improved: *At the end of the course,* the student who does his work conscientiously will have a broad and thorough education.

> Misleading: A system which can accomplish this *certainly* is far better than one which scatters the energies of the student.
> Improved: A system which can accomplish this is *certainly* far better than one which scatters the energies of the student.

Placing a comma before the ambiguous modifier does not remedy the fault. The sentences require a different arrangement.

The Split Infinitive

E3. **As a general rule, avoid placing a modifier between the *to* and the verb-form in an infinitive.**

The indiscriminate use of the split infinitive is objectionable. If used at all, this construction should be reserved for particular cases where it expresses the idea more effectively than some other construction does. These cases will not occur frequently.

> Questionable: The captain ordered us *to immediately report* at camp.
> Improved: The captain ordered us *to report* at camp *immediately*.

> Awkward and Objectionable: He is sure *to not be* ready.
> Improved: He is sure *not to be* ready.

> Awkward and Objectionable: They promised *to at once bring* us the report.
> Improved: They promised *to bring* us the report *at once*.

In order to avoid an objectionable split infinitive it is sometimes necessary to recast the sentence.

> Objectionable: They promised *to at once bring* us the report that we wanted.
> Improved: They promised that they would *at once* bring us the report that we wanted. (If *at once* were placed at the end of the original sentence, the phrase would seem to modify *wanted*.)

Position of Correlative Conjunctions

E4. **Correlative conjunctions should be placed immediately before the words or groups of words to which they belong.**

Correlative conjunctions (such as *either—or, neither—nor, both—and, not only—but also,* etc.) are used in pairs to introduce two related words or groups of words, and to emphasize the relationship between the two. Ordinarily the related parts will be parallel in form: two verbs, two infinitive phrases, two adverbial clauses, and so on.

Right: You may either *go* or *stay* (two verbs).

Right: Neither *John* nor *Harry* will be there (two nouns).

Right: These conditions are found both *in the city* and *on the farm* (two phrases).

Right: They told us not only *where we should go* but also *what we should do* (two clauses).

The following examples show the incorrect and correct placing of correlative conjunctions:

Not Good: This statement *not only* applies *to the employee but also to the young man* engaged in business for himself.

Improved: This statement applies *not only to the employee but also to the young man* engaged in business for himself.

Not Good: The child must then attend a "continuation" school, where he *either* prepares himself *for the university or for his future vocation.*

Improved: The child must then attend a "continuation" school, where he prepares himself *either for the university or for his future vocation.*

Not Good: *Not only* is the work *interesting but also instructive.*

Improved: The work is *not only interesting but also instructive.*

Exercise in Sections E 1–E 4

Are any related parts unnecessarily separated? Are all modifiers so placed that they unmistakably modify the correct word? Are correlative conjunctions properly placed?

Point out the faults definitely; then restate the sentences correctly.

1. I had been thinking about the trip that I was about to take for almost a year.

2. He promised when a vacancy occurred to consider me for the position.

3. It is a sinister tale related in the semi-darkness beneath the thatched roofs of peasant hovels with bated breath.

4. He found a dog in the boat, which was dark brown in color with a white tail.

5. They were so excited that they didn't even hear me when I shouted.

6. He said that he would either see you at home or at the office.

7. Current magazines are available in the reading room of the club, as well as many of the latest novels.

8. It is advisable for you to at least send a small deposit with the order.

9. At last they discovered who the man that wrote the threatening letter to the boy's parents was.

10. I told you to come home early at least three times before you left the house this morning.

11. In 1819 resolutions calling on Calhoun, Secretary of War, to report on plans for national defense, were passed.

12. He seemed at first to conscientiously try to carry out the captain's instructions.

13. You should not only give your address but also your phone number.

14. He carried a cane on his arm which he had picked up in Ireland.

15. They were friends of my father whom I had met a year before I left home.

16. I only bought one of the textbooks and that nearly took all my money.

17. We decided to go shopping that morning, for we wanted to buy several people back home gifts.

18. They are related both to the Marlows and the Bairds.

19. A group of Camp Fire Girls presented the president with a bag of cookies, two feet long, baked by themselves.

20. Mr. Blair made a fair living after he graduated on the proceeds of his fiction writing.

PARTICIPLES

A Participle is a verbal adjective: that is, it is a form of a verb used as an adjective—to modify a noun or a pronoun.

Though it is derived from a verb, a participle alone is never used as a verb: that is, it cannot, by itself, make a statement about a subject. In order to do this, it must be combined with some form of the verb *be* (*is going, will be working*) or *have* (*have seen, had finished*).

Participle and Gerund. A verb plus *-ing*, like *read-ing*, is not always a participle. It is a participle only when it is used as an adjective. When it is used as a *noun*, it is a Gerund (also called a *Verbal*, or *Verbal Noun*).

Participle—used as an adjective:

There was a sound of *marching* feet.
The boy *reading* the report is a senior.

Gerund—used as a noun:

Reading is beneficial (subject of verb).
He enjoys *reading* (object of verb).
He spends his time in *reading* (object of preposition).

Forms of the Participle. The most important forms of the participle are:

Present Participle:	*seeing, bringing, working* (active voice).
	being seen, being brought (passive voice).
Past Participle:	*seen, brought, worked* (passive voice).
Perfect Participle:	*having seen, having brought* (active voice).
	having been seen, having been brought (passive voice).

The Active Voice indicates that the noun which the participle modifies is doing something; the Passive Voice indicates that the noun is being acted upon—receiving the action.

The man *throwing* the ball is the pitcher (active).
The ball *thrown* by the pitcher was lost (passive).

Exercises

A. Point out the participles and gerunds. Tell how each is used in the sentence.

1. An imposing structure, built of stone and marble, now stands on the spot once occupied by the fort.
2. The leader, thinking that the marchers were tired, insisted on stopping at the nearest inn.
3. After reading the book, we wrote a report summarizing the points made by the author.
4. Having made the trip before, we were driving fast without looking at the road signs.
5. Collecting rare plants was his hobby, and he enjoyed walking through the tropical jungles.
6. Having been warned beforehand, we were prepared for the worst.
7. Thinking back, he remembered seeing a man trying to unlock the door.
8. The hardest part of the work was loading the machine on the truck.
9. The swimming instructor also gave lessons in diving.
10. He walked home slowly, thinking about what he should do.

B. Give the present and past participles for the following verbs, and use each in a sentence.

    write   bring   catch   burn   play

C. Give the perfect active and perfect passive participles for the following verbs, and use each in a sentence.

    select   break   send   hang   take

D. Make sentences using the following words as participles and as gerunds (a separate sentence for each use).

    wearing   thinking   talking   rowing   paying

Position of Participles

E5. A participle should be so placed that it clearly refers to the right noun.

1. A single participle is generally placed just before the noun that it modifies.

The *foaming* water poured from the *broken* pipe.

2. A participial phrase usually follows the noun.

The man *carrying the banner* rode in a wagon *drawn by four horses.*

A few intervening words are permissible if they do not cause ambiguity.

The *foreman* of the mill, *hearing the noise,* ran into the office.

3. A participle or participial phrase modifying the subject may be placed before the subject (see Sec. **E 6**).

4. A participle or participial phrase modifying the subject may be placed after the verb, if there is an uninterrupted path to the subject.

The *men* stood at ease, *resting* their guns on the pavement.

Care should be taken, however, that there is no intervening word to which the participle might seem to refer.

Ambiguous: The *boy* watched the approaching officer, *whistling* to keep up his courage. (Was the officer whistling?)

Improved: *Whistling* to keep up his courage, the *boy* watched the approaching officer.

A participle which does not modify a definite noun or pronoun is called a "dangling" or "hanging" participle. Two particularly common types of this faulty construction are discussed in the following sections.

Dangling Participle Preceding the Subject

E6. A participle at the beginning of a sentence or clause should modify the subject of that sentence or clause.

If a participle in this position does not modify the subject, it is an incorrect, dangling construction. The remedy for the fault is to—

1. Change the subject so that it will be the word which the participle should modify; or

2. Change the participial phrase into a clause.

Wrong: *Driving* home that night, the *road* seemed endless. (Was the *road driving?*)

Improved: *Driving* home that night, *he* thought that the road was endless. (*He* was driving.) (Or)

Improved: *As he drove home that night,* the road seemed endless.

Wrong: *Having passed* through the rapids safely, a long *stretch* of clear water lay before us.

Improved: *Having passed* through the rapids safely, *we* had a long stretch of clear water before us.

Wrong: *Being built* on solid rock, the *engineers* knew that the building would not settle. (Were the engineers built on solid rock?)

Improved: *As the house was built on solid rock,* the engineers knew that it would not settle.

Wrong: There was no one at home, but *finding* a window unlocked, *it* took us only a minute to climb into the basement.

Improved: There was no one at home, but *finding* a window unlocked, *we* quickly climbed into the basement. (Participle modifies the subject of the second clause.)

A few participles when placed before the subject and used in absolute constructions (such as *generally speak-*

ing, strictly speaking, and the like) and a few old participles which have now become practically equivalent to prepositions (such as *during, regarding, concerning,* etc.) do not need to modify the subject.

Correct: *Generally speaking,* there are two sides to a question.

Correct: *Concerning* the theory itself, scientists are agreed that it is objectionable in some important details.

Dangling Participle— Implied Reference

E7. A participle should refer to a definite noun— not to a statement as a whole.

This type of faulty reference may be corrected—
1. by supplying a noun for the participle to modify; or
2. by eliminating the participle and changing the construction.

Not Good: The city is very unhealthful, *caused* by its location near a swamp. (*Caused* refers to the whole preceding statement.)

Improved: The city is very unhealthful, a *condition* caused by its location near a swamp. (The statement is summed up in the noun *condition,* which the participle modifies.) (Or)

Improved: The city is very unhealthful, because of its location near a swamp. (The participle is eliminated.)

Not Good: The theme should then be revised, *giving* special attention to sentences and punctuation. (The noun that *giving* should modify is not in the sentence.)

Improved: The theme should then be revised, special *attention being given* to sentences and punctuation. (*Giving* is changed to *being given,* a participle modifying *attention.*)

Dangling Participle Indicating Result. Dangling participles indicating result or purpose are frequent offenders.

This construction is often, but not always, introduced by *thus* or *thereby*.

The fault may be corrected:

1. by making the participial phrase into a co-ordinate statement introduced by *therefore, and therefore, and thus, and as a result,* etc.;

2. by recasting the sentence.

Not Good: No one was at home, *making* it impossible for me to deliver the package.

Improved: No one was at home; therefore it was impossible for me to deliver the package. (Or)

Improved: No one was at home, and therefore it was impossible for me to deliver the package. (Or)

Improved: As no one was at home, it was impossible for me to deliver the package. (Or)

Improved: I found it impossible to deliver the package, for no one was at home.

Not Good: We came early, *thus assuring* ourselves of ringside seats.

Improved: We came early, and were therefore able to get ringside seats.

Not Good: We started at ten o'clock, *thereby avoiding* the mid-day rush.

Improved: We started at ten o'clock, and *thus avoided* the mid-day rush.

Not Good: The audience became restless and inattentive, *causing* the chairman to rap for order.

Improved: The audience became so restless and inattentive that the chairman had to rap for order.

Exercises in Sections E 5–E 7

A. Point out the faulty participles; explain why they are faulty; and restate the sentences in proper form.

1. Looking over the edge of the pool, large bass and pike could be seen swimming among the weeds.

2. Having failed in two courses, the dean canceled my registration in the school.

3. The notes should be kept in a loose-leaf note book, thus making them convenient for ready reference.

4. With a little care a good sentence can be written by the student, having all its parts in the proper order.

5. Riding through the country today, the fields were beautiful in their white blanket of snow.

6. The speed of the fan is quickly reduced, caused by the pressure of the air.

7. Having been baked for two hours in a hot oven, we were sure that the potatoes were thoroughly done.

8. Swimming in the icy water brought on an attack of rheumatism, making it necessary for him to go to the hospital for a few days.

9. Lying on the sand at ebb tide, one can find many interesting specimens of marine life.

10. Standing there in the Roman Forum, it was easy to imagine what it looked like in Caesar's time.

11. Finally, the container must be sealed, being careful to make it airtight.

12. Seated on the platform of the observation car, the flat prairie covered with purple sage stretched as far as we could see.

13. Shrieking and shouting, the gendarmes forced the women rioters into a cell.

14. The theme should be neatly typed, leaving a generous margin on each side.

15. A table of contents was added to the book, giving all the main headings and a page reference for each.

16. Having spent several years in Samoa, the writer's account of his experiences there gave me a feeling of nostalgia.

17. He has been ill for several weeks, caused by worry and overwork during the bankruptcy proceedings.

18. Being made of glass, we thought that the container would be airtight.

19. The fish was forty-two inches long, measuring it from tip to tip.

20. Exhausted by the long struggle, our troops forced the enemy into a headlong retreat.

B. Complete the following sentences by adding main clauses having proper subjects:

1. Looking from the upper window, ...
2. Being written in French, ...
3. Being a native of France, ...
4. Having read the report, ...
5. Having been sent by registered mail, ...
6. Armed with bows and arrows, ...
7. Having been detected early, ...
8. Taken as a whole, ...
9. Riding through the main street, ...
10. Being a newcomer in town, ...

DANGLING PHRASES AND ELLIPTICAL CLAUSES

E8. Be sure that an elliptical clause (like *while looking, when in the city*, etc.), or a phrase containing a ger-
und or an infinitive, refers to a definite noun.

An elliptical clause is one in which part of the words
are omitted, only a partial framework being retained. For
example, "while reading the book" is an elliptical clause
condensed from "while he was reading the book."

These constructions are subject to the rules which
govern the use of participles. When placed at the beginning of a sentence, they should refer definitely to the
subject of the following clause.

Not Good: *While visiting* in New Orleans, the old
French quarter was the place where I spent most of
my time. (Was the *French quarter* doing the *visiting?*)

Improved: *While visiting* in New Orleans, *I* spent most
of my time in the old French quarter. (*I* was *visiting*.)

Not Good: *When only six years old*, his *parents* sent
him to a boarding school in London.

Improved: *When only six years old*, *he* was sent to a
boarding school in London. (Or)

Improved: *When he was only six years old*, his parents
sent him to a boarding school in London.

Not Good: *After rinsing* the clothes in cold water, *they*
are hung on a line to dry.

Improved: *After rinsing* the clothes in cold water, the *laundress* hangs them on a line to dry. (Or)

Improved: *After being rinsed* in cold water, the *clothes* are hung on a line to dry.

Not Good: *To get the most benefit* from the course, the *written work* should be handed in regularly.

Improved: *To get the most benefit* from the course, the *student* should hand in his written work regularly. (The *student gets* the benefit.)

When placed elsewhere in the sentence, these constructions should refer logically to the right noun.

Not Good: The proofs must be carefully corrected before *returning* them to the printer. (The proofs do not do the *returning;* they are *returned.*)

Improved: The proofs must be carefully corrected before *being returned* to the printer.

Not Good: These *packages* are entirely too heavy *to handle* by children.

Improved: These *packages* are entirely too heavy *to be handled* by children. (Or)

Improved: These packages are entirely too heavy for *children to handle.*

Exercises in Section E 8

A. Point out the dangling phrases and elliptical clauses; explain why they are faulty; then restate the sentences in proper form.

1. While living in Philadelphia, the home of the poet was in what is now the factory district.

2. The mountains were too far away to see them distinctly.

3. Hunting boots should be well oiled before using them.

4. The room was comfortable enough while moving around, but it was too cold to sit and read.

5. When very ill, the physician is doubly alert for changes in the patient's condition.

6. To profit fully from these corrections, a list of the errors should be kept in a notebook.

7. Before arriving at this conclusion, a thorough investigation was made by the engineers.

8. The letters are usually kept in the current files for a year before transferring them to the "dead" files.

9. Upon graduating from high school last June, my father took me for a month's motor trip.

10. While enjoying a life of luxury, the bank of which Mr. Emory was the president failed.

11. If kept in a sealed container, you will find that these specimens will be preserved almost indefinitely.

12. After jotting down a few sentences from the lecture, the girl's mind wandered to the letter which she had just received.

13. When painted red, his wife thought that the cabinet would be more attractive.

14. To get the best results, the juice should be strained before putting it into jars.

15. While talking with one of the early settlers, he told us about the building of the first railroad in that territory.

16. Upon consulting a lawyer, he told me to pay the bill and forget it.

17. Before taking the medicine, the physician advised me to add some orange juice.

18. The particles are too small to detect with the naked eye.

19. If questioned by the customs officers, we advise you to answer them frankly.

20. Though presented as facts, we later discovered that these reports were only rumors.

B. Complete the following sentences by adding main clauses having the proper subjects.

1. When fully completed, ...
2. Upon striking a match, ...
3. By adding a little more salt, ...
4. When only a small child, ...
5. While in college, ...
6. After being told of the accident, ...
7. After being placed in position, ...
8. Before moving to the city, ...
9. While working in a factory, ...
10. When in trouble, ...

PRONOUNS

The *Personal Pronouns* are *I, you, he, she,* and *it,* with their various forms indicating case and number, such as *me, us, their, him,* etc.

The *Relative Pronouns* are *who, whose, whom, which,* and *that.* The compound relatives are *whoever, whatever, whichever, what,* etc.

The *Demonstrative Pronouns* are *this* and *that;* plural, *these* and *those.*

The relative pronoun *who* refers to persons; *which* refers to non-persons (such as animals and inanimate objects); *that* refers to persons or non-persons.

> The *boy who* was here
> The *horse which* ran away
> The *purse which* was lost
> The *boy that* was here
> The *purse that* was lost

Position of Pronouns. A Relative Pronoun must be in the same sentence with its antecedent, and usually follows immediately after it (see Sec. **E 2a**).

A Personal or a Demonstrative Pronoun may be placed at some distance from its antecedent—and even in a different sentence—provided there is no intervening noun to which the pronoun might seem to refer.

> He took the *books* from the case and placed *them* on the table.
> Harry won the second *prize,* but he was not satisfied with *that.*

Reference of Pronouns

E9. Generally speaking, personal, relative, and demonstrative pronouns should refer unmistakably to a definite antecedent: that is, to a definite noun or pronoun.

The general rule given above needs some qualification. The pronouns *I* and *you* rarely have an antecedent expressed in the sentence. The other personal pronouns do not always require an expressed antecedent *in conversation,* where the person or thing to which they refer may be indicated by a gesture or a look. The compound relative pronouns do not have antecedents.

a. Avoid Double Reference for a Pronoun. Double reference occurs when there are two possible antecedents in a sentence and the pronoun does not unmistakably refer to the right one. The reader should be spared even a momentary hesitation in seeing the connection.

The fault may be corrected by dropping the pronoun and repeating the noun, or by using a synonym for the noun, or by changing the construction of the sentence so as to remove the ambiguity.

> Ambiguous: When a *student* hands in a theme to the *instructor, he* is not always satisfied with it.
> Improved: A *student* is not always satisfied with a theme when *he* hands it in to the instructor.

> Ambiguous: We took the *oranges* out of the *boxes,* and threw *them* into the furnace.
> Improved: We took out the oranges, and threw the *boxes* into the furnace.

> Ambiguous: There are several *inconsistencies* in the new football *rules,* and the coaches say that *these* must be changed before *they* are adopted.
> Improved: There are several *inconsistencies* in the new football rules, and the coaches say that these *inconsistencies* must be removed before the *revised code* is adopted.

An Inconspicuous Antecedent. A pronoun should not be made to refer to an antecedent placed inconspicuously in the sentence, if another noun is so prominent that the reader naturally connects the pronoun with it.

Other things being equal, a pronoun should usually refer to the nearest noun in the sentence, but mere proximity is not always a guarantee of clear reference. For instance, the subject of the sentence may stand out so prominently that the reader unconsciously assumes it to be the antecedent of a pronoun which was intended by the writer to refer to a nearer but less conspicuous noun.

> Not Clear: The hive is constructed so that the bee may work all around each frame and so that *it* may be removed, when full, without disturbing the others. (Is the bee removed?)
>
> Improved: The hive is constructed so that the bee may work all around each frame, and so that the *latter*, when full, may be removed without disturbing the other frames.

b. Avoid Implied Reference for a Pronoun. Implied reference occurs when the antecedent of a pronoun is not expressed in the sentence, but is implied in some word or group of words.

> Not Good: Girls, sitting at both sides of a table, wrap the margarine in thin paper and then put *them* in pasteboard cartons.
>
> Improved: Girls, sitting at both sides of a table, wrap the margarine in thin paper and then put the *packages* in pasteboard cartons.

> Not Good: If a person sees an advertisement for help, and thinks *it* worth applying for, he must do so immediately.
>
> Improved: If a person sees an advertisement for help, and thinks *the position* worth applying for, he should do so immediately.

1. *Which* **Referring to a Whole Statement.** Using the relative pronoun *which* to refer to a whole statement is a form of implied reference that is very common among inexperienced writers.

This fault may be remedied: (a) by summing up the idea of the preceding statement in a single noun, which is made the antecedent of the relative (*a fact which, a*

condition which, etc.); (b) by making the two statements co-ordinate and thus discarding the relative; (c)
by recasting the sentence.

> Not Good: Some students leave their themes until the
> last minute, *which* results in their having to do the
> work hastily.
>
> Improved: Some students leave their themes until the
> last minute, *a practice which* results in their having
> to do the work hastily. (Or)
>
> Improved: Some students leave their themes until the
> last minute, and *as a result* they have to do the work
> hastily.

> Not Good: He was always friendly and good-humored,
> *which* made everybody like him.
>
> Improved: His friendliness and good humor made every-
> body like him.

2. *This* and *That* Referring to a Whole Statement.
The demonstrative pronouns *this* and *that* are often misused in a similar manner.

> Not Good: He once lost some money that he had in-
> vested in farm mortgages and *this* made him sus-
> picious of all investments.
>
> Improved: He once lost some money that he had in-
> vested in farm mortgages, and *this experience* made
> him suspicious of all investments.

Note. Even good writers sometimes make *which, that,* and
this refer to a whole statement, and there is no particular
objection to the occasional use of this construction, if it does
not result in an ambiguous reference or an awkward expression. However, until the writer is sure of his judgment, he
should avoid this construction, and under no circumstances
is it to be used frequently.

3. Indefinite *They*. Avoid the indefinite use of *they* to
refer to people in general.

> Not Good: In India *they* have many curious customs.
> Improved: In India there are many curious customs.

Agreement in Number

E10. A singular pronoun is used with a singular antecedent, a plural pronoun with a plural antecedent.

> Wrong: Very few *landowners* will grow timber to be used for lumber, because about forty years must elapse before *he* can get a profit.
>
> Improved: Very few *landowners* will grow timber to be used for lumber, because about forty years must elapse before *they* can get a profit, (or) before a profit can be realized.

> Wrong: The aim of the commission is to stimulate the physical growth of the *child* and to improve *their* morale.
>
> Improved: The aim of the commission is to stimulate the physical growth of the *children* and to improve *their* morale.

a. *Each, Everybody, Anybody.* A singular pronoun must be used with *each, everybody, anybody, somebody,* etc., or with a word or series of words introduced by *each, every,* etc.

> Wrong: When the meeting began, *everybody* took *their* seats at the desks assigned to *them.*
>
> Improved: When the meeting began, *everybody* took *his* seat at the desk assigned to *him,* (or) *all the members* took *their* seats at the desks assigned to *them.*

> Wrong: If *anybody* heard this story, *they* would probably doubt my veracity.
>
> Improved: If *anybody* heard this story, *he* would probably doubt my veracity.

> Wrong: *Every dentist and physician* in the city will be asked to give some of *their* time to the children's clinic.
>
> Improved: *Every dentist and physician* in the city will be asked to give some of *his* time to the children's clinic.

Even in cases where the antecedent includes persons of both sexes, custom has decreed that a singular, masculine pronoun—*he, his,* or *him*—shall be used, as in the sentences above. If this seems awkward, the antecedent should be changed to one that does not require a singular pronoun, or the sentence should be reconstructed.

Except in formal documents where absolute accuracy is required, the awkward combinations *he or she* and *his or her* should be avoided.

> Awkward: Every student should apply these principles to *his* or *her* own business or profession, or *he* or *she* will not derive the full benefit from the course. (Use *his* and *he.*)

b. Pronoun Referring to a Collective Noun. When a noun like *firm, company,* etc., is the subject of a verb and also the antecedent of a pronoun, care should be taken not to make the verb singular and the pronoun plural, or vice versa. Both should be singular, or both plural. The choice will depend on the meaning. (See Sec. **C 1i.**)

> Not Good: The company *has* shown that *they* are interested in the welfare of *their* employees.
> Improved: The company *has* shown that *it* is interested in the welfare of *its* employees.

Exercise in Sections E 9–E 10

See that each pronoun refers clearly to a definite antecedent and that it agrees in number with its antecedent. Point out the faults, and restate the sentences correctly.

1. It was an old letter written by my father to his brother when he was living in Australia.
2. When we got back from fishing, we showed our catch to the girls and then buried them in the icehouse.
3. The sheriff had seen the stranger when he passed the bank.
4. Everybody in the room was startled when they heard the door slam.

5. He spent over two hours in writing the letter, which was very unusual for him.

6. He hesitated for a moment before answering and this gave me a chance to observe him more closely.

7. The committee has announced that their future meetings will be open to the public.

8. After the parents of the children died, the relatives sold the furnishings of the house and sent them to an orphanage.

9. I took three cents from my pocket and offered it to the newsboy.

10. A lawyer or a physician must keep themselves informed on the latest developments in their field.

11. She had traveled extensively in many countries and was constantly talking about it.

12. He refused to borrow the money, which we thought was the wise thing to do.

13. In some parts of Canada they call a pickerel a "jack."

14. When the passengers were seated, I undid the rope that was fastened from one end of the boat to the dock, and prepared to slide into it.

15. The dietician ate two sandwiches, pronounced them good, and promised to give them to her patients for lunch.

16. An instructor should be ready to help a student when he feels that he needs it.

17. A person either votes the ticket that the machine presents, or they don't vote at all.

18. When the results of the election were tabulated, it showed that his opponent had a majority of the votes.

19. In this school they have classes in the evening as well as during the day.

20. We usually bake the fish instead of frying it, which gives it a better flavor.

PARALLEL CONSTRUCTION

E11. **Statements that are co-ordinate in use should be made parallel in form.**

In this way the equality in use and rank is emphasized by the similarity in form.

For example, a noun should be co-ordinated with a

noun, an infinitive with an infinitive, a prepositional phrase with a prepositional phrase, or a clause with a clause—not a noun with a phrase, an infinitive with a clause, or a phrase with a clause.

A simple working rule that covers most of the applications of this principle may be stated as follows: *The co-ordinate conjunctions* and *and* or *should be used only between statements that are parallel in form.*

> Not Good: None of the leaders realized the *difficulty* of the work, or *how much time it would take* (a noun and a clause).
>
> Improved: None of the leaders realized the *difficulty* of the work, or the *amount* of time that it would take (two nouns). (Or)
>
> Improved: None of the leaders realized *how difficult the work was* or *how much time it would take* (two clauses).

> Not Good: We stopped at the nearest garage *for gasoline* and *to inquire about the road to Stevens Point* (a prepositional phrase and an infinitive phrase).
>
> Improved: We stopped at the nearest garage *to buy gasoline* and *to inquire about the road to Stevens Point* (two infinitive phrases).

> Not Good: He said *that we should go north for a mile* and then *to turn west on a gravel road* (a clause and an infinitive phrase).
>
> Improved: He told us *to go north for a mile* and then *to turn west on a gravel road* (two infinitive phrases).

> Not Good: *On account of the steep trail* and *because we were carrying heavy packs,* we made slow progress up the mountains (a phrase and a clause).
>
> Improved: *Because of the steep trail and our heavy packs,* we made slow progress up the mountain.

a. The *And-Which* Construction. The so-called *and-which* construction consists in using an *and, but,* or *or* between a relative clause and another modifier of a different form.

The general rule is: Do not use *and which* or *and who* (*but which, but who,* etc.) unless there is a preceding *which*-clause or *who*-clause, respectively, modifying the same word.

> Not Good: We came to another hill, much steeper than any of the others *and which* seemed to stretch endlessly before us.
>
> Improved: We came to another hill *which* was much steeper than any of the others, *and which* seemed to stretch endlessly before us. (*And* now joins two *which*-clauses.) (Or)
>
> Improved: We came to another hill which was much steeper than any of the others, and seemed to stretch endlessly before us. (*And* joins two verbs, *was* and *seemed.*)

> Not Good: He is a man over eighty years of age, *but who* is still active and strong.
>
> Improved: He is a man *who* is over eighty years of age, *but who* is still active and strong. (Or)
>
> Improved: He is over eighty years of age, but is still active and strong.

b. Parallelism in a Series. The members of a series of co-ordinate elements should be made parallel in form.

> Not Good: He is *honest, courageous,* and *of an optimistic turn of mind* (two adjectives and a phrase).
>
> Improved: He is *honest, courageous,* and *optimistic.*

c. Parallelism by Repetition of a Connective. Repeating a preposition or a conjunction before co-ordinate elements often produces a clearer and more emphatic statement, for this repetition emphasizes the fact that the elements are parallel in use.

> Ordinary: Complaints poured into the office from France, Italy, and China.
>
> More Emphatic: Complaints poured into the office *from* France, *from* Italy, and *from* China.

> Not Entirely Clear: He said that he would be in Boston today and we should meet him there.

Improved: He said *that* he would be in Boston today, and *that* we should meet him there.

d. Parallelism in Comparisons. As a rule, the parts of a comparison should be parallel in form.

Not Good: *To see* a play is more interesting than *reading* it (an infinitive and a gerund).
Improved: *Seeing* a play is more interesting than *reading* it (two gerunds).

Exercise in Section E 11

See that co-ordinate parts are made parallel in structure.

1. The flagman signaled that the road was clear and for us to proceed.

2. You should practice faithfully, giving attention to the pronunciation of each word and make sure that no syllable is slighted.

3. The speaker was a man apparently well acquainted with the subject but who lacked the ability to present it clearly.

4. This discussion covers three main topics: the history of the club, its present status, and what its plans are for the future.

5. The main entry to the mine varies greatly in width; in some places it is very narrow, and others being much wider.

6. We used the canvas as a tent at night and to cover the food by day.

7. He had no intention of doing the work and not get paid for it.

8. In the evening I went to the club for dinner and to hear a lecture on Mexican pottery.

9. Most people considered him discourteous, selfish, and a person without refinement.

10. At last we came to a log cabin on the shore of a small lake and which seemed to be deserted.

11. He decided that to pay the debt was easier than contesting it in court.

12. In this story the reader is shown how the better class of Englishmen lived, and their attitude toward less favored classes.

13. He has been with the company ten years—clerking, as assistant manager, and finally being made general manager.

14. You make the batter by adding water to the flour and then stir the mixture until it is smooth and creamy.

15. Ralph entered the office with his overcoat on and was carrying his hat in his hand.

16. It was a first edition of *Kim*, autographed by Kipling himself, and which had formerly been in the Logan collection.

17. The committee was directed to study the local tax situation and how the money was being spent.

18. The chorus was made up of boys dressed like girls but whose voices betrayed them.

19. On the hill I saw a barn and what I thought was a corral but which later proved to be the walls of an old log fort.

20. At first, typing my themes seemed harder than to write them by hand.

Exercises in Chapter VI

A. Point out the mistakes, and restate the sentences in correct form.

1. Being a sickly child, her mother had humored her until now she was thoroughly spoiled.

2. This was done for the purpose of forestalling complaints and to create good will for our products.

3. It is a house formerly owned by Abraham Lincoln and which is now used as a Lincoln museum.

4. One girl wore a ring on her finger which looked like it was made of brass.

5. While in the city, I hope that you will come to see us.

6. I offered to pay him for the work, but he refused it.

7. Usually there is either too much rain or there is not enough.

8. He could see even in the semi-darkness of the tropical night a band of horsemen riding down the trail.

9. These trees are only found in marshes and on the banks of streams.

10. When thoroughly baked, we removed the potatoes from the oven and served them piping hot.

11. The instructor told us to seat ourselves at any desk and that he would assign us to permanent places later.

12. After breaking my arm, my father refused to allow me to play football.

13. The prospector told us about finding the gold and how it was mined.

14. Not until the last paragraph was the name of the leader who had made the expedition a success mentioned.

15. John told his brother that he was responsible for the mistake.

16. After he has completed the course, he is given a certificate at the end of the six-week term.

17. The driver can slow this car down to two miles an hour without killing the engine, which is highly desirable in congested traffic.

18. Being practically airtight, moths cannot enter the chest when it is closed.

19. When she was put on board the train she was cautioned not to speak to any man she had not been introduced to by her mother.

20. The medicine should be shaken thoroughly before using it.

B. Follow the instructions given for Exercise A.

1. It was a tiresome meeting both for the speakers and audience.

2. At first everybody was sure that they had an answer to the problem.

3. He would have gladly and without any pity sacrificed all his friends.

4. The divers carry a basket fastened to a girdle about their waists in which they place the oysters.

5. All my classes were in the morning, thus allowing me to do some outside work in the afternoon.

6. Just outside the city we took the wrong road and did not discover it until we had driven ten miles.

7. He explained the error and what we should do to correct it.

8. He will either sell the house or he will rent it.

9. It was an old-fashioned picnic and everyone was supposed to bring their own food.

10. The police found a revolver in the alley which the bandit had dropped from his pocket.

11. When you do a person a favor you expect them to at least show some sort of appreciation.

12. The settlers thought that the Indians could be trusted since they had offered to help them.

13. While the jury was listening to the testimony, they seemed to be favorably impressed.

14. In shipping enameled brick, straw is placed between the faces so as not to scratch them.

15. I had only read the poem twice but I could almost repeat half of it word for word.

16. In writing a theme, you can save time by first analyzing the subject and then make an outline.

17. From the ceiling a chandelier made of an old oxbow and two kerosene lanterns is suspended.

18. Special attention should be given to the correct placing of the parts of a sentence, and also be sure to make co-ordinate statements parallel in form.

19. As a prospective student in our school, I am sure that you will be interested in looking through the enclosed bulletin.

20. Cotton is a staple product of this district, and also tobacco.

Exercises in Words

A. The following words are often confused. Look them up in the dictionary and use them in sentences.

adopt, adapt	council, counsel,	detract, distract
conscience, conscious	consul	convene, convoke
monograph, mono-	proscribe, pre-	sit, set
gram	scribe	

B. Look up the following words and use them in sentences.

cynical	precocious	antipathy	tyro
equivocal	thwart	puppet	acrid
churlish	agnostic	baleful	obsess

C. Learn the third five pairs of synonyms on page 288, and use them in sentences.

Review Exercise in Sentences

The following sentences have some of the faults discussed in preceding chapters. Point out the mistakes, and correct them.

1. We soon gave up hope of reaching camp that night. The snow having completely covered the trail.

2. In a small town the chances for advancement in his profession were limited, therefore he decided to go to Chicago.

3. He protested the decision of the court, and he believed it to be unconstitutional.

4. For this course we had to buy two textbooks. Each of which cost five dollars, plus the sales tax.

5. Last summer we spent our vacation in the West and were camping in the Rockies, and it was here that I had a thrilling adventure with a grizzly bear.

6. After his visit to New York, he has been thinking of getting a position with some firm in that city.

7. The other members of the class were younger than him, and he felt very much out of place.

8. If I was him, I would not try to go.

9. We asked them who they wanted to see.

10. I wish that he was here to talk to the collector.

11. This is no time for we Americans to be complacent and self-satisfied.

12. We ate two of the sandwiches when I noticed that the meat was moldy.

13. Please send the goods to my home, charging them to my account.

14. On one side of the main street is a store and a barber shop.

15. It was him and not me that you should have seen.

16. Have either of the patients improved since yesterday?

17. It seems as if the water in the lake is several inches higher this summer.

18. Who do you think that the club will send as its delegate?

19. They were not near finished with dinner when we arrived.

20. We would like to have the book when you are through reading it.

Chapter Seven

CLEARNESS IN THE SENTENCE

(*Continued*)

OMISSION OF WORDS

Omission of a Verb

F1. **Do not omit a verb or a part of a verb that is needed to make the sentence logically and grammatically complete.**

A verb should not be omitted in one part of a sentence unless the same form of the verb is used elsewhere in the sentence and can be readily supplied at the place of omission.

Not Good: The work *is* interesting and the opportunities for advancement very good (opportunities *is* good?).

Improved: The work *is* interesting and the opportunities for advancement *are* very good.

Not Good: He always *has* and always *will take* a personal interest in municipal affairs (*has take*?).

Improved: He always *has taken,* and always *will take,* a personal interest in municipal affairs.

Not Good: The voters *have* not *approved* this plan, and they do not intend *to.*

Improved: The voters *have* not *approved* this plan, and they do not intend *to approve* it (or, do not intend *to do* so).

Even when the form of the verb is the same in two parts of a sentence, it should not be omitted in either part if it is used as a complete verb in one place and as an auxiliary verb in the other.

Not Good: The program *was* excellent and thoroughly enjoyed by the audience.

Improved: The program *was* excellent, and *was* thoroughly *enjoyed* by the audience.

(In the first part, *was* is a complete verb; in the second part, it is an auxiliary verb.)

A verb form should not be omitted anywhere in a sentence if the omission will cause ambiguity or awkwardness.

Not Good: These social affairs *are* a source of great pleasure and of no little importance (a source of no little importance?).

Improved: These social affairs *are* a source of great pleasure, and *are* of no little importance.

Omission of a Connective

F2. Do not omit a connective that is needed to complete a grammatical or logical statement, or to make the meaning clearer.

a. Omission of a Preposition.

Incomplete: She had great respect and unlimited faith *in* her physician. (Not respect *in* her physician.)

Improved: She had great respect *for* her physician and unlimited faith *in* him.

Incomplete: These advertisements will appear *in* the leading magazines and billboards throughout the country. (Not *in* billboards.)

Improved: These advertisements will appear *in* the leading magazines and *on* billboards throughout the country.

Incomplete: He has promised to buy stock *in* whatever company you are interested. (A second *in* is required: "to buy stock *in* whatever company you are interested *in*.")

Improved: He has promised to buy stock *in* any company *in* which you are interested.

Incomplete: For a person my age, it was a foolish dream.
Improved: For a person *of* my age, it was a foolish dream.

b. Omission of *Who*, *Which*, or *That*. In the more formal types of writing it is better not to omit a relative pronoun or the conjunction *that* before a clause.

Incomplete: As a result of the war, some of the European countries now possess territory they have long coveted.
Improved: As a result of the war, some of the European countries now possess territory *which* they have long coveted.

Incomplete: The election showed the great mass of the people in this country want Congress to retain the power originally vested in it.
Improved: The election showed *that* the great mass of people in this country want Congress to retain the power originally vested in it.

The last "incomplete" example is particularly bad, for at first sight the expression, "the great mass of the people in this country," is almost certain to be regarded as the indirect object of the verb *showed*, instead of being recognized as the subject of the following clause.

In less formal writing and in conversation, the connective is often omitted.

Allowable: Is this the book you want (*that* you want)?
Allowable: He knew they were coming (*that* they were coming).

c. Omission of *And* in a Series. In a series of words or phrases do not omit an *and* that is needed to show the proper grouping of members.

Usually this faulty omission occurs when the series is followed by an *and* belonging to another construction in the sentence. This *and* does not affect the series; the latter should be complete.

Not Clear: The sale of Defense Bonds furnished our boys with food, kept them in ammunition, in clothes, and paid their salaries.

Improved: The sale of Defense Bonds furnished our boys with food, kept them in ammunition *and* in clothes, *and* paid their salaries. (*In ammunition* and *in clothes* constitute a series within the other series.)

Not Clear: We bought clothing, food, fuel, and ordered them delivered to his home.

Improved: We bought clothing, food, *and* fuel, *and* ordered them delivered to his home.

Omission of an Article

F3. Do not omit an article (*a, an, the*), if the omission causes awkwardness or ambiguity.

Not Good: Please send check for amount due.
Improved: Please send *a* check for *the* amount due.

Not Good: We shall be glad to give you full information regarding financial condition of bank.
Improved: We shall be glad to give you full information regarding *the* financial condition of *the* bank.

Ambiguous: On the street I met a grocer and butcher. (One person?)
Improved: On the street I met *a* grocer and *a* butcher.

If there is no danger of ambiguity or awkwardness, the article may be omitted.

Right: He owns a horse and wagon.

Exercise in Sections F 1–F 3

Point out any illogical or ungrammatical omissions in the following sentences, and make the corrections.

1. One of the rioters was killed and three wounded in the fight with the police.

2. The two little girls carried on their conversation in loud, shrill tones and many giggles.

3. He is engaged in social welfare work, and the author of a number of books in that field.

4. When he is "roughing it" in the North Woods, he always has a cook and valet with him.

5. She knew the man who lived in the large brick house on the corner was a clerk in the mayor's office.

6. He takes pride in whatever work he is engaged.

7. The company has, or at least will, increase its appropriation for advertising.

8. The novelist must have a complete understanding and sympathy with his characters.

9. His savings are wiped out, his self-respect gone, and he is quite unfit for work.

10. We hope this question is settled and nothing more will be said about it.

11. The majority of the stock is owned by the secretary and treasurer.

12. He refused to say whether he was opposed or in favor of the plan.

13. The cars are then coupled together, the air hose connected, and the engine and caboose attached.

14. A house that size sells for two thousand dollars.

15. Our chief concern was where to spend the evening—at a show, a dance, or a last-minute date.

16. She ate a piece of apple pie and chocolate sundae for dessert.

17. I never had but always wanted to take a motor trip through Mexico.

18. She has not seen anyone since the funeral but she will me.

19. In many respects life moves more swiftly in New York than smaller cities.

20. We saw the man at the top of the ladder was going to fall.

FAULTY COMPARISONS

F4. Avoid illogical, incomplete, and ambiguous comparisons.

a. **Comparative and Superlative Degrees.** The comparative degree should be used in comparing two things;

the superlative degree in comparing more than two (see page 82).

Wrong: John is the *tallest* of the *two* boys.
Right: John is the *taller* of the *two* boys.
Right: John is the *tallest* of *all* the boys.

b. Comparison of a Part with a Whole. Do not compare some characteristic or quality of one object with another object as a whole. Compare characteristic with characteristic, or object with object.

Wrong: The climate of Atlantic City is more pleasant than inland resorts.
Right: The climate of Atlantic City is more pleasant than *that* of inland resorts.

Wrong: The purposes of this school are different from most commercial schools.
Right: The purposes of this school are different from *those* of most commercial schools.

c. The Use of *Other* in Comparisons. When the comparative degree is used in comparing objects belonging to the same class, the word *other* is necessary.

Wrong: Texas is *larger* than *any* state in the Union.
Right: Texas is *larger* than *any other* state in the Union.

With the superlative degree, *other* is not used.

Wrong: Texas is the *largest* of *all the other* states in the Union.
Right: Texas is the *largest* of *all the states* in the Union.
(Or) Texas is the largest state in the Union.

d. *As Good—If Not Better*. In expressions like *as good as, as far as, as large as,* followed by *better, farther, larger,* etc., do not omit the second *as*.

Not Good: My plan is *as good, if not better than* yours.
Correct, but Awkward: My plan is *as good as, if not better than,* yours.

Improved: My plan is *as good as* yours, *if not better*.
(Complete one comparison before beginning the
second.)

In certain similar expressions, *than* is sometimes incorrectly omitted.

Not Good: He is *larger, or at least as large,* as his
brother. (Not larger *as* his brother.)
Improved: He is *larger than* his brother, or at least *as
large.*

e. *One of the Best—If Not the Best.* In expressions like
one of the best (*first, latest,* etc.)—*if not the best* (*first,
latest,* etc.), do not omit the plural noun. Supply that
noun, and omit the singular noun in the second part.

Not Good: This is one of the smallest, if not the smallest,
specimen in the museum.
Improved: This is one of the smallest *specimens* in the
museum, if not the smallest.

Note. Notice that it is permissible to omit words more
freely at the end of a sentence than in the middle. When the
omission comes at the end, the syntax of the main part is
complete and the omitted part in the elliptical phrase can be
readily supplied by the reader.

f. Ambiguous Comparison. A word or words necessary
for a clear understanding of a comparison should not be
omitted.

Ambiguous: The boy likes the dog better than his
mother.
Improved: The boy likes the dog better than his mother
does.

Ambiguous: The editor was better acquainted with the
minister than the lawyer.
Improved: The editor was better acquainted with the
minister than *with* the lawyer. (Or)
Improved: The editor was better acquainted with the
minister than the lawyer *was.*

Exercise in Section F 4

Point out the faulty comparisons, and restate the sentences correctly.

1. They found themselves in competition with men who were as good and often better than themselves.
2. The president, of course, has more authority than any man in the organization.
3. We have not found the winters here to be as cold as Illinois.
4. The Salem church is one of the oldest, if not the very oldest church in the state.
5. The Bible has been more widely read than any book ever published.
6. I tried on both dresses and finally decided to buy the most expensive one.
7. His latest novel is as long, if not longer, than the previous ones.
8. Girls usually like candy better than boys.
9. Our prices are considerably lower than our nearest competitor.
10. The convenience of a modern automobile may be compared with a well-appointed drawing room on a transcontinental train.

VERB WITHOUT A LOGICAL SUBJECT

F5. Be sure that each verb has a definite, logical subject.

A phrase or a clause used as a subject must logically express the subject relation.

> Wrong: Situated as it is in the heart of the residential district of Chicago makes the school easily accessible.
> Improved: Situated as it is in the heart of the residential district of Chicago, the school is easily accessible.
> (Or)

Improved: Because of its location in the heart of the residential district of Chicago, the school is easily accessible.

Wrong: With Russia pushing southward and Austria thrusting eastward at the same time, caused an inevitable conflict.

Improved: With Russia pushing southward and Austria thrusting eastward at the same time, a conflict was inevitable.

a. *Because*-Clause. A *because*-clause should never be used as the subject of a verb.

Wrong: *Because a man talks glibly* does not necessarily mean that he talks intelligently.

Improved: The fact that a man talks glibly does not necessarily mean that he talks intelligently.

b. Compound Predicate. Be sure that the second verb in a compound predicate refers to the right subject.

The careless writer sometimes forgets what the real subject is, and makes the verb refer to a nearer noun.

Wrong: The high school *student* gets a distorted picture of college life from these books, and *make* him feel that a university is merely a place to have a good time.

Improved: These *books* give the high school student a distorted picture of college life, and *make* him think that a university is merely a place to have a good time.

Wrong: The *outline* of the picture is now visible on the negative, and *is* almost ready to be removed from the developing solution.

Improved: The outline of the picture is now visible on the negative, and the *plate is* almost ready to be removed from the developing solution.

Wrong: The *diamond,* when first mined, has a greasy coating, and *gives* the stone the appearance of a drop of gum.

Improved: The diamond, when first mined, has a greasy coating *which gives* the stone the appearance of a drop of gum.

Exercise in Section F 5

Point out the mistakes, and restate the sentences correctly.

1. Barton's house was almost surrounded by giant pines, and made it look dark and gloomy.

2. Because he failed in a course is no reason for his leaving school.

3. The larger a business is determines the number of executives needed to control its operations.

4. There are two bedrooms in each cottage and also contains a very large living room.

5. Being built of tough oak logs makes this cabin a safe refuge from the winter storms.

6. Your description of the trouble you are having is not serious and can be remedied by a few minor adjustments.

7. The two teams being evenly matched adds to the excitement of the game.

8. There were many sailors on the street and gave this inland town the appearance of a seaport town.

9. Because you got an A in the examination is no reason for bragging.

10. In shady spots along the swamp are usually the best place for blueberries.

11. The superstition regarding the lucky horseshoe arose in ancient Greece, and is regarded as a lucky symbol because it resembles the crescent moon.

12. Here is a sure method of preventing the loss of class notes and also enables you to keep them in systematic order.

13. The color of the moon was a golden red and was just rising above the tree tops.

14. On a fishing trip is a good time to learn the real character of a man.

15. From boyhood Carlyle suffered from chronic indigestion and caused him to be moody and irritable.

16. The title of the book is *Tom Sawyer* and tells of the life of a boy in a river town.

17. Because he was elected president does not mean that he is the most popular man in the class.

18. Wrapped in cellophane keeps the cigarettes from becoming dry.

19. It was just before dinner and was raining hard.

20. The style of his writing makes the story interesting, but seems too long.

GRAMMATICALLY UNRELATED OR UNFINISHED STATEMENTS

F6. Be sure that every statement is completed and is grammatically related to the rest of the sentence.

The majority of unrelated elements occur because the writer forgets how he began a statement and shifts to another construction. Each element must be complete and be in grammatical harmony with the context.

Wrong: The second-growth timber, if it is treated scientifically, the owner can get an income in ten years (a confusion of two constructions).

Improved: The second-growth timber, if it is treated scientifically, will yield the owner an income in ten years. (Or)

Improved: From the second-growth timber, if it is treated scientifically, the owner can get an income in ten years.

Wrong: He must be courteous to everybody, but undue familiarity with none.

Improved: He must be courteous to everybody, but not unduly familiar with anyone.

ILLOGICAL STATEMENTS

F7. Each statement should be logically related to the rest of the sentence and should be phrased in such a manner that the relation is evident.

Illogical: On some days the student has *more* time to prepare his work than on others, and the instructor will have to forbear with him.

Improved: On some days the student has *less* time to prepare his work than on others, and on these occasions the instructor will have to forbear with him.

Illogical: The Holstein breed of cows is the oldest breed of dairy cattle in the world, *originating* in Schleswig-Holstein; it is *therefore* the purest dairy breed in the world.

(This sentence implies that the breed is the oldest because it originated in Schleswig-Holstein, and says that it is the purest because it is the oldest and originated there.)

Improved: The Holstein breed of cows, which originated in Schleswig-Holstein, is the oldest and purest dairy breed in the world.

Intermediate Step Omitted. Frequently an illogical statement results from the omission of an intermediate step—an omission which brings together two unrelated thoughts.

Illogical: Inasmuch as we asked you whether there was any mistake in our bill, we assume that the amount is correct.

Improved: Inasmuch as we asked you whether there was any mistake in our bill, *and you did not reply,* we assume that the amount is correct.

a. Faulty Predication. Be sure that a construction used after *is, was,* and other similar verbs has the proper logical and grammatical relation with the subject.

These verbs may be followed by a predicate noun, which names the same thing as the subject; by a predicate adjective, which modifies the subject; or by an adverbial element.

Illogical: The mixture is stirred until it is a creamy consistency. (A *mixture* is not a *consistency.*)

Improved: The mixture is stirred until it *has* (or *is of*) a creamy consistency.

Reason Is Because. Avoid saying, *"The reason is because* of something." A reason is not *because* of something; it *is* something. The idea of cause is included in the word *reason*.

Wrong: The reason for the increased dues *is because* the expenses of the club are heavier this year.

Right: The reason for the increased dues *is that* the expenses of the club are heavier this year. (Or)

Right: The dues will have to be increased *because* the expenses of the club are heavier this year.

Is When, Is Where. Be careful of *is when, is where.*

Wrong: Nine o'clock *is when* we start work.

Right: Nine o'clock *is the time* when we start work. (Or) We start work at nine o'clock.

Wrong: Chicago *is where* he lives.

Right: Chicago *is the city* where he lives.

Wrong: Astronomy *is where* one learns about the stars.

Right: Astronomy *is the study* in which one learns about the stars.

b. Illogical Classification. In naming a series of objects or persons, be sure that the members of the series do not overlap—that they are mutually exclusive.

Wrong: The program consisted of recitations, singing, and music. (*Singing* is included in *music*.)

Improved: The program consisted of recitations, singing, and *instrumental* music.

Wrong: Invitations were sent to the mayor, the members of the city council, and men interested in the welfare of the community.

Right: Invitations were sent to the mayor, the members of the city council, and *other* men interested in the welfare of the community.

Exercise in Sections F 6–F 7

Point out any incomplete, unrelated, or illogical statements, and restate the sentences correctly.

1. Mr. Crandon knew all about the Chicago fire, because he was just a small boy when it occurred.

2. Economics is where I had my greatest difficulty in my junior year.

3. The school offers courses in sewing, cooking, and subjects of a practical nature for girls.

4. Drew Park field house is open seven days a week; therefore it is the recreation center for the whole neighborhood.

5. The reason for the accident was because the local train was late.

6. After dinner is when he is most likely to be at home and in good humor.

7. This container is usually the shape of a cone and is made of steel.

8. It was through the close relationship I developed with Baxter by playing golf that finally led to my getting the position.

9. The reason that the car would not start was because he had left the emergency brake on.

10. If you expect to take the civil service examination, it will be given in the city hall at 3 o'clock Monday afternoon.

11. He spends his leisure time reading Kipling or Conrad, or some good author.

12. Gunn had found the treasure and therefore he had hidden it in his cave.

13. The instructor had promised that if all my themes were in on time, to excuse me from the final examination.

14. Christmas is when we all like to be at home with our own families.

15. *Vanity Fair* made Thackeray famous, as it came out in installments stretching over a period of two years.

16. The membership of the club is made up of chemists, physicists, and men who are experts in the natural sciences.

17. The shark was fully the length of an oar and had enormous teeth.

18. One reason for his success was due to his personal popularity with the voters.

19. Everything that you do, it should be done carefully.

20. The leader of this revolt, when the investigation is completed, it will be found that he is a member of the leftist group.

DOUBLE NEGATIVE

F8. **Do not use a double negative in making a negative statement.**

> Wrong: He *can't* do *nothing.*
> Right: He *can't* do *anything.* (Or) He *can* do *nothing.*

> Wrong: They *aren't* allowed to go *nowhere.*
> Right: They *aren't* allowed to go *anywhere.*

Be especially careful to avoid the use of the adverb *not* with words like *hardly* and *scarcely,* which convey a negative meaning.

> Wrong: He *wouldn't hardly* do that.
> Right: He *would hardly* do that.

> Wrong: I *don't scarcely* think so.
> Right: I *scarcely* think so.

Correct Double Negative. A double negative is correctly used to make a weak or modified affirmative statement.

> Right: This book is *not unlike* that one.
> Right: The boy was *not unhappy.*

The first sentence, for example, makes an affirmative statement which is weaker than the positive assertion, "This book is like that one."

THE RIGHT CONNECTIVE

F9. **Choose the connective that expresses the logical relation between thoughts.**

1. Do not use *and* (same line of thought) for *but* (contrast), or vice versa (see page 57).

> Questionable: The house is very old *and* is well preserved.
> Right: The house is very old *but* is well preserved.

2. Do not overuse:
if for *whether* (see Sec. **H 10**)
while for *and* or *whereas* (see Sec. **H 10**)
so for *therefore* or *consequently* (the "so-habit").

Questionable: Please let us know *if* the goods arrived safely. (Don't let us know if they did not arrive?)
Right: Please let us know *whether* the goods arrived safely.

Questionable: This paper is white, *while* the other is gray.
Right: This paper is white, *and* the other is gray. (Or) This paper is white; *whereas* the other is gray.

3. Do not use prepositions in the wrong sense.

Wrong: The examiner then makes inquiries *of* the financial condition of the firm.
Right: The examiner then makes inquiries *about* (or *regarding*) the financial condition of the firm.

Wrong: These trips are written up fully *by* the monthly bulletin.
Right: These trips are written up fully *in* the monthly bulletin.

AWKWARD AND MISLEAD–ING CHANGES IN CON–STRUCTION

F10. In two successive statements, the subject should not be needlessly changed.

If the subject of the first clause (or an equivalent word) can logically be carried over into the second, a smoother and clearer construction is generally produced.

Frequently, the change in subject is accompanied by a shift in voice—from the active to the passive, or vice versa. This combination is almost always awkward.

Not Good: When *we* reached the stadium, *half an hour* was lost in looking for a place to park the car.

Improved: When *we* reached the stadium, *we* lost half an hour in looking for a place to park the car.

Not Good: *Betty* is fond of music, and every spare *moment* is devoted to practicing on the piano.

Improved: *Betty* is fond of music, and devotes every spare moment to practicing on the piano.

Note. For a discussion of the weak use of the passive voice, see Sec. **G 9.**

Unnecessary Change in Person and Mood

F11. An unnecessary change in person and mood should be avoided.

Not Good: The study of English is important for *everyone*, even if *you* do not intend to be a professional writer (a shift from the third to the second person).

Improved: The study of English is important for *everyone*, even if *he* does not intend to be a professional writer.

Not Good: The line *should be wound* twice around the post; then *tie* it securely in a double knot (a shift to the imperative mood).

Improved: The line *should be wound* twice around the post, and *tied* securely in a double knot.

Exercise in Sections F 8–F 11

Point out the faults. Then restate the sentences correctly.

1. If a student is unable to attend the chapel services, you are supposed to get an excuse from the dean.

2. The batter attempted to bunt the ball, but it was missed completely.

3. Take the film from the camera in a dark room; then it should be packed in a light-proof container and sent to be developed.

4. We searched for the purse all over the house, and it was finally found behind the piano.

5. He would like to know if you approve of his plan.

6. A nickel is put in the slot at the top of the machine; then pull down the lever as far as it will go.

7. One might live for months in this neighborhood without knowing a single person who would be interested in your welfare.

8. If you plan your theme carefully, much rewriting and revising will be avoided.

9. The captain told Jim Hawkins to watch for an old sailor with a wooden leg; moreover, Jim should notify the captain when the sailor arrived.

10. The reader goes through each paper carefully, and the mistakes are marked in red ink in the margin.

11. The play was interesting but it didn't hardly seem convincing.

12. The speaker talked in a low voice, and he could be heard distinctly even by people in the second gallery.

13. She looked at me like I was a worm.

14. When a person is in doubt as to the pronunciation of a word, a good dictionary should be consulted.

15. She couldn't scarcely recognize him when he came to the door.

16. The coach was crowded and I was fortunate enough to get a seat for myself and baggage.

17. Some of the officers wore civilian clothes, while others were in uniform.

18. I saw in this morning's paper where the mayor's house had been robbed.

19. The mechanic says that he can't find nothing wrong with the motor.

20. He never finds much enjoyment from going to the theater.

Exercises in Chapter VII

A. Point out the mistakes, and make the necessary corrections.

1. The car is waiting for us, and we can't stay but a minute.

2. The foliage of the maple is darker in color and denser than the poplar.

3. The reason we went was because we wanted to visit the catacombs.

4. This principle should be observed and not try to evade it.

5. They did not object to the length of the drive as much as the monotony of the scenery.

6. He has done more than anyone to make the fair a success.

7. It would be dangerous to rely or put our trust in the loyalty of this group.

8. Because the work is difficult is no reason for you to neglect it.

9. The orders are then numbered and the date stamped on each.

10. This tax is levied on pianos, silverware, antique rugs, and articles of household use.

11. His latest book is one of the most interesting, but not the best-written novel of the year.

12. The first inning was when most of the runs were made.

13. If you look on p. 145, there is a graphic description of this phenomenon.

14. Tonight the audience was as large if not larger than previous nights.

15. The cause of the increased brilliance of Mars is perhaps due to its unusual closeness to the earth.

16. The soldiers were more friendly to the marines than the sailors.

17. On these short trips he usually carries a volume of poems and dictionary.

18. Next, the inspector asked us if we were American citizens.

19. These items are arranged in alphabetical order and makes reference to them easy.

20. Any man, when you get to know him better, you will find that he has some good traits.

B. Follow the instructions given for Exercise A.

1. The steak was tough and the potatoes only half done.

2. The country people had come early—on horseback, buggies, and decrepit Fords.

3. The cover was discolored, the pages torn, and the printing almost illegible.

4. At present the First Ward is Republican, while the Third always goes Democratic.

5. He is one of those men that can't do but one thing at a time.

6. This plan, when you examine it closely, will not work.

7. The class spent more time on the problems than the material in the text.

8. He never has and never will agree to a compromise on this important issue.

9. The meeting is open to the faculty, students, and people connected with the university.

10. We sent two samples to the laboratory to be tested and were found to be high-grade copper ore.

11. They decided that if they were too late for the train, to go home by bus.

12. Since you asked me, I am only a freshman.

13. Woman's place in the age of chivalry was very different from modern times.

14. We never had no doubt as to the outcome of the trip.

15. The apples should be picked when they begin to turn red and not let them get too ripe.

16. During Mardi Gras street dancing and open-air entertainments are held all over the city.

17. The reason for his refusal was due to his having some work to do at home.

18. Because he took too much of the sedative is why he slept all the next day.

19. Although we looked carefully in every room, no trace of the missing purse could be found.

20. In my vest pocket is where I keep my small change.

Exercises in Words

A. The following words are often confused because of their similarity in form. Look them up in the dictionary and use them in sentences.

observance, observation	beside, besides
imply, infer	exceptional, exceptionable
most, almost	egoist, egotist

B. Look up the following words and use them in sentences—and in your own writing.

cursory	lucid	expedient	grandiose
crestfallen	placid	precarious	agenda
desultory	irksome	garrulous	anachronism

C. Select any two pages of a good book or magazine. Make two lists of words that you find there:

1. Words which you recognize, but which you yourself do not use.

2. Words which you do not know. Look these up in the dictionary.

Review Exercise in Sentences

The following sentences have some of the faults discussed in preceding chapters. Point out the mistakes and correct them.

1. This is a vital matter touching the lives of all citizens and which no one can afford to neglect.

2. We arrived at the farm early Saturday morning, this was the beginning of what proved to be a delightful vacation.

3. In these alcoves the books which are used by graduate students doing research work are placed.

4. These lathes turn down the steel rods to their exact size. So that they fit to a thousandth of an inch.

5. Having access to the code book, the deciphering of the message was easy for us.

6. One of the duties of the auditor is to carefully and systematically examine the books of the company.

7. The instructor told us that there would be no class and for us to spend the hour in the library.

8. When thoroughly stewed, you will find that these apples make a delicious sauce.

9. Almost every day we went squirrel hunting for they were plentiful that winter.

10. It was just before dinner time and everybody was lounging about the camp and somebody proposed a game of poker.

11. He went to the door, locking it and putting the key in his pocket.

12. He struck out the two men who were leading the team in hitting in the fifth inning.

13. You will find roses and other flowers among the rocks which you should gather and bring to camp.

14. The interest as well as the principal on these bonds are guaranteed by the government.

15. He wrote that he is sending the package by express.

16. He reminded us that the ocean was salty.

17. She asked me to come to see her twice, but I was too busy.

18. I wrote a long theme on this subject which the instructor thought was excellent.

19. He is only in this country a year.

20. The water in the lake is very clear. Vegetation on the bottom being visible at a depth of ten feet.

Chapter Eight

EFFECTIVENESS IN THE SENTENCE

CONCISENESS

G1. Cultivate conciseness of expression; avoid wordiness.

Conciseness does not necessarily mean brevity. It means getting rid of all superfluous words—finding the shortest way of expressing an idea accurately and completely, without sacrificing any essential thought or part of a thought. A statement one hundred words in length may be concise; it will be if the thought cannot be adequately expressed in fewer words. A sentence ten words in length may be verbose; it will be if the thought can be adequately expressed in five words.

> Wordy: Perhaps not one tenth of the people who have occasion to listen to a good symphony orchestra render a selection worthy of commendation have a clear understanding of the organization of the modern full orchestra. (35)
> More Concise: Perhaps not one tenth of the people who listen to a good symphony orchestra have a clear understanding of its organization. (21)

> Wordy: There is a considerable amount of time needed for doing the work in an adequate manner. (16)
> More Concise: To do the work adequately will require considerable time. (9)

> Wordy: These difficulties can be avoided, or at least a large percentage of them can be. (15)
> More Concise: Most of these difficulties can be avoided. (7)

A sentence can often be made more concise by reducing a main clause to a subordinate clause, a subordinate clause to a phrase, or a phrase to a single word.

Wordy: One feature which this machine has and which makes it particularly desirable is that it is economical of fuel.

More Concise: One particularly desirable feature of this machine is that it is economical of fuel.
(One clause reduced to a single adjective and an adverb; another to a phrase.)

Wordy: If you ask him a few questions which are pertinent to what he is telling you, all that you have to do is sit back and listen.

More Concise: If you ask him a few pertinent questions, you have only to sit back and listen.
(Two clauses reduced to a single word; another reduced to a phrase.)

a. Tautology. The principle of conciseness is violated by the use of tautology, which consists in the needless repetition of an idea in different words. For example, in the sentence, "A crowd had *gathered together* to hear the speaker," *gathered together* is tautological, for the idea of *together* is covered by *gathered*. The proper form of the sentence is, "A crowd had *gathered* to hear the speaker."

Tautological: It is not *generally* known *by most people* that this plant is poisonous.

Improved: It is not *generally* known that this plant is poisonous. (Or)

Improved: *Most people* do not know that this plant is poisonous.

Tautological: A *widow woman* named Hicks lives there now.

Improved: A *widow* named Hicks lives there now.

Tautological: The book *bound in a cover made of buckram* is mine.

Improved: The book *bound in buckram* is mine.

Exercises in Section G 1

A. Restate the following sentences more concisely.

1. The reason that this method is preferable is due to the fact that it is cheaper and simpler.

2. Beside her lay a poodle that was shaved in such a fashion that it resembled a lion.

3. He tried with all the strength that he was able to muster to drag his companion from the position where he was lying under the fallen tree.

4. This transcontinental railroad is noted for the excellent passenger and freight service that it is accustomed to give to its patrons.

5. Before a pilot is hired or permitted to fly a plane at all, he is subject to and must pass tests that are very extensive and exacting.

6. The committee made a survey in order that they might find out in what way these families that are destitute could be helped in the most effective manner.

7. I was in Chicago last week, and while I was in the city I took occasion to go out to Lincoln Park where I wanted to see the statue of Lincoln, which is the work of the sculptor St. Gaudens.

8. One fault that this writer is frequently guilty of and that makes his style seem heavy and awkward, is his use of long parenthetical expressions.

9. In the case of many students, the writing of a term paper is a difficult thing for them to do, especially if the subject is of such a nature that a considerable amount of reading in the library is required.

10. He was living in Richmond, which is a suburb of London, and he invited me to have dinner with him in his home.

B. Point out the tautology and wordiness, and recast the following sentences.

1. Certain essential qualities are necessary for a successful after-dinner speaker.

2. The yard was completely surrounded on all sides by a high board fence.

3. It was a futile attempt, and nothing came of it.

4. He referred back to a previous statement that I had made in an earlier talk.

5. The two twins were named Mary and Ruth.

6. Without any previous preparation he spoke extemporaneously for over an hour.

7. *Paradise Lost* is written in blank verse without rhyme.

8. At the end of his speech he concluded his remarks with an apt quotation from Browning that was right to the point.

9. In his later years he wrote his own autobiography.

10. One distinctive feature that made this house different from the others was that it had seven gables.

11. Locally he is highly esteemed by the people of his own community.

12. It is a common belief in the minds of many people that a toad if it is handled will produce warts.

13. It was a frequent practice among the early settlers to plant a row of trees along the north side of their homes in such a way that they would be protected from the prevailing winds which were usually from the north.

14. The word *cute* is a shortened form of *acute* which has been abbreviated by dropping the initial *a* at the beginning.

15. On every side and on every hand instances of the inequalities of the present system of taxation now in force can be found by anyone who cares to take the trouble to look for them.

16. The foundation must be built in such a manner that it will have a sufficient amount of strength to bear the burden of supporting the massive machinery.

17. The fireplace was made of bricks which were a golden brown in color and were arranged in formations having the shape of triangles and squares.

18. Never before during all the twenty years he had served his State in the Senate had a proposal of this sort ever been presented to him.

19. None of the former tenants who had occupied the cabin before we came had paid the slightest bit of attention to the condition of the roof or anything about the place.

20. When I first began to write the report it occurred to me that one way by which I could make it more intelligible would be to include a series of diagrams.

EFFECTIVE USE OF SHORT SENTENCES

G2. The short sentence, when properly used, is a means of effective expression.

a. A Single, Short Sentence. An important thought may be made to stand out prominently by placing it in a single, short sentence.

> Ordinary: He felt sure that the voters would soon forget his misuse of public funds; but he was mistaken, for they did not forget.
>
> Emphatic: He felt sure that the voters would soon forget his misuse of public funds, but he was mistaken. They did not forget.

b. A Series of Short Sentences. A series of short sentences is valuable in making a rapid summary, in taking the reader quickly over a series of events, or in emphasizing a series of important thoughts.

> Ordinary: In order that this result may be accomplished, a number of matters will have to be adjusted. These include arranging a peace, solving economic problems, and settling differences with European countries. In fact, we have to re-establish ourselves in the reconstructed world.
>
> Emphatic: In order that this result may be accomplished, a number of matters will have to be adjusted. We have a peace to arrange. We have economic problems to solve. We have differences with European countries to settle. In fact, we have to re-establish ourselves in the reconstructed world.
>
> Emphatic: To this great conflict for human rights and human liberty America has committed herself. There can be no backward step. There must be either humiliating and degrading submission or terrible defeat or glorious victory. It was no human will that brought us to this pass. It was not the President. It was not

Congress. It was not the press. It was not any political party. It was not any section or part of our
people.[1]

The habitual use of short sentences is to be avoided,
for this practice results in a jerky, disconnected style.
As a general rule, they are to be reserved for passages
which require special emphasis. (For a discussion of
short, choppy sentences, see Sec. **D 3**.)

Exercise in Section G 2

In a book or a magazine article find five examples of
the effective use of short sentences.

VARIETY IN SENTENCE
STRUCTURE

G3. **Effective writing requires variety in sentence
structure. Monotony is to be avoided.**

1. Do not begin a number of successive sentences
with the same word, like *the, this, he, we,* etc., and do not
place the subject at the beginning of every sentence.

Awkward: The tendency at present is to move the iron
and steel mills from inland towns to lake points, such
as Cleveland, Chicago, and Gary. *This* is due to the
economy that results from having the blast furnace
close to the ore dock where the steamer unloads.
This was an important factor in causing the United
States Steel Corporation to locate at Gary. *This* plant
is the largest and most complete in the world for the
manufacture of steel.
(Each sentence begins with the subject, and the last
three begin with the same word.)
Improved: At present, the tendency is to move the iron
and steel mills from inland towns to lake points, such
as Cleveland, Chicago, and Gary. In these cities the

[1] Elihu Root. Reprinted by permission of the author.

blast furnace can be placed close to the ore dock where the steamer unloads, and as a result the ore can be handled more economically. It was this important factor that caused the United States Steel Corporation to locate at Gary, where it has erected the largest and most complete plant in the world for the manufacture of steel.

Note. The same structure is sometimes used in successive sentences for the purpose of emphasizing similarity or parallelism in thought.

Sherman had the qualities of a great leader. He was courageous. He was resourceful. He could win and hold the confidence of his followers.

2. Avoid "seesaw" sentences: that is, a series of sentences, each consisting of two co-ordinate statements connected by *and, but,* or *or.*

Awkward: Directly above us, a star is faintly visible, *and* after an imperceptible growth it becomes a flashing jewel in the black velvet of the sky. A half-burned log settles itself noisily in the fire *and* a flurry of sparks spin upward through the trees. The lone cry of a loon comes from the lake, *and* his mate answers from the other shore. We talk lazily of many things, *and* gradually our voices become quieter. Finally conversation ceases, *and* we lie there on the sand, just thinking.

Improved: Directly above us, a star—only faintly visible at first—brightens almost imperceptibly until it becomes a flashing jewel in the black velvet of the sky. A half-burned hickory log settles noisily in the fire, sending a flurry of sparks spinning upward through the trees. From the lake comes the lone call of a loon, echoed by the cry of his mate from the opposite shore. We talk lazily of many things, but as the evening advances our voices grow indistinct, and at last we lie there on the sand, just thinking.

3. Avoid a series of sentences containing main clauses followed by subordinate clauses having the same form.

Awkward: The fireplace was built of rocks *which* had been gathered from every state in the Union. These rocks were arranged in patterns *which* made irregular designs of different colors. The mantel over the fireplace was an oak beam *which* had been a part of the old capitol building at Vandalia.

Improved: The fireplace was built of rocks which had been gathered from every state in the Union. These were arranged in irregular designs of different colors. Over the fireplace was a mantel made of an oak beam from the old capitol building at Vandalia.

To avoid monotony, the writer should make himself familiar with the various possible ways of expressing an idea. The following example will suggest some of the possibilities:

1. He could find his way through the woods even on the darkest night, for he knew every foot of the trails.

2. Finding his way through the woods was easy even on the darkest night, for he knew . . .

3. It was easy for him to find his way through the woods even on the darkest night, for he knew . . .

4. Easy it was for him to find his way . . .

5. Knowing every foot of the trails, he could find . . .

6. As he knew every foot of the trails, he could find . . .

7. With his sure knowledge of every foot of the trails, he could find . . .

8. Being familiar with every foot of the trails, he could find . . .

9. Every foot of the trails being familiar to him, he could find . . .

10. Because of his familiarity with every foot of the trails, it was easy for him to find . . .

Exercises in Section G 3

A. Rewrite the following passages so that the sentence pattern will be less monotonous. Make any needed changes in arrangement or structure or number of sentences.

1. The shutters were hanging from their hinges and part of them were off entirely and lying on the ground. Windows were broken and some were without any glass. The small porch leading to the kitchen was sagging and several of the boards were missing. The three steps were in a state of collapse and the treads were unsafe to step on.

2. In three of the walls there are windows, and in the fourth are two solid wooden doors. Against the walls are eight bunks, over each of which is a box for a shelf. Near one of the walls there is a cast-iron stove, which has a pipe going straight up through the roof. In the middle of the room there is a big, square table, around which there are boxes to sit on.

3. The gnarled hands held a newspaper and quivered a little as the clock struck three. The pages crackled slightly as the hand turned and folded them. The wad of paper came to rest on crossed legs and the old man sighed. He touched his left hand to his breast pocket, and frowned for an instant. The fingers shot up to his ear and came down with a yellow stub of a pencil.

4. The captain ordered everyone on board to don life belts soon after leaving the harbor. Most of the passengers scoffed at this precaution, for the lake appeared no rougher than usual. Two ladies took it for granted that the ship was sinking and became panic-stricken. They were reassured after a time by the captain's eloquent description of the seaworthiness of the ship and the reliability of the crew. Their fears were again aroused a few minutes later as the ship began to pitch and roll. We were approaching the tumultuous stretch of water known as Death's Door.

5. A new parade, the result of a year of careful planning, is seen each night during Mardi Gras. Historical and legendary themes are chosen and executed with breathless beauty. The brilliantly colored floats, drawn by mules and lighted by torches, thread their way for miles through the crowded streets. Street dances and other open-air entertainments are found all over the city. Mardi Gras is the time when a whole city plays in the streets.

B. State the thought in each of the following sentences in five different ways.

1. John was the favorite son, and he received the largest share of the estate.

2. It had been raining steadily all day, and the dirt roads were almost impassable.

3. He read the letter for the fourth time, but he was still unable to understand it.

4. Writing the term paper meant that he had to spend considerable time in the library, for he had to go through many old periodicals in order to get the necessary data.

5. We had never been in this part of the country before, but we followed the trail maps carefully and were able to find our way through the forest without a guide.

REPETITION

Careless repetition—the kind that results from a limited vocabulary or from unwillingness to spend the energy necessary for finding a substitute—is always objectionable. On the other hand, intelligent and intentional repetition is often used for emphasis.

Careless and Awkward Repetition

G4. Avoid the careless and awkward repetition of words.

This caution applies to all classes of words—to prepositions and conjunctions as well as to the more conspicuous parts of speech, such as nouns and verbs.

The remedy is to substitute a synonym or a pronoun for the repeated word, or to change the construction of the sentence.

Awkward: The boards are then passed on to the different *cutters* who *cut* them into certain lengths. One set of men *cuts* boards for the sides and tops, while another *cuts* the end boards.

Improved: The boards are then passed on to different cutters, who saw them into certain lengths. The pieces for the sides and tops are cut by one set of men; those for the ends by another group.

Awkward: The tenderfoot soon *finds* that it is not easy to *find* the trail at night.

Improved: The tenderfoot soon *learns* that it is not easy to *find* the trail at night.

Awkward: The student is asked *to* read the poem aloud *to* enable him *to* become accustomed *to* hearing his own voice.

Improved: The student is asked to read the poem aloud so that he may become accustomed to hearing his own voice.

Awkward: That winter many families suffered because *of* the lack *of* foresight *of* the officials *of* the charitable organization.

Improved: That winter many families suffered because the officials of the charitable organization were lacking in foresight.

a. Repetition of a Word in Different Senses. Do not use a word in two different senses close together in the same sentence.

Awkward: The town was *but* a mile away, *but* the roads were almost impassable.

Improved: The town was *only* a mile away, *but* the roads were almost impassable.

b. Tandem Clauses and Phrases. As a general rule, do not use two or more successive clauses or phrases introduced by the same connective, unless they are intended to be parallel in form (see Sec. **G 5a**).

Awkward: Between the walls is a two-inch space *which* is packed with granulated cork, *which* is the most effective non-conductor of heat yet discovered.

Improved: Between the walls is a two-inch space packed with granulated cork, which is the most effective non-conductor of heat yet discovered.

Awkward: The upper floors of the building were completely destroyed, *for* the firemen were unable to
reach the flames, *for* the water pressure was too weak.

Improved: The upper floors of the building were completely destroyed, for the water pressure was so weak
that the firemen were unable to reach the flames.

c. Redundant Repetition of *That*. In a noun clause
introduced by *that*, the writer should be careful not to
repeat the conjunction after a number of intervening
words which are likely to make him forget that it has
already been used.

Wrong: It is evident *that* with improved roads in the
country districts *that* the price of farm lands will increase.

Improved: It is evident *that* with improved roads in
the country districts the price of farm lands will increase.

Wrong: We have decided *that* since labor and materials
are sure to be lower within a few months *that* it
would be inadvisable to begin the construction now.

Right: We have decided *that*, since labor and materials
are sure to be lower within a few months, it would
be inadvisable to begin the construction now.

Exercise in Section G 4

Point out awkward and careless repetition of words;
then correct the sentences.

1. I have an idea that his present ideas of social justice
are too visionary.

2. He had but one arm, but he played a good game of
golf in spite of it.

3. I took the next car for home, for it was time for me to
begin reviewing for the mid-semester examination.

4. The landlord said that in that case the lease that we
had signed would be returned.

5. We thought that if we took the first road to the right,
that we would soon come to the main road.

6. I made a box of strong oak boards, and then when it was made, I found that it was too small.

7. There were many people there from many parts of the country.

8. I enjoy horseback riding and I know that riding is good exercise, but it is hard to find time to ride in the winter time.

9. The architect showed us a model which he had made for the gymnasium which the college was building.

10. We selected this place for a camp because it was private and it was a good place for fishing.

11. The instructor told the class to come prepared to take a trip to the Dells to study the rock formations there.

12. It is a common belief that when anyone has accidentally spilled some salt, that he should pick some up and throw it over his left shoulder.

13. They came wading toward us in water that came up to their shoulders.

14. By noon by actual count he had gone by the house ten times.

15. We had to select the model that we wanted to make and then get the material from which to make it.

16. The manager promised that if a new shipment of goods arrived that he would notify us.

17. He thought that he had found a new way for hardening steel, but later it was found that this way had been patented years before.

18. In building this house he tried to build a house that was different from any that he had ever built before.

19. In this room there was just room enough for a bed and a small dresser.

20. I felt just the way you felt, and his next remark didn't make me feel any better.

Effective Repetition

G5. An important word is sometimes purposely repeated for emphasis.

Right: They were *starving—starving* in a land of plenty.

Right: It [the work of the Peace Conference] is full of *perils; perils* for this country, *perils* for all lands,

perils for the people throughout the world. (Lloyd George.)

Right: We *wish peace;* but we *wish* the *peace* of justice, the *peace* of righteousness. (Theodore Roosevelt.)

a. Effective Repetition of the Same Form of Construction. Emphasis, as well as clearness, may be secured by repeating the same form of construction—noun clause, adverbial clause, infinitive phrase, prepositional phrase, and the like—introduced by the same connective.

This device should be used only when the expressions are parallel: that is, when they perform the same function in the sentence.

Right: *If you believe* that honesty and industry are needed in city government, *if you believe* that faithful service to the public should be rewarded, you should work for the re-election of this alderman.

Right: Any sort of restraint, whether *by* military force, *by* legislation, or *by* public opinion, is obnoxious to this group of radicals.

Right: The objects of this science are *to determine* the constituents of which the material is composed, *to reduce* these constituents to their simplest forms, and *to build* up new chemical compounds from them.

In these cases the connective should be conscientiously repeated wherever the repetition will make the statement clearer or more emphatic.

Not Clear: The stability of a nation depends more *upon* the loyalty of its citizens than the form of government.

Improved: The stability of a nation depends more *upon* the loyalty of its citizens than *upon* the form of government.

Not Clear: The prisoner says *that* he has been betrayed by his associates, and his revenge is therefore justified. (Does the writer or the prisoner think that the revenge is justified?)

Improved: The prisoner says *that* he has been betrayed by his associates, and *that* his revenge is therefore justified.

b. Balanced Constructions. For special emphasis, two contrasted thoughts or two similar thoughts are sometimes placed in balanced constructions.

Balanced constructions are similar in form and are built in such a way that one seems to be weighed against the other. Unlike the expressions in the preceding section, they do not necessarily begin with the same word.

Not Balanced: A man's character is the sum total of his real qualities, while his reputation only bears witness to the impression that he makes on other people.
Balanced—More Emphatic: Character is what you are; reputation is what people say you are.

Not Balanced: Invitations were sent to a good many people, but there were only a few persons present.
Balanced: Many people were invited, but only a few came.

Exercises in Sections G 4–G 5

A. In some of these sentences repetition is intentionally used for emphasis and clearness; in others it is careless and awkward. Identify the two classes. Correct the faulty repetition.

1. A ball player, if he is good, can usually command a good salary.
2. One of the hunters had a sort of horn which made a sound which resembled the call made by a moose when mating.
3. This is a novel which the critics will praise but which the average reader will avoid.
4. Because of his daring, because of his skill, and also because of his luck, the bandit had never been caught.
5. This machine is the product of the genius of one of the leading scientists of the country.

6. Typing is of value to a student, whether he is in grammar school, in high school, or in college.

7. Such teachers are the kind that develop the right kind of boys.

8. It is a long walk, and when I say long, I mean long.

9. Before long an inspector came along and told us that we were taking too long for this work.

10. It is a large house intended for a large family.

B. In a book or a magazine article, find five examples of effective repetition.

EMPHATIC POSITION

The most prominent positions in a sentence are the beginning and the end. Ideally, therefore, these positions should be reserved for statements which the writer wishes to make emphatic. Practically, however, this procedure is not always possible—especially at the beginning.

The beginning of a sentence has two functions to perform. (1) It is the place where a clear transition from the preceding sentence must be made. (2) It affords a convenient and necessary place for adverbial clauses and phrases that would otherwise pile up after the verb and cause ambiguity (see Sec. **E 2**). These are matters of clearness in presentation of the thought, and as a general rule the question of emphasis is secondary to them.

Emphatic Beginning

G6. **For emphasis an important word or statement may be placed at the beginning of a sentence.**

a. Transposed Elements. A word may be emphasized by transposing it—giving it a position different from its normal one.

This is especially true of direct objects (words or clauses), predicate adjectives, and adverbs placed at the beginning of the sentence. Direct objects and predicate adjectives normally follow the verb; adverbs either precede or follow the verb. When they are transposed to the beginning of the sentence, the unusualness of the position serves to attract the reader's attention to them.

Normal: Although he was *tired,* he refused to rest.
More Emphatic: *Tired* as he was, he refused to rest (predicate adjective).

Normal: We always have *the poor* with us.
More Emphatic: *The poor* we always have with us (direct object).

Normal: He is willing to admit *that he has failed.*
More Emphatic: *That he has failed,* he is willing to admit (clause as direct object).

Normal: The procession moved *slowly* through the crowded street.
More Emphatic: *Slowly* the procession moved through the crowded street (adverb).

b. Connectives. As a general rule, formal connectives— such as *nevertheless, therefore, consequently, however,* etc.—should be "buried" within the sentence, instead of being placed at the beginning.

Questionable: *However,* government officials believe that the plane will be found.
Improved: Government officials, *however,* believe that the plane will be found.

Emphatic Ending

G7. A sentence should end with a worth while statement.

Stated negatively, this principle means that a sentence should not end with a weak, straggling phrase or clause. This caution does not apply to a phrase or clause which makes a definite contribution to the thought. It refers to those expressions which contain cautious qualifications of the main idea, or give the impression of being afterthoughts. Familiar examples are *as a rule, in some cases, I think, you may be sure, at least,* and others of similar nature. These expressions should be "buried" within the sentence, or if this procedure is impractical they should be placed at the beginning, rather than at the end.

Weak: Our future prosperity depends upon the co-operation of capital and labor, *to a large extent.*

More Emphatic: Our future prosperity depends, *to a large extent,* upon the co-operation of capital and labor.

Weak: An excess of magnesia in the cement will cause it to expand and crack *in time.*

More Emphatic: An excess of magnesia in the cement will, *in time,* cause it to expand and crack.

Weak: This device is adapted for use only with plate cameras having removable holders, *for reasons which will be explained later.*

More Emphatic: *For reasons which will be explained later,* this device is adapted for use only with plate cameras having removable holders.

a. A Preposition at the End of a Sentence. As a general rule, a preposition makes a weak ending for a sentence.

Weak: The parlor, a medium-sized room, artistically decorated, makes a very attractive place to entertain your guests *in.*

More Emphatic: The parlor, a medium-sized room, artistically decorated, makes a very attractive place *in* which to entertain your guests.

In some cases, however, a preposition may properly stand at the end of a sentence. This is especially true in certain questions, which, as a matter of fact, lose much of their effectiveness if another construction is used.

Emphatic: Where did you come *from?* (*"From* where did you come?" would be awkward and less effective.)

Emphatic: What did you do that *for?* (More emphatic than *"Why* did you do that?")

Certain sentences like those below are also allowable in speaking and, within reason, in the more informal types of writing.

Allowable: This is the article that you were talking *about.*

Allowable: He is the man that you asked *for.*

In these cases the sentence is usually short, and the preposition follows immediately after the verb or is separated from it by only a small word.

Allowable: This is a good country *to live in.*

Awkward and Weak: This is a poor country *to spend* the best years of one's life *in.* (*In* is too far from *to spend.*)

b. The Periodic Sentence. For special emphasis, the main thought may be placed at the end of the sentence. This type of construction produces what is known as the Periodic Sentence.

Not Periodic: Four members sprang to their feet as soon as the chairman finished his remarks.

Periodic—More Emphatic: As soon as the chairman finished his remarks, four members sprang to their feet.

In practice, not all sentences, or even the majority of them, are made periodic. The constant use of this type would mean a stiff and monotonous style, but when employed judiciously, it is a valuable aid to emphasis.

Note. Strictly speaking, a periodic sentence is one in which the grammatical construction is not complete until the end of the sentence is reached. For practical purposes, however, a sentence in which the main clause is placed last may be regarded as periodic.

Effective Arrangement in the Sentence—Climax

G8. In a series of words and phrases which vary considerably in relative importance, the members should be arranged with the weakest first and the strongest last.

Anti-climax: He was an eminent jurist, a distinguished lawyer, and a skillful politician.

Improved: He was a skillful politician, a distinguished lawyer, and an eminent jurist.

a. The Shorter Element Before a Longer One in a Series. As a general rule, the shorter member of a series should precede the longer member. In this way one form of climactic arrangement is secured.

Awkward: The book is beautifully illustrated in colors and *interesting*.

Improved: The book is *interesting* and is beautifully illustrated in colors.

b. A Negative Statement Before a Contrasted Affirmative One. In many cases, the placing of a negative statement before an affirmative contrasted statement makes a more emphatic sentence.

Less Emphatic: He failed because he was over-confident, *not because he was over-trained*.

More Emphatic: He failed, *not because he was over-trained*, but because he was over-confident.

Less Emphatic: His actions were guided by a desire for power, *not by love of humanity*.

More Emphatic: His actions were guided, *not by love of humanity*, but by a desire for power.

Exercises in Sections G 6–G 8

A. Rearrange these sentences for greater emphasis, giving special attention to the italicized parts. Make any necessary changes in the structure of the sentences.

1. His latest book is not his best, *however*.

2. *However*, we soon realized that the case was hopeless.

3. The army forced its way through the jungle *relentlessly*.

4. It is true that the campaign has not been pushed very vigorously *in some cases*.

5. His latest book is *inspiring*, interesting, and well written.

6. He accepted the position because he felt it was his duty, *not because he wanted the money*.

7. The time has *never* passed so slowly.

8. We do not know *what his motive was*.

9. He could do *nothing* that would relieve the pain.

10. This explanation is easy to understand and *concise*.

11. Most of us have had experiences as harrowing as this one, *to some extent at least*.

12. He had his *luck* with him that day.

13. Although the situation is *serious*, it is not entirely hopeless.

14. This book is an outstanding contribution to our knowledge of mass psychology, *if we are to believe the critics*.

15. He was *considerate of the rights of others*, modest, and generous.

16. As he was *hungry and discouraged*, he gave up the fight.

17. Each of us was given a small chest to stow our clothing away *in*.

18. This money was given to the precinct captain as a contribution to the campaign fund, *not as a bribe*.

19. He replied, "*No*, I won't do it."

20. We had eggs fried in rancid bacon grease *every morning, noon, and night*.

B. In a book or a magazine article find:

1. Five examples of emphatic elements transposed to the beginnings of sentences.

2. Five examples of transitional devices buried within sentences.

3. Five examples of climactic arrangement within sentences.

AWKWARD AND INDEFI-NITE USE OF THE PASSIVE VOICE

G9. Do not use the passive voice when the active voice would be more natural and definite.

Especially avoid the passive voice when it does not clearly indicate the person or thing to which the statement refers.

> Awkward: You know that your efforts *are appreciated* by us.
> Improved: You know that *we appreciate* your efforts.

> Awkward and Indefinite: The committee has worked faithfully and a number of reforms *have been effected.* (Who effected the reforms?)
> Improved: The committee has worked faithfully and *has effected* a number of reforms.

SPECIFIC VS. GENERAL STYLE

G10. For emphasis, make a statement definite by the use of specific words, details, and examples.

General statements have a legitimate use in carrying the reader over less important parts of an article, but they are not suitable for passages that need to be emphasized. The specific style is more vivid and therefore more stimulating to the reader's imagination and thought.

> General: This machine is guaranteed not to *injure any fabric.*
> Specific—More Effective: This machine is guaranteed not to *tear* the *finest chiffon* or the *most delicate lace.*

General: By means of moving pictures you can become familiar with the *manufacturing processes* used in *different lands*.

Specific—More Effective: By means of moving pictures you can become familiar with the process of manufacturing *steel rails in Pittsburgh, silk in Japan, and laces in France.*

General: Everybody uses this car.

Specific—More Effective: Everybody uses this car—*bankers, lawyers, farmers, business men, mechanics, United States Senators.*

General: We pay little attention to correct standards in writing, and are careless in our use of words.

Specific: We smile at the mention of standards, for these are old-fashioned; we use "don't" for "doesn't," even when we pretend to be educated; and not one college graduate out of a hundred, I venture to say, could use correctly the word "only." (C. H. Towne.)

General: In the courtyard stood two bullocks, and nearby was a servant guarding Holden's horses.

Specific: The two sleek, white well-bullocks in the courtyard were steadily chewing the cud of their evening meal; old Pir Khan squatted at the head of Holden's horses, his police sabre across his knees, pulling at a big water-pipe that croaked like a bullfrog in a pond. (Kipling.)

For a further discussion of specific style, see Sec. **H 2a.**

Exercises in Section G 10

A. Improve the following general statements by using specific words, or specific details and examples, or both.

1. He has been before the traffic court several times recently for infractions of the law.

2. John is an excellent student. (What makes you think that he is excellent?)

3. It was a typical October morning. (What constitutes a typical October morning?)

4. He has been with the company for many years.

5. The letter had been carelessly typed.

6. The factory covered considerable ground and was several stories in height.

7. The meat was not fit to eat and the pastry that we had for dessert was terrible.

8. At last everything about the camp became quiet.

9. Fifty years ago this part of the state was wild and sparsely settled.

10. In class today the professor was absent-minded.

11. This apartment is commodious and pleasant.

12. As I opened the gate a big dog came toward me menacingly.

13. The door opened, and an overdressed woman came into the office.

14. The office boy was ambitious to better his position.

15. It was a typical mid-Victorian parlor.

16. John is ungrammatical in his speech.

17. I heard a queer sound outside the room.

18. Many people are superstitious about black cats.

19. She wore a queer-looking hat and shoes that were not suitable for hiking.

20. The teacher punished Harry because he was a bad boy in school this morning.

B. In a book or a magazine article find ten examples of specific statements.

DEFINITE, DIRECT STATEMENTS

G11. Make definite, direct, straightforward statements. Do not be satisfied with an approximate statement of a thought. Avoid awkward and involved expressions.

Not Definite: Because of recent conditions, Europe is very limited in the industry producing wool.

Improved—More Direct: Because of the war, Europe is producing but little wool.

Improved—More Direct and Specific: Because of the war, Europe is producing only five per cent of its normal amount of wool.

Not Definite: A notable difference between bank panics and industrial depressions is the length of time of each.

Improved: A notable difference between bank panics and industrial depressions is that the latter cover a longer period of time.

Awkward and Involved: Here the student will get instruction which cannot help being an aid to him in the betterment of the daily pursuance of his duties.

Improved: Here the student will get instruction which will be of benefit to him in his daily work.

Exercises in Chapter VIII

A. Point out the faults, and restate the sentences more effectively.

1. The days were hot, but the nights were cool as a general rule.

2. A course of six months in typewriting was next taught to me.

3. There was only one excuse that he could give for acting as he did and that was that he was ill.

4. His friends are confident that when the returns of all the precincts are in, that he will be the winner.

5. The few who went, went from a sense of duty.

6. In our study of the work done by this artist it was interesting to compare the painting which he did in his early years with that which was done when he was seventy years old.

7. She accepted the invitation, but she did not come to the dinner for some reason.

8. Each guest was given one guess as to what the soup was flavored with.

9. There were not many people there when we arrived.

10. I put the residue in a pan and proceeded to wash the coloring matter and other foreign matter out.

11. The success of the club depends upon the co-operation of all the members, not on the efforts of a few officers.

12. It was a bird which resembled nothing which I had ever seen.

13. This plan made our work much easier, and of course it was heartily approved by us.

14. He was tall and slender. His high forehead was that of a scholar. His dark eyes looked out keenly from their deep sockets. His shoulders were stooped from too much bending over his books and manuscripts. He was a medieval recluse transplanted into the modern world.

15. We entered the hall right from the street, and knocked at the first door on the right.

16. He knew that when the books were audited at the end of the month that the deficit would be discovered.

17. The instructor put special emphasis on another point that we should observe when we were writing, and that was that we must be concise in our writing and not use unnecessary words.

18. She was constantly criticizing the other members and made herself thoroughly disliked as a result.

19. He had but little money but it was enough for his simple needs.

20. Most of the specimens which made up the collection we found when we examined them more closely were imitations which were made of wood and wax.

B. Follow the instructions given for Exercise A.

1. Your message was received by me this morning.

2. Evidently, this is not the course that you do your best work in.

3. You should be able to read the book in less than an hour, it seems to me.

4. We stayed for over an hour, for we wanted to find out her reason for refusing our invitation.

5. So much noise so early in the morning was unusual, so I went to the window to see what was happening.

6. A man is judged by what he does, not by what he wants to do.

7. The other model is stronger and more efficient than this one, of course.

8. We knew that if we were late to class again, that the instructor would not excuse us.

9. I couldn't imagine what he should be angry with me for.

10. During the present term I am taking only required courses which I must take in order to get my degree.

11. All during the time that he was a student in college, he was forced by circumstances over which he had no control to do a great deal of outside work in order to pay his expenses.

12. Instead of living on a farm he would have liked to live in a big city, like New York for example.

13. This is the source that they expected to get the greater part of the supplies from.

14. The house had been lived in by many families.

15. Washington was first in the hearts of his countrymen, first in peace, and first in war.

16. This car is the same as the older models to all intents and purposes.

17. For additional protection heavy insurance had been carried by him for many years.

18. At first the police made no attempt to regulate the so-called taverns at all.

19. Mr. Atkins as well as his family is always well dressed.

20. They promised that after the ice went out in the spring, that the ferry service would be resumed.

Exercises in Words

A. The following words are often confused because of their similarity in form. Look them up in the dictionary, and use them in sentences.

lose, loose	practical, practicable	diary, dairy
deadly, deathly	luxuriant, luxurious	credible, credulous

B. Look up the following words and use them in sentences—and in your own writing.

cryptic	authentic	intrinsic	unctuous
gregarious	antithesis	austere	bucolic
philander	insidious	fatuous	berserk

C. Open the dictionary at random. Make a list of any words cited there which you do not now use, but which you think would be useful additions to your vocabulary.

Review Exercise in Sentences

The following sentences have some of the faults discussed in preceding chapters. Point out the mistakes and correct them.

1. After telling my story to the ticket manager, he assured me that my money would be refunded.

2. The liquid soon begins to boil, and is accompanied by violent frothing.

3. The audience was made up of men, women, and musicians.

4. Before anyone attempts these repairs, they must be familiar with the engine's construction.

5. We couldn't hardly wait for the performance to begin.

6. The second solution should be as strong if not stronger than the first.

7. You will either find him at the store or the post office.

8. As winter came on my mother planned a trip, this was to be to California, also including a visit to Mexico.

9. My father drove the car out of the garage and I took my seat behind the wheel, and I felt like I was queen of the world.

10. My friend only had one leg which, however, did not prevent him from playing a fairly good game of golf.

11. I was walking along a street in Paris and someone called my name.

12. On Sunday we visited the Tower and St. Paul's Cathedral. After which we had dinner at the old Cheshire Cheese.

13. The jury believed the testimony of the witness was false.

14. At that time knighthood was in flower, and they spent their days riding around and rescuing damsels in distress.

15. Two men have been arrested by the police who are believed to be involved in the robbery.

16. Each of the players are required to buy their own uniforms.

17. They sent for John and I to finish the assignment.

18. We knew the general location of the camp but not how to get there.

19. He speared the big fish that was swimming near the shore with a sharp hickory pole.

20. When frozen, you can keep the fish in edible condition for months.

Chapter Nine
DICTION

The choice of words that are appropriate for a given occasion depends upon the subject, the type of readers or hearers, and the conditions under which a person is writing or speaking.

In the discussion of a philosophical problem, for example, his vocabulary will of necessity be different from that which he uses in telling about a fishing trip. An article which he writes for readers professionally interested in the field will contain technical words that would not be suitable in an article intended for the general reader. And in talking about the same subject he will be less meticulous in his choice of words than he would be in writing about it.

Levels of Usage. Various classifications or levels of usage for words may be made—based on their appropriateness under different conditions.

Standard Words are those which are in general use by good writers and speakers. They are appropriate on all occasions, and furnish the bone and sinew of all communication.

Colloquialisms are admissible and even desirable in conversation, in familiar letters, and in other types of informal writing, but are questionable or objectionable in formal writing. (For examples, see Section **H 3**.)

Slang is defined in Webster's dictionary as "Language comprising certain widely current but usually ephemeral terms (esp. coined or clipped words, or words in special senses, or phrases, usually metaphors or similes) having a forced, fantastic, or grotesque meaning, or exhibiting eccentric or extravagant humor or fancy." Slang occupies a lower social level than colloquialisms. (For examples, see Section **H 4**.)

Technical Words are essential for discussions of technical subjects among specialists, but are likely not to be intelligible to the general reader. Included in this group are the professional vocabularies of the physician, the lawyer, the engineer, the scientist, the mechanic, and the members of other trades and professions.

| caducous | peropodous | damascenine |
| gelseminine | entoplastron | chondrophyte |

Dialectal Words—also called *Provincialisms* and *Localisms*—are those which are current in certain sections, but not in the country at large. In formal writing they are usually out of place.

redd up (put in order)	reckon (suppose)	out of kilter
kine	greet (lament)	buss (kiss)
boughten	complected	bairn
pieplant (rhubarb)	poke (paper bag)	

Obsolete Words are relics of an earlier time and are not now in good use. *Archaic* words are on the way to becoming obsolete. Under ordinary conditions the writer will have no need for them.

homely (homelike)	trow	whilom	meed (wages)
leech (physician)	quoth	wot	becall (summon)
knave (boy servant)	prithee	ween	amuse (bewilder)
churl (a man)	bourne	bedight	

Some of this group are archaic or obsolete only in certain of their meanings: as *homely* and *amuse*. They are in current good use in other meanings.

These are not hard-and-fast classifications; they are flexible and subject to change. A slang expression of yesterday may be a colloquialism today and a standard term tomorrow. A word that was once highly technical may become familiar to the general reader. Nor are the contents of each class all on the same level. Some colloquialisms are close to standard; others verge on slang. In slang, also, there are different grades.

Moreover, as has already been suggested, levels of usage vary with the sort of writing that one is doing. In standard English the measuring sticks are different from those that apply in the more informal writing intended for popular consumption—as in articles for newspapers and popular magazines, stories, advertising, and similar fields. Technical writing also presents its own problems of word choice.

With all these variations, it is impossible to formulate any rule that will infallibly guide the writer in his choice of words for all occasions. Standard words are, of course, in good repute always and everywhere. For the other classes the most definite rule that can be given is that a writer shall make his selection intelligently—with proper consideration of his subject and his readers. He should use with discretion words in classes other than standard. If he is uncertain about the standing of any word, he should look it up in the dictionary, where he will find it labeled colloquial, slang, dialectal, etc., if it is not in standard use.

Exercise

Look up the following words in Webster's unabridged dictionary. Note their standard, colloquial, slang, technical, obsolete, and archaic uses.

set	give	turn
make	pull	draw

THE CORRECT WORD

H1. Use words in their correct meaning.

Mistakes are frequently made in the following classes of words. Unless the student is sure of a word, he should look it up in the dictionary:

1. Words which are somewhat similar in appearance or sound, but are different in meaning: as, *affect, effect; credible, credulous; exceptional, exceptionable.*

Wrong: They finally *affected* a compromise.
Right: They finally *effected* a compromise.
Right: This failure *affected* his whole life.

Right: He has *exceptional* ability as a leader (= out of
the ordinary).

Right: His conduct at the meeting was very *exceptionable* (= objectionable).

2. Words which have a similar basic meaning, but
which express quite different phases of that meaning: as,
*noted, notorious; enormity, enormousness; disinterested,
uninterested.*

Wrong: He was *notorious* for his good deeds.
Right: He was *noted* for his good deeds.
Right: He was *notorious* for his evil deeds.

Right: The *enormity* of the crime is now fully realized.
Right: The *enormousness* of this world-wide campaign
for democracy can now be understood. (Better: the
vast extent or the *enormous possibilities.*)

3. One part of speech loosely used for another:

a. Adjectives used as adverbs: as, *real* (for *really* or
very).

b. Prepositions used as conjunctions: as, *like* (for *as* or
as if); *without* (for *unless*).

Wrong: He was *real* glad to see us.
Right: He was *really* (or *very*) glad to see us.

Wrong: He acted *like* he was ill.
Right: He acted *as if* he were ill.

Wrong: He talks just *like* his father does.
Right: He talks just *as* his father does. (Or)
Right: He talks just *like* his father.

Wrong: She will not go *without* she is invited.
Right: She will not go *unless* she is invited. (Or)
Right: She will not go *without* an invitation.

4. Ungrammatical forms: as, *ain't, I seen, I done, could
of, had went, throwed, hisself.*

Wrong: That problem *ain't* right.
Right: That problem *isn't* right.

Wrong: Those men *ain't* officers.
Right: Those men *aren't* officers.

Wrong: I *ain't* ready yet.
Right: *I'm not* ready yet.

Wrong: I am right, *ain't* I?
Right: What I said is right, *isn't* it?

5. "Words" which are not words: as, *irregardless,* *irevelant, undoubtably.*

Wrong: He will go *irregardless* of the expense.
Right: He will go *regardless* of the expense.

Wrong: Your statement is *irrevelant* to the subject.
Right: Your statement is *irrelevant* to the subject.

Exercises in Section H 1

A. The following words are frequently misused, in most cases because of their similarity in form. Look them up in the dictionary, carefully distinguish the difference in the meaning, and use them in sentences.

accept, except
adverse, averse
affection, affectation
ancient, antiquated
avocation, vocation
cannon, canon, canyon
casual, causal
censor, censure
cite, site, sight
comprehensive, comprehensible
contemptible, contemptuous
debase, demean
difference, deference
disability, inability
disinterested, uninterested
distinct, distinctive
divers, diverse
economic, economical
elicit, illicit
eminent, imminent
emigrant, immigrant

endurable, durable
expect, suspect, suppose
formerly, formally
historic, historical
idol, idle, idyl
imposition, imposture
later, latter
leave, let
liable, likely
lie, lay
moral, religious
ordinance, ordnance
person, personage
profit, prophet
rein, reign
relieve, alleviate
respectfully, respectively
rise, raise, rear
than, then
transpire, happen
valuable, invaluable
willfully, willingly

B. Review the words in the list below, which have been given in the exercises at the ends of previous chapters.

adopt, adapt
affect, effect
allusion, illusion
amend, emend
artisan, artist
balance, remainder
beside, besides
compliment, complement
conscious, conscience
convene, convoke
council, counsel, consul
credible, credulous
deadly, deathly
detract, distract
diary, dairy
dual, duel
egoist, egotist
exceptional, exceptionable
feminine, effeminate
healthy, healthful
human, humane

hung, hanged
imply, infer
ingenious, ingenuous
judicial, judicious
loath, loathe
lose, loose
luxurious, luxuriant
monograph, monogram
most, almost
observance, observation
overlook, look over
practical, practicable
principal, principle
proscribe, prescribe
prosecute, persecute
rhyme, rhythm
sensual, sensuous
sit, set
stationary, stationery
troop, troupe

C. Point out the faulty diction, and supply the correct words.

1. Most of the class were disinterested in the theoretical discussions.

2. Jerry made an exceptionally good record in his aptitude tests.

3. If he don't finish the work today, he will come back tomorrow.

4. We don't want to lay here in the sun all day.

5. The official stationary should not be used by students in their personal correspondence.

6. I am always here on time, ain't I?

7. Half of the audience left before the ball game was finished.

8. He will not do the work without he gets paid for it.

9. The dust laid like a thick film over the carpets and cushions.

10. Larry wrote to her real often for a year after he left town.

11. She was always singing Polish songs like she was the happiest girl in the world.

12. I asked the sheriff to leave me talk to the prisoner.

13. She likes queer foods: for instants, she is crazy about cucumber and watermelon salad.

14. We have less students in school this year than last.

15. Baseball attracts larger audiences than hockey.

16. The teacher talked continuously about my use of *ain't*.

17. He is an imminent statesman and a notorious diplomat.

18. I felt that most anything could happen in a place like that.

19. Until I went over it in an airplane, I had not realized the enormity of the territory covered by the city.

20. A number of days have lapsed since the child disappeared.

D. Supply the correct word in the following sentences:

1. John made some .... remark and turned away (irrevelant, irrelevant).

2. The boys seemed .... interested in the story (real, really).

3. The student actors gave a very .... performance (creditable, credible).

4. His coat looked .... he had slept in it (like, as if).

5. We gave the .... of the clothing to the Red Cross (remainder, balance).

6. The new .... a number of drastic changes in the school (principle, principal; effected, affected).

7. These changes .... the students' attitude toward their work (effected, affected).

8. An optimist usually has a .... disposition (sanguinary, sanguine).

9. He .... know the difference between *don't* and *doesn't* (don't, doesn't).

10. This is a (an) .... specimen, the only other one being in the British Museum (unique, unusual).

11. We caught some bass and pike .... a number of pan fish (besides, beside).

12. The enemy gave way before the .... attack of our marines (unrelentless, relentless).

13. Why not .... the older boys finish the work? (let, leave).

14. Some people call jazz .... but I like it (barbaric, barbarous).

15. The books were .... on the table when I left (laying, lying).

16. He talked .... about amateur acting (contemptuously, contemptibly).

17. At first I didn't .... that he was an officer (suspect, suspicion).

18. Their treatment of the children was .... and cruel (barbaric, barbarous).

19. He is a senior this year, ... he? (aren't, ain't, isn't).

20. The speaker .... that his hearers were ignorant (inferred, implied).

E. Go through the themes that you have written. Make—and keep—a list of the words that you have misused. Keep the list up-to-date.

THE EXACT WORD

H2. Choose the word that exactly expresses your idea.

The writer should not be satisfied with a "blanket" word that only approximates the idea. Blanket words are general terms used loosely to cover a multitude of ideas which can be and should be expressed definitely: as—

Thing (for almost any object or idea).

Proposition (for *plan, proposal, scheme, device, problem, difficulty,* and a host of other words).

Nice (as general term of approval: a *nice* time; a *nice* dinner; a *nice* speech).

Indefinite: Tennis is a *thing* that appeals to the young man.

Improved: Tennis is a *sport* that appeals to the young man.

Indefinite: He made a *nice* speech to the students.

Improved: He made an *instructive* (*helpful, friendly, interesting,* etc.) speech to the students.

To this class also belong *splendid, grand, gorgeous, fine:* as, a *grand* time, a *fine* man; and general terms of disapproval like *bad, awful, terrible:* as, an *awful* lesson, a *terrible* time.

a. Specific Words. Specific words bring a definite mental image to the reader. They are therefore more vivid and more expressive than general words.

Specific verbs and specific nouns are particularly effective.

General: Above the desk was a *picture* of a *building.*

Specific: Above the desk was an *etching* of *Westminster Abbey.*

General: He *went* to the window and *looked* at the crowd outside.

Specific: He *strode* (*tiptoed, sprang, stole*) to the window and *stared* (*glared, peeped, peered, glowered*) at the crowd outside.

General: At the last moment a *puff* of wind *extinguished* the light.

Specific: At the last moment a *tongue* of air *scurried* in and *licked* out the *flame* of the lamp. (Conrad.)

General: The candle *flickered* by the side of my bed.

Specific: The *nervous* candle flame *shuddered* by my bedside. (Tomlinson.)

General: The rain was *beating* on the window.

Specific: The rain *kept tapping* with a *million nervous fingers.* (McIntyre.)

Exercises in Section *H 2*

A. For each italicized "blanket" word substitute a more definite, specific one; then give two or three other specific words that might also be used: thus, "He was a *good* leader" might be changed to "He was an *inspiring* leader" (*resourceful, courageous, magnetic*).

1. It was a *good* book.
2. It was a *good* steak.
3. It was a *good* speech.
4. It is a *bad* day.
5. He was a *bad* boy.
6. We had a *grand* time at the picnic.
7. I made an *awful* mistake at the party.
8. She has a *nice* voice.
9. He had an *unpleasant* voice.
10. He has an *unpleasant* manner.
11. She wore a *reddish* dress.
12. She wore a *light-colored* dress.
13. It was a *noisy* crowd.
14. Quinine is the best *thing* for a headache.
15. Algebra is the *thing* I dislike.
16. His fingerprint was the *thing* that led to his arrest.
17. Happiness is the *thing* we all want.
18. The noise was *terrible*.
19. He made a *weak* answer to the accusation.
20. He gave some *good* arguments for the plan.

B. For each italicized word or group of words substitute a more specific word. Then give three or four more specific words that might be used: thus, "He *cut* a limb from the tree" might be changed to "He *chopped* a limb from the tree" (*hacked, clipped, hewed, lopped, pruned*).

1. He *walked slowly* down the street (one word for the two).
2. He *went rapidly* down the street (one word for the two).
3. He *put* the pencil on the table.
4. She *looked* at her friend.
5. He *looked* at the unwelcome intruder.
6. She *took* the book from the rack.
7. We made the trip down the *stream* in a *boat*.

8. We heard a *faint sound* in the next room (one word for the two).

9. He was awakened by the *sound* of rain on the tin roof.

10. The *animal came* toward me (a noun and a verb).

C. For each word in the following list, give a series of terms each of which is more specific in meaning than the preceding one: thus, *building, house, cottage, colonial cottage, Dutch colonial cottage, Mr. Snyder's Dutch colonial cottage.*

school	book	meat	dessert	clothing
doctor	vehicle	confectionery	weapon	animal

D. In your latest theme find five words which could profitably be made more specific.

COLLOQUIALISMS

H3. In formal writing, avoid colloquialisms.

A colloquialism is a word or expression which is suitable for conversation, but which is usually out of tone in formal writing. In their proper place, colloquialisms give a touch of informality that is often desirable. The question of how far one is to go in this direction is a matter of considered individual judgment based on the kind of subject, the readers, and the occasion.

Colloquialisms differ widely in their social status: some are on the verge of standard use; others are on the fringe of slang or illiteracy. It would be hopeless to attempt to classify the thousands of words in this group according to their relative respectability, but some idea of the range may be suggested by a simple example. In the following series there is obviously a down grade from *homey* and *folks,* with their intimate associations—through *chipper* and *mean*—to *cussed* and *plumb crazy.* These different gradations should be felt by the writer when he comes to using words from the colloquial group.

The words in the list below are labeled colloquial in the latest (second) edition of Webster's International Dictionary (unabridged).

fix (for *repair*)
a lot of (for *many*)
a bad lot (for *a bad sort*)
fellow (for *a beau*)
loud (colors)
out loud (for *aloud*)
lose out (for *fail*)
a try (*an attempt*)
deal (for *transaction*)
folks (*relatives*)
kind of
tight (*stingy*)
chipper
bank on
pernickety
plumb crazy
tasty
bunch (of friends)

heap (of trouble)
cheek (*audacity*)
date (*appointment*)
turn in (*go to bed*)
turn out (for the game)
go back on (*turn against*)
go in for (debating)
mighty (for *very*)
homey
tuckered out
slant (*attitude*)
mean (*ill-tempered*)
cadge (*beg*)
dander (*temper*)
duds (*clothes*)
cussed (that *cussed* theme)
spruce up

Colloquial: The students all *turned out* for the game, for they wouldn't *go back on* the team.
Standard: The students all *went* to the game, for they had to *support* the team.

Colloquial: I made *a try* for a position on the college paper but *lost out*.
Standard: I *tried* to get a position on the college paper, but *failed*.

Another group of colloquialisms consists of: (a) words loosely used in a sense different from their legitimate meaning; (b) words made by using one part of speech for another.

(a) balance (for *remainder*)
claim (for *maintain*)
funny (for *odd, strange*)

(b) to suicide (for *to commit suicide*)
to enthuse (for *to be enthusiastic*)
plenty (for adverb

locate (for *settle*)

"amply"—as, *plenty good*)

an invite (for *an invitation*)

Since words of this sort add little if any spice to the writing, and since the words for which they are substituted express the ideas more accurately, there would seem to be no justification for their use, even as colloquialisms.

Colloquial: We spent the *balance* of the afternoon at the theater.

Standard: We spent the *remainder* of the afternoon at the theater.

Contractions and Abbreviations. Contractions and abbreviations should be used sparingly, if at all, in formal writing: as *ad* (for *advertisement*), *phone, gym, exam, auto, lab.*

Colloquial: The *prof* threatened to give us an *exam* the next day.

Standard: The *instructor* threatened to give us an *examination* the next day.

Contractions like *isn't, aren't, haven't,* and *don't* are proper, and even desirable, as colloquialisms.

SLANG

H4. Slang should be avoided in serious writing.

Some slang is picturesque and lively; when used in the proper setting it adds spice to one's speech. If it fits a real need it may live and finally enter into the family of standard words. Other slang is cheap and commonplace. It has no particular fitness or point. It springs up, flourishes for a time, and then dies, to be replaced by a new crop.

Slang is likely to develop into a lazy habit. If used to

excess, it becomes a rubber stamp—a weak substitute for the direct, exact statement.

Each person must be his own judge as to the place that he gives to slang in conversation and informal writing. In serious writing it is to be avoided.

a drool	jive	what's cookin'?
a goon	slap-happy	cooking with gas
a jerk	a wolf	on the beam
wacky	a wolfess	wise guy
corny	a good Joe	fall for it

Exercises in Sections H 3–H 4

A. Point out the colloquial and slang expressions, and restate the sentences in standard English.

1. The consul gave us the latest dope on the European situation.

2. The invite read eight o'clock at the Parker Hotel.

3. It was a bum steer that he gave us but we were wise to him.

4. She looks awful tacky in that sports outfit.

5. We tried to contact the president but he had vamoosed.

6. I enjoy Bach's music but I can't enthuse over Wagner.

7. It is a wacky play, but it makes a hit with students.

8. I had a hunch that it was a phony deal.

9. After our hike the bunch were sure all in but we decided to take in a movie before we hit the hay.

10. The audience was aggravated by the speaker's mannerisms.

11. That day we had a date to see the pope.

12. The dean fixed it so my classes came early.

13. The coach was peeved because I cut practice.

14. The nurse doctored me up with some vile-smelling dope.

15. He's one of those wise guys, but he'll have to go some to put that plan over.

16. We couldn't buy a paper any place in town.

17. The dog was barking and I knew he wanted in.

18. The garage man fixed the carburetor and it worked swell.

19. He's a good Joe and is always on the beam.

20. He thought he was taking me for a ride, but I was wise to him.

21. I almost passed out when I saw the size of the check.

22. I made a try at writing the report but it was no go.

23. The oranges are small and kind of tasteless at this time of the year.

24. His mother took on terribly when he was hurt.

25. I didn't plan on buying a suit till fall.

B. Look up the following verbs in Webster's unabridged dictionary, and list the colloquial and slang uses that are given there.

take	get	put	hold
go	pass	come	play

TRITE EXPRESSIONS

H5. Avoid trite expressions—expressions that have been worn threadbare by constant repetition.

It should be remembered that any expression, no matter how picturesque it may have been originally, loses its effectiveness through constant use.

aching void	clinging vine
along these lines	conspicuous by its absence
bated breath (with)	dead as a doornail
bathed in tears	deaf as a post
beggars description	eyes like stars
better half (my)	fair sex (the)
bitter end (to the)	feather in his cap
blind as a bat	fell with a dull thud
bounteous repast	fill a long-felt want
brave as a lion	goodly number
brown as a berry	green with envy
busy as a bee	heartfelt thanks
checkered career	honest as the day is long

host of friends
hungry as a bear
last but not least
last sad rites
mad as a wet hen
method in his madness
nipped in the bud
pretty as a picture
proud possessor
quick as a wink
reigned supreme
riot of color
satisfy the inner man

sea of faces
sigh of relief
soul of honor
straight as an arrow
too full for utterance
too numerous to mention
unguarded moment
view with alarm
weaker sex (the)
wended my way
worse for wear
wreathed in smiles

Exercises in Section H 5

A. Make a list of trite expressions that you are in the habit of using.

B. In the following sentences, translate the trite expressions into more original form.

1. The foliage was a riot of color, and over the forest silence reigned supreme.

2. The plot was nipped in the bud by the secret police and the leader ended his checkered career in a federal prison.

3. In his palatial residence on Park Avenue we partook of a bounteous repast.

4. The sunset was a gorgeous sight that beggared description.

5. In his own domicile Fritz was monarch of all he surveyed.

6. The master of the house was conspicuous by his absence, but his better half was very much in evidence and was the life of the party.

7. He is brave as a lion and generous to a fault.

8. At last he retired, full of years and honors; he was gone but not forgotten.

9. In a few well-chosen words he introduced the pianist who proceeded to favor us with a few selections.

10. He could not express his heartfelt thanks, for he was too full for utterance.

POMPOUS OR AFFECTED DICTION

H6. Avoid pompous or affected diction.

There is no objection to a long word simply because it is long. There is no virture in a short word simply because it is short. But if two words, one long and the other short, will express an idea equally well, the short one is usually preferable.

Pompous: Yesterday I *witnessed* two newsboys having a *pugilistic encounter* over a penny.

Improved: Yesterday I *saw* two newsboys *fighting* for a penny.

Pompous: Last week we *inaugurated* a new checking system.

Improved: Last week we *started* a new checking system.

Especially objectionable is the overloading of a passage with a number of heavy words.

Foreign Words. As a general rule, foreign words should be avoided if there are adequate English equivalents.

The frequent use of foreign expressions is a mark of the affectation which sometimes results from a little learning.

Affected: Because of a slight attack of *mal de mer*, I was unable to partake of the *pièce de résistance* which the *garçon* placed before me.

Improved: Because of a slight attack of *seasickness*, I could not eat the *beef pie* which the *waiter* placed before me.

Exercise in H 6

Rephrase the following sentences; make them direct and natural.

1. This proposition is not conspicuous for its practicability.

2. Because of my financial status it was incumbent upon me to procure employment.

3. At last I was successful in making a business connection with a merchandising firm in the retail dry goods field.

4. The recurrence of this accident does not appear to lie within the realm of probability.

5. He was apprehensive of reprisals on the part of the proponents of the plan.

6. He has been the target for frequent criticism concerning his dereliction in the performance of his official duties as mayor.

7. The desirability for closer co-operation has become increasingly obvious.

8. During my sojourn at the resort certain circumstances necessitated my avoidance of physical exercise.

9. This concern is notoriously prone to delinquency in the settlement of its financial obligations.

10. A vast assemblage had congregated to witness the ceremony attendant upon placing the cornerstone in its position.

IDIOM

H7. Do not violate the requirements of English idiom.

Idiom requires that certain words shall be used together. The reason is often unexplainable; in fact there is generally no reason other than that usage has established the form.

In the following sentence, for example, the two words *up* and *down,* which are logically opposite in meaning, may be used interchangeably to express the same idea: "He slowed *up* (slowed *down*) as he drove into town." Again, in "He likes to show *off* his new clothes" and "He failed to show *up* for practice," the words *off* and *up* do not convey their customary idea of direction. These are idiomatic expressions—the distinctions have to be "felt," not analyzed.

Certain idioms do not conform with the principles of present-day English grammar. Some are the remains of older expressions that were once grammatical; some are the result of ellipsis; and others have made their way into good use through a long period of time in spite of their irregularity.

For instance, in the sentence, "He is a friend of *mine*," the object of the preposition is in the possessive case. (Compare the modern slogan, "Buy it at your drug-gist's.") In a "*five-mile* walk," *five* modifies *mile*, which is singular. In "I am not *to blame*," the strictly logical and grammatical form would require a passive infinitive: "I am not *to be blamed*." The sentence, "I had better go," contains the combination *had go*. All of these are ac-cepted as standard forms. They are idioms—outside the ordinary rules.

1. Some words are followed by an infinitive, others by a gerund or a phrase containing a gerund.

> Wrong: He is *capable to go*.
> Right: He is *capable of going*.
> Right: He is *able to go*.

The following combinations are correct:

like to sing (singing)	insisted on going
enjoy singing	was determined to go
help to make	a desire to go
aid in making	desirous of going
assist in making	
	refused to go
expect to go	objected to going
anticipate going	
look forward to going	intend to go
	no intention of going
is difficult to find time	
had difficulty in finding time	had a notion to go
	had no notion of going
am pleased to meet you	is a privilege to go
is *a* pleasure to meet you	have the privilege of going
had *the* pleasure of meet-ing you	

Sometimes the infinitive and the gerund express different meanings.

He is sure *to win*. (I know it.)
He is sure *of winning*. (He thinks so.)

He was afraid *to go* overboard.
He was afraid *of going* overboard.

2. Idiom requires that certain prepositions be used with certain words.

Right: He was free *from* his troubles (not *of*).
Right: I was ashamed *of* the mistake (not *at*).
Right: His work is different *from* mine (not *than*).
Right: This author treats *of* many subjects (but deals *with* many subjects).

Other correct idiomatic combinations are:

accede *to* (not *with*)
accused *of* (not *with*)
agreeable *to* (not *with*)
angry *with* a person (not *at*)
comply *with* (not *to*)
contrast *with* (not *to*)
die *of* (not *with*)
disagree *with* (not *to*)
entertain *at* (not *to*)
frightened *by* or *at* (not *of*)
full *of* (not *with*)

identical *with* (not *to*)
in search *of* (not *for*)
independent *of* (not *from*)
interest *in* (not *for*)
listen *to* (not *at*)
of his own accord (not *on*)
plan *to go* (not *on going*)
stay *at* home (not *to*)
superior *to* (not *than*)
unequal *to* a task (not *for*)
unmindful *of* (not *about*)

3. Different prepositions are associated with the same word in different idioms.

Right: I agree *with* you.
Right: I agree *to* your proposal.

Right: He compared his coat *with* yours.
Right: He compared the road *to* a silver ribbon.

Right: We couldn't *make out* the address.
Right: We had to *make up* the deficit.
Right: She *made over* the dress for me.

Right: He waited *for* us an hour.
Right: The clerk waited *on* the customer.

4. With many adjectives, *very* may be used alone; with others—especially with past participles—*very much*, *very well*, and similar combinations with *very* are required (see Glossary, page 275).

Right: I am *very* happy.
Right: I am *very* tired.

Not Good: I am *very* contented.
Right: I am *very well* contented.

Not Good: She is *very* interested in the work.
Right: She is *very much* interested in the work.

Exercises in Section H 7

A. Point out the faulty idioms, and correct them.

1. I don't remember of hearing about the accident.
2. We succeeded after some difficulty to quiet the unruly group.
3. She was a plump little French woman of about fifty years old.
4. There is no definite way in arriving at a reasonable solution.
5. We were very pleased to see you at the reception.
6. They have no intention to sell their home.
7. Our opinions are due to a great extent upon what we read in the papers.
8. He was unable to assist his brother get a high school education.
9. In this situation we must consider carefully about our next step.
10. There was a scarcity of officers capable to train the recruits.

11. The speaker gave us an excellent insight on the customs of the natives.

12. A lie is something said for the purpose to deceive someone.

13. I was very amused at what she was saying.

14. Especially I enjoy to read a good detective story.

15. Intellectually, the natives are on a very low status.

16. The instructor stressed largely on the importance of grammar.

17. Reynolds had no expectation to be elected.

18. They accused us with taking the books.

19. This plan is not in accord to the wishes of the majority.

20. After the operation he was practically free of pain.

B. Supply the correct idiomatic form.

1. She did not feel . . . . home in the city (to, at).

2. He is . . . . satisfied with it (very, very well).

3. The arrival of the ships . . . . their destination was uncertain (to, at).

4. It was . . . . this prison that the governor threw his enemies (into, in).

5. He was infatuated . . . . a beautiful woman in Paris (with, by).

6. The proof . . . . this statement is easily available (to, of).

7. I was ashamed . . . . what you said (of, at).

8. There is little prospect . . . . the law repealed (to have, of having).

9. Smoking is often condemned because of its bad effect . . . . the heart (on, to).

10. I derive a good deal of pleasure . . . . attending football games (by, from).

AWKWARD COMBINATIONS

H8. Avoid awkward combinations of words and letters.

Awkward combinations frequently result from the careless repetition of words which are similar in sound, or from the use of a series of words which begin with the same letter or end with the same suffix.

Planned rhyme and alliteration belong to the technique of poetry; the careless and unintentional use of these devices is out of place in ordinary prose.

Awkward: He tried to *row* and *tow* the other boat behind him, but the wind was *blowing* too hard.

Improved: He tried to row and pull the other boat behind him, but the wind was blowing too hard.

Awkward: This attachment *sl*ides in the *sl*ot between the *sl*abs on the top.

Improved: This attachment moves in the slot between the plates forming the top.

Awkward: In this way, one is able to foretell the trend of business *a*ctivity *a*ccurate*ly*, *a*pproximate*ly* four months ahead.

Improved: In this way, one is able to foretell what the trend in business will be for approximately the next four months.

Awkward: An important factor affec*ting* the shipp*ing* is the pack*ing*.

Improved: An important factor in shipping is the method of packing the goods.

Exercise in Section H 8

Point out awkward combinations of letters and words; recast the sentences.

1. The enemy made a counterattack on the extreme right extremity of our line.

2. My felt hat felt hot and uncomfortable.

3. The sound of hurrying feet resounded in the silent corridor.

4. Clinging to a swinging rope hanging from the upper window, the fireman slowly made his way to safety.

5. One of the crew called to the captain to come out of his cabin.

6. For days he moped about the house as if in a daze.

7. He knew a few of the new songs, and many of the old favorites.

8. His elation over his promotion was an indication of his strong ambition.

9. She smiled smugly and shrugged her shoulders.

10. The maid made an effort to make the house presentable but she made little progress.

11. The cook took one look at the venison and pronounced it unfit to cook.

12. Finding his footing insecure in the shifting sand, he tried walking on the firmer stretch of beach above the ebbing tide.

13. When he jumped he bumped his head against the stump.

14. How can a queen bee be distinguished from other bees?

15. You should have let her send the letter by registered mail.

16. The frail fabric failed to hold the torn pieces together.

17. Before long a man came along and took my ticket.

18. Before they went they paid the rent and the grocery bill.

19. A solid oak spoke in the wheel was broken into pieces.

20. At any rate it was too late to make a date for that evening.

MIXED FIGURES
OF SPEECH

H9. Avoid mixed or incongruous figures of speech.

Confused: A new leaf is to be turned over; every man should put his shoulder to the wheel and all pull together.

Improved: A new policy is to be adopted; every man should put his shoulder to the wheel and all push together.

Confused: Let us put our hands to the plow and climb the ladder of success.

Improved: Let us put our hands to the plow and finish this work.

Confused: Golf now occupies the seat of honor as the national game of America.

Improved: Golf now has the honor of being the national game of America. (Or) Golf is now the national game of America.

When properly used, figures of speech add color and life to one's style.

"I am Lord Tilbury," he said, looking like a man unveiling a statue of himself. (Wodehouse.)

He was the black sheep of a rather greyish family. (Munro.)

His face was as long as an after-dinner speech. (Baldwin.)

He had a good memory and a tongue hinged in the middle of it.

Beyond the street rose many hills, and the town was thrown like a broken set of dominoes over all. (Kipling.)

It was a mouth big enough to sing duets. (Cantor.)

It was a face filled with broken commandments. (Masefield.)

GLOSSARY OF FAULTY OR COLLOQUIAL DICTION

H10. Observe the distinctions in usage in the following expressions.

Above. To be used sparingly as an adjective; it is properly an adverb or a preposition. Questionable: The *above* statement is true (*above-mentioned, foregoing,* or *preceding* is preferable).—The following use is correct: "The room *above* is for rent"; here *above* may be regarded as the equivalent of a phrase, *above this one.*

Accept, except. As verbs, *accept* means *to receive, to take; except* means *to throw out, to reject.* As a preposition, *except* means *excluding, with the exception of.* Correct: Everyone was there *except* John.

Advise. Properly means *to give counsel* or *advice*. Use sparingly as a substitute for *say, tell, inform*. Questionable: He *advised* us that the goods had been lost. Better: He *informed* us that the goods had been lost.

Affect, effect. *Affect* means *to have some influence on*. *Effect* means *to accomplish, to bring about some definite result*. Correct: The sunlight *affected* his eyes. Correct: The physician *effected* a cure.—The verb *effect* is correctly used when *accomplish* can be substituted for it.—*Effect* may also be used as a noun. Correct: They did not know what *effect* the law would have. Correct: The *effect* of the medicine was soon felt.—*Affect* is never a noun.

Aggravate. Means *to make worse, to increase in severity*. Dialectal and questionable when used for *annoy* or *irritate*. Questionable: His insolence *aggravated* me (use *annoyed* or *made me angry*). Correct: The damp air *aggravated* his cough.

Ain't. A branded outlaw. *Isn't* is the correct contraction for *is not; aren't* for *are not*.

All ready, already. These two forms should not be confused. *Already* means *by this time*. *All ready* means *entirely ready*. Correct: He has *already* finished the work. Correct: He is *all ready* to begin the work.

All the farther, all the higher. Incorrect for *as far as, as high as*, etc. Incorrect: This is *all the farther* we went. Correct: This is *as far as* we went.

All together, altogether. *All together* means *taken collectively*. (*All together*, the load weighed a ton.) *Altogether* means *completely*. (You are *altogether* right.)

Alright. Incorrect for *all right*.

Among. See *Between*.

Amongst. *Among* is simpler and preferable. Preferable: He lived for twenty years *among* the Indians (not *amongst*).

Amount, number. *Amount* refers to bulk or mass; *number* to individuals or units. "A large *amount* of sugar; a large *number* of cars."

And etc. *Etc.* is the abbreviation for *et cetera*, meaning *and others*. *Et* is the Latin word for *and*; hence do not use *and etc*. That would mean *and and others*.

Anybody else's, anybody's else. Both are correct.

Any place, every place, some place. Colloquial when used as adverbs instead of *anywhere, everywhere, somewhere.* Preferable: I couldn't find him *anywhere* (not *any place*). —The expression "I couldn't find him in *any place* where I looked" is correct; here *place* is a noun, object of the preposition.

Anywheres, everywheres, somewheres. Incorrect for *anywhere, everywhere, somewhere.* Drop the final *s.*

Approach. A pompous and indefinite substitute for *speak to, appeal to, ask, consult,* and the like. Choose the simpler and more direct statement. "We *spoke to* (or *consulted with*) the manager about this plan" is better than "We *approached* the manager about this plan."

As. Not to be used for *that* or *whether* in a noun clause. Correct: I don't know *that* he can come (not *as*).

At. Not to be used in sentences like "Where did you find him *at?*" or "Where is he *at?*" Correct: Where did you find him? Where is he?

A ways. An ungrammatical colloquial combination of the singular article *a* and a plural noun. Use *a way.* Correct: He lives *a* long *way* from here (not *a* long *ways*).

Awfully, dreadfully, terribly. Not to be used in serious writing for *very.* Inaccurate: I'm *terribly* glad to see you (use *very*).—If you must use these words in this sense, restrict them to the platitudes of conversation.

Balance. Carries the idea of *equilibrium,* of the actual *balancing* of one thing against another. Not to be used in general writing as a substitute for *remainder, the rest,* and the like. Correct: The *remainder* of the day was devoted to golf (not *balance*).—It is correctly used in commercial expressions like the *balance on the books, the balance in the bank,* and similar ones.

Beg. To be avoided in expressions like "We *beg* to say," "We *beg* to advise," and others of similar nature. This faulty use is especially common in business letters. *Beg* is allowable in certain statements where real deference or regret is expressed: as, "I *beg* to differ with you."

Between, among. *Between* is correctly used in referring to two objects; for more than two, *among* is preferable. "A discussion *between* two members; a discussion *among* all the members."

Blame it on. Colloquial: They *blamed it on* me. Standard: They *blamed me* for it. (Or) They laid the *blame on me.*

Bursted. The past tense and past participle are *burst.* Correct: The pipe has *burst* (not *bursted* or *busted*).

But what. Colloquial in expressions like "I don't know *but what* you are right." Standard: I don't know *but that* you are right.—A simple rule is this: Do not use *but what* unless *but that which* can be substituted for it. Correct: I have said nothing *but what* I believe (*but that which* I believe).

Can, may. *Can* denotes *ability, power.* It should not be used for *may* to denote *permission* or *possibility.* Incorrect: *Can* I go? (use *may*).

Cannot help but. A colloquial substitute for two standard idioms. Colloquial: I *cannot help but feel* sorry for him. Standard: I *cannot help feeling* sorry for him. I *can but feel* sorry for him.

Can't hardly, couldn't hardly. Incorrect double negatives. Incorrect: I *can't hardly* (*couldn't hardly*) read the letter. Correct: I *can hardly* (*could hardly*) read the letter.

Can't seem. Colloquial for *seem unable.* Colloquial: I *can't seem* to recall the incident. Standard: I *don't* recall the incident. (Or) I *seem unable* to recall the incident.

Claim. Properly used when there is a definite idea of demanding what is one's own. Correct: He *claimed* one half of the estate. Used colloquially as a substitute for *say, contend,* or *maintain.* Colloquial: He *claimed* that the story was exaggerated.

Complected. Not good: He was dark *complected.* Correct: He was dark *complexioned.* (Or) He had a dark *complexion.*

Contact. The use of *contact* as a verb is labeled slang in Webster's unabridged dictionary. It is properly used as a noun. Not Good: I *contacted* the manager about the new ruling. Better: I *spoke to* the manager (*talked with, made an appointment with*).

Data. A Latin plural form (singular *datum*). Strictly speaking, it should be used as a plural noun. "*These data are* reliable." The singular *datum*, however, is now rarely, if ever, used in the sense of a *fact*, and *data* is thought of as a collection of facts. It would seem, therefore, that there is some justification for the growing tendency to regard the word as singular in nature, though not in form, and to use it in expressions like "*This data is* reliable."

Different than. The American idiom is *different from.* Unidiomatic: This book is different *than* yours. Idiomatic: This book is different *from* yours.

Disregardless, irregardless. Not legitimate words. The suffix *-less* conveys the negative idea; hence the prefixes *dis-* and *ir-* are superfluous. Say "*regardless* of conditions," not "*disregardless* (or *irregardless*) of conditions."

Don't. *Don't* is a legitimate colloquial contraction of *do not;* it is incorrect as a contraction of *does not.* Incorrect: He *don't* care. Correct: He *doesn't* care (contraction of *he does not*). Correct: They *don't* care (contraction of *they do not*).

Dove. A colloquial past tense for the verb *dive.* Colloquial: He *dove* into the water. Standard: He *dived* into the water.

Due to. Much overworked as a substitute for *because of* or *on account of.* Avoid, as a general rule, expressions like "*Due to* a misunderstanding, I did not meet him" (say "*Because of* a misunderstanding"). A safe rule to follow is this: Use *due to* only after some form of the verb *be.* Correct: My failure to meet him *was due to* a misunderstanding.

Equally as. Not to be used for *just as.* Not good: This lesson is *equally as* difficult as that one (use *just as*).

Except. See *Accept.*

Expect. Carries the idea of *looking into the future;* not a synonym for *suppose* or *think.* Inaccurate: I *expect* he is at home (use *suppose* or *think*).

Favor. Not to be used as a substitute for *letter* in expressions like "Your *favor* of July 15 has been received" (use *letter*).

Fewer, less. *Fewer* refers to units or individuals; *less* to bulk or mass. Correct: *fewer* pennies; *less* money.

Fine, nice, grand, splendid, glorious, elegant. In serious writing do not use these words to express general approbation: as, a *fine* time, an *elegant* dinner. Reserve them for places where they accurately convey your thought. Their more accurate meanings are as follows: *Fine*—delicate, excellently made: as, a *fine* watch, a *fine* piece of silk. *Nice*—accurate, discriminating: as, a *nice* adjustment, a *nice* distinction. *Grand*—conveys the idea of largeness and magnificence: as, a *grand* estate. *Splendid* —shining, brilliant: as, *splendid* moonlight. *Glorious*— somewhat like *splendid,* but adds the idea of color: as, a *glorious* sunset. *Elegant*—emphasizes the idea of refinement, propriety: as, an *elegant* gown.

First, firstly. *First* is both an adjective and an adverb. In a series the customary forms are *first, secondly, thirdly;* or *first, second, third. Firstly* is an adverb, but is now seldom used.

First-rate. Properly an adjective. Correct: He is a *first-rate* bookkeeper. Colloquial when used as an adverb. Colloquial: He feels *first-rate.* Standard: He feels *well.*

Fix. Colloquial when used for *repair* or *mend,* or as a noun in the sense of a *predicament.* Colloquial: He tried to *fix* the broken lock. They were in a pretty *fix.*

From hence, from thence. *Hence* means "*from this* place"; *thence,* "*from that* place." *From* is therefore incorrectly used with these words.

Funny. Properly means *laughable, droll.* Colloquial as a synonym for *odd, unusual.* Standard: I saw an *unusual* funeral today (not *funny*).

Got, gotten. The shorter form, *got,* is generally preferred as the past participle of *get: get—got—got.*

Guess. Colloquial when used for *think* or *suppose.* Colloquial: I *guess* they will be there. Standard: I *suppose* (*think*) they will be there.

Had better, had rather. Correct in sentences like "You *had better* come at once" and "I *had rather* ride than walk." These are idiomatic expressions.

Had ought, hadn't ought. Incorrect for *ought* and *ought not.* Incorrect: They *had ought* to tell us. Correct: They *ought* to tell us. Incorrect: He *hadn't ought* to do that. Correct: He *ought not* to do that.

If. Questionable when used for *whether* to introduce a noun clause. Doubtful: Let us know *if* you can come. Better: Let us know *whether* you can come.

In back of. An awkward colloquial substitute for *behind*. Not good: The barn is *in back of* the house. Better: The barn is *behind* the house.

Inside of. Omit the *of*. Say "*inside* the house," not "*inside of* the house."

Irregardless. See *Disregardless*.

It's, its. *It's* is a contraction of *it is*: *It's* raining. *Its*, without an apostrophe, is the possessive case of *it*: Everything is in *its* place.

Kind of, sort of. Colloquial when used before an adjective in the sense of *rather*. Colloquial: I feel *kind of* tired. Standard: I feel *rather* tired.—These expressions are correctly used before a noun. This *kind of* man; this *sort of* candy.

Kind of a, sort of a. The *a* is superfluous. Say "this *kind of* apple," not "this *kind of an* apple."

Later on. The *on* is superfluous. Correct: I will see you *later* (not *later on*).

Leave, let. Never use *leave* in the sense of *allow*. Very bad: *Leave* me get the book. Correct: *Let* me get the book.

Less, fewer. See *Fewer*.

Liable, likely. *Liable* and *likely* both convey the idea of probability. *Liable*, however, is used when there is a probability that something disagreeable or unpleasant will happen. Correct: It is *likely* to be a pleasant day (not *liable*). Correct: It is *liable* to rain tonight.—In the latter sentence *likely* could also be used, for it is broad enough to cover the meaning of *liable*.

Lie, lay. The principal parts are *lie, lay, lain* (*lying*, present participle); *lay, laid, laid* (*laying*, present participle). The verbs of the first group do not take an object; those of the second have an object. Correct: The book *lies* on the table. The book *lay* on the table yesterday. The book has *lain* on the table all week. The book is *lying* on the table. Correct: He *lays* the book down. He *laid* the book down. He has *laid* the book down. He is *laying* the book down.

Like, as, as if. *Like* is equivalent to a preposition and is followed by a noun or pronoun used as its object. It should not be used as a conjunction to introduce a clause. Correct: He looks *like* a tramp. Correct: I did the work *as* you directed (not *like*). Correct: You act *as if* you were tired (not *like*).

Lots of, a lot of. Colloquial, to be avoided in serious writing. Use *considerable, many, a large amount of, a number of,* and similar expressions. Colloquial: He had *lots of* friends. Better for writing: He had *many* friends.

Most, almost. *Most* means *in the highest degree; almost* means *nearly.* They are not interchangeable. Not good: I am *most* ready to go (say *almost* or *nearly*). Correct: He was *most* happy to see me (meaning *happy in the highest degree*).

Nice. See *Fine.*

Nowhere near. Colloquial for *not nearly.* Colloquial: He was *nowhere near* ready. Standard: He was *not nearly* ready.

Nowheres. See *Anywheres.*

Number. *A number of* takes a plural verb; *the number of* takes a singular verb. Correct: *A number* of accidents *have* occurred. Correct: *The number* of accidents *has* increased.

Of. An illiterate substitute for *have* in *could of, would of, might of, ought to of,* etc. Illiterate: He *could of* done it. Correct: He *could have* done it.

Off of. The *of* is superfluous. Correct: He pulled the cloth *off* the table (not *off of* the table).

Other times. The proper form is *at other times.* Not good: *Other times* he was quite normal (say *"at other times"*).

Outside of. Omit the *of* in expressions like *"outside of* the house"; say *"outside* the house."

Party. A *party* consists of a number of persons. In general writing and speaking, the word should not be used in referring to a single person. Not good: When I met this *party* yesterday, he didn't recognize me (say *man* or *person*).—In legal documents, such as contracts and the like, *party* is correctly used to mean a single person.

Per, as per. In general writing use *a* instead of *per* in expressions like *a day, a week, a yard.* Preferred: two dollars *a day* (not *per day*); ten cents *a yard* (not *per yard*). *As per* is commercial jargon for *according to.* Say *"according to* your letter of the fifth" (not, *"as per* your letter"). *Per diem* and *per annum* are in good standing.

Phenomenon. *Phenomenon* is the singular form; *phenomena* is the plural form.

Plan on. Omit the *on*. Correct: We had *planned* a smaller house (not *planned on*). I had *planned* to drive (not *planned on* driving).

Previous to. A pretentious commercial substitute for *before*. Say "*before* receiving your letter" (not "*previous to* receiving your letter").

Prior to. *Before* is simpler, and is usually preferable. See *Previous to*.

Proposition. A much-overworked word. Do not use it constantly in place of *plan, proposal, suggestion, scheme*.

Raise, rise. *Raise* is transitive (requires an object); *rise* is intransitive (does not take an object). Correct: He *raised* the window. Correct: He *rose* from his chair.—The principal parts are *raise, raised, raised; rise, rose, risen*.

Raise, rear, bring up. Not good: He was *raised* in Chicago. Better: He was *brought up* in Chicago (or *reared*).— In standard English, chickens are *raised;* children are *reared* or *brought up*.

Rarely ever. *Ever* is superfluous. The better form is *rarely* or *seldom*. Not good: An accident of this sort *rarely ever* happens. Better: An accident of this sort *rarely* (or *seldom*) happens.

Real. An adjective, not an adverb. Not good: I am *real* glad to be here. Correct: I am *very* glad to be here.— The adverb *really* would also be correct in this sentence, but it expresses a somewhat different meaning.

Regard, regards. Do not use *regards* (with an *-s*) in the phrases *in regard to* or *with regard to*. Correct: *In regard to* (or *Regarding*) this matter he said nothing.— The expression *as regards* is correct.

Same. Do not use *same* as a substitute for *it, they, them*, and other pronouns. Not good: Please send us the following items and charge *same* to our account. Correct: Please send us the following items, and charge *them* to our account.

Second-handed. Say "*second-hand* book," "*second-hand* car" (not *second-handed*).

Seldom ever. Omit *ever*. Correct: This room is *seldom* used (not *seldom ever* used).—The sentence, "This room is *seldom, if ever,* used," is also correct, but the meaning is somewhat different.

Sit, set. *Sit* never takes an object; *set* regularly has an object. Correct: He *sits* in the house all day. Correct: Please *set* the box on the floor.—In a few idiomatic expressions *set* is used without an object: as, "The sun *sets* in the west." "Concrete *sets,* or hardens." The principal parts are *sit, sat, sat; set, set, set.*

Size, sized. *Size* is the noun; *sized,* the adjective. Incorrect: I shall need a smaller *size* kettle. Correct: I shall need a smaller *sized* kettle.

So, such. Colloquialisms for *very* in the following sentences: "I am *so* glad to see you." "He is *such* a polite man." To be avoided in serious writing or speaking. These words are correctly used when they are accompanied by an explanatory expression: for example, "He was *so* tired *that he could scarcely walk.*" "There was *such* a noise *that we could not hear the speaker.*"

Some. *Some* is an adjective or a pronoun; colloquial when used as an adverb. The standard adverbial form is *somewhat* or *a little.* Correct: I am *somewhat* worried (not *some*). Correct: He plays the piano *a little* (not *some*).

Sort of, sort of a. See *Kind of, kind of a.*

Subsequent to. A pretentious substitute for *after.* Say, "This occurred *after* your recent visit" (not *subsequent to* your recent visit).

Such. See *So.*

Suspicion. Webster labels *to suspicion* (for *to suspect*) as dialectal. Its use as a verb is to be avoided. Not good: I *suspicioned* that he was a tramp. Correct: I *suspected* that he was a tramp.

These here, this here, that there, those there. Illiterate: I want some of *these here* apples. *That there* book is mine. Correct: I want some of *these* apples. *That* book is mine.

These kind, those kind. *These* and *those,* being plural, cannot grammatically be used with the singular noun *kind* or *sort.* Use *this* or *that.* Incorrect: *These kind* of people should not be invited. Correct: *This kind* of people should not be invited.—*These* (or *those*) *kinds* is correct, since both the pronominal adjective and the noun are plural.

Transpire. Means *to become known.* It does not mean *to* *happen* or *to occur*. Correct: It *transpired* yesterday that a merger of the three companies had been effected. Incorrect: A decisive battle *transpired* yesterday. Correct: A decisive battle *occurred* yesterday.

Underhanded. *Underhand* is the preferred form: He resorted to *underhand* methods (not *underhanded* methods).

Very much, very. As a general rule, use *very much, very well*, etc. (not *very* alone) with a past participle. Correct: *Very much excited, very much surprised, very well pleased, very much shaken* (not *very excited, very pleased*, etc.).—With a few past participles, however, which have practically lost their participial nature and have come to be regarded almost as simple adjectives, *very* is used without *much*: as, *very tired, very conceited*.

Way. See *A ways*.

While. (a) Properly used to introduce an adverbial clause of time; means *at the same time*. Correct: He studied art *while* he was in Paris. (b) The use of *while* as a substitute for *although* frequently results in ambiguity and should generally be avoided. Doubtful: *While* the report may be true, the conclusions might be expressed more tactfully. Better: *Although* the report may be true, the conclusions might be expressed more tactfully. (c) *While* is to be used sparingly, if at all, between co-ordinate statements. Not good: This building is five stories high, *while* the other is only four (use *and* or omit the conjunction). Not good: He has always been a stanch supporter of a protective tariff, *while* his brother believes that free trade will be the salvation of the country (use *whereas* or omit the conjunction).

General Exercises in Diction

A. Point out the faulty diction, and restate the sentences correctly.

1. This invention allows you to talk to people most any place in the world.

2. He didn't know if the police were looking for him or not.

3. Our repair department dissembled the watch and found two jewels broken.

4. An audience of half-crazed zealots had gathered about the guillotine to jeer at the condemned man.

5. With this amount of members the society should be prosperous.

6. After our long walk we laid down and took a nap.

7. John took the bull by the horns and butted into the president's office.

8. Why didn't you leave the book lay where I put it?

9. Important in every home is the dining room which carries the burden of festive occasions.

10. He tried to put something over in the quiz but the prof was wise to him.

11. Alice knew perfectly well that she had been a perfect failure in her chemistry course.

12. He don't have a chance to escape without somebody helps him.

13. Meanwhile the nobles were living in luxuriant villas and stately palaces.

14. He was glad of an opportunity of increasing his mentality by going to night school.

15. I was boiling inwardly at the suggestion, and proceeded to throw cold water on the plan.

16. The young doctor came to the village with high ideals but he was soon disallusioned.

17. To me it seemed like the ship was being sucked down into a whirlpool.

18. His eagerness and ambition are a premonition of a successful future career.

19. The warden suspicioned that I didn't have no fishing license.

20. A predominate human instinct is that of self-preservation.

B. Follow the instructions given for Exercise A.

1. John is liable to get first prize in the spelling contest.

2. He is well known for his liberalism to the hospital and other local charities.

3. We had an awfully good time but I never felt quite to home there.

4. A few of the officers were in uniform, but the balance wore civilian clothes.

5. This text was quite different than the one we had been using.

6. The citizens of the town boast of its healthy climate and fine scenery.

7. They are living some place in Virginia but I disremember where.

8. Bob had ran all the way home to fetch the luncheon.

9. He fell for her talk hook, line, and sinker.

10. These trips can be terribly dangerous due to the bad roads.

11. Naturally, he was anxious to make a good impression on the balance of the guests.

12. I expect you felt very concerned when you got the message.

13. He was working for an advance degree in economics.

14. The driver of the small car was undoubtably responsible for the accident.

15. A party named Thompson is coming to the office to contact you about the new tax bill.

16. The members of the crew fought between themselves after they had came to the island.

17. We swum out to the raft and dove off into deep water.

18. It seemed like the whole town was laying around on the sand.

19. The bombing of defenseless cities is a barbaric thing.

20. The eats were the swellest part of the picnic.

IMPROVING YOUR VOCABULARY

H11. **Make use of the various means of improving your vocabulary.**

Getting a better working vocabulary requires constant effort and watchfulness. It means:

1. Avoiding the mistakes that are prevalent in careless writing and speech.

2. Knowing accurately the words which you already use, but about which you are not entirely certain.

3. Adding new words which you do not now use. These will be of two kinds:

a. Words which you recognize when you meet them in your reading. The members of this group number into the thousands. They are in common use by writers and speakers. You have seen or heard them again and again. They are not pedantic. Most of the improvement in your command of words will come from transferring members of this group from your reading vocabulary to your working vocabulary.

b. Words which you do not know when you meet them in your reading. You should look them up in a dictionary and make use of those which fit your needs.

Learning to Know Words

It is not enough to add words to a list in your notebook. You must get to know them—make yourself acquainted with the various points of interest connected with them. Then you should employ them in your own writing.

a. **Background of Words.** Form the habit of looking for the background, or etymology, of words. Etymology is concerned with analyzing them into their constituent parts, and tracing their original form and meaning. For the numerous words taken into English from foreign sources—from Latin, Greek, French, and many others— the original form and meaning should be traced back to these languages.

Families of Words. The same root often appears in a number of English words—some of which, at first sight, may seem unrelated. You should train yourself to identify the members of the different families.

The recognition of these groups—and the study of etymology in its wider sense—frequently will enable you to determine, at least approximately, the meaning of an unfamiliar word. Moreover, a knowledge of the background and associations of a word will give a feeling of intimacy that makes for accuracy and confidence in its use.

b. Synonyms. Make—and study—lists of words that express the same idea or different degrees and phases of the same idea. This work will not only enlarge your vocabulary, but will also give valuable practice in distinguishing the finer shades of meaning and thus aid you in using the exact word that the thought requires.

c. Reading Good Literature. Begin at once to read each day, or at least two or three times a week, a short passage from some good writer, not for the purpose of securing amusement or information, but with the idea of finding new words. Put down in a notebook kept for that purpose each word that is new or only vaguely familiar. Then look up its exact meaning or meanings in a good dictionary. Note also its etymology, pronunciation, and spelling.

d. Browsing in the Dictionary. Make a habit of browsing in the dictionary. Open it at any place and see what it offers. Some of the words that you find may be ignored, for the dictionary contains many technical and obsolete terms which you will probably never have an occasion to use. But on almost every page there will be others which you may profitably add to your vocabulary.

e. Deliberate and Conscious Effort to Use New Words. Finally, whenever or wherever you find a new word, put it to work as soon as possible. Use it every time you get the opportunity—and if an opportunity fails to present itself, make one. A word becomes a habit through use.

A. BACKGROUND OF WORDS

In the study of background or etymology, two points are to be kept in mind:

1. The structure of the word, as revealed by an analysis of the parts from which it is built.

2. The meaning—including both the original meaning and the changes, if any, which it has undergone.

Structure of Words

Structurally, a word consists of one or more of the following three elements: prefix, root, suffix. A root is always present, but one or both of the other parts may be lacking.

The *root* gives the basic meaning.

The *prefix* shows some particular modification or application of the basic idea.

The *suffix* shows the part of speech under which the word is classified, and sometimes is also indicative of some phase of the meaning.

For example, take *reference*, *preferred*, and *inferring*. The root *fer-* (from the Latin *fero*) means "to bear, carry." The prefixes *re-*, *pre-*, and *in-* express the idea of "back" or "again," "before," and "in" or "into," respectively. The suffixes *-ence*, *-ed*, and *-ing* indicate that the words are respectively noun, past tense or past participle, and present participle.

Use the Dictionary. The dictionary gives the language from which an English word is derived; its form and meaning in that language; and usually the root and prefix by means of which it was formed. If this information is not given under the entry for which you are looking, try a more basic form of the word. For instance, if you are unsuccessful under *information*, try *inform*.

Lists of Prefixes and Roots

The student should learn the more common prefixes and roots—those which occur frequently in English (suffixes are not included in our study, since they are of less importance in determining the meaning of words).

Some of the more important prefixes and roots are listed below.

LATIN PREFIXES

PREFIX	MEANING	EXAMPLES
a, ab	from, away	avert, abnormal, abduct
ad, ac	to	administer, accede
ante	before	antedate, anteroom
bene	well	benefactor, benefit
bi, bis	two, twice	bisect, biscuit
circum	around	circumnavigate, circumscribe
com, con, col, cor	together, with	combine, concur, collect, correspond
contra	against	contradict, contrary
de	down, from, off	degrade, dejected
dis	away, general negation	dissatisfy, disrobe
e, ex	out, from	evaporate, exclude, exile
extra	beyond	extraordinary, extravagant
in, im, il, ir	not	infirm, impossible, illegal, irresponsible
in, im	in, into	invade, inmate, impress
inter	between, among	international, interchange
intra, intro	within	intramural, introduce
male, mal	bad, ill	malefactor, malpractice
mis	wrong, ill	misfortune, misbehave
multi	many	multitude, multimillionaire
non	not	nonsense, non-essential
ob, op	against	object, oppose
per	through, fully	pervade, perform, perfect
post	after	postpone, post-mortem
pre	before	predict, predestined
pro	for, forward	pronoun, produce, proceed
re	back, again	return, rebound, recur
retro	backward	retrograde, retroactive
se	from	seclude, secede
semi	half	semiannual, semicircle
sub, sup	under	subordinate, support
super	above	superhuman, superior
trans	across, beyond	transatlantic, transfer
ultra	beyond	ultra-conservative
un	not	unable, unpleasing
uni	one	uniform, unify

LATIN ROOTS

The following list of Latin roots is divided, for convenience, into two groups: verbs, and nouns and adjectives. Any root in either list, however, may appear in different parts of speech in English.

Verbs. For each verb, the first form given is the first person, singular number, present tense (*ago*—I do). If only two forms are given, the second is the past participle (*actus*—done). If three are given, the last one is the past participle, and the middle one is the first person, singular number, perfect tense—similar to the present perfect tense in English (*cepi,* I have taken).

ROOT	MEANING	EXAMPLES
ago, actus	to do	agent, action
amo, amatus	to love	amorous, amateur
audio, auditus	to hear	audience, audible
capio, cepi, captus	to take	captive, receptive
cedo, cessus	to go	recede, procession
credo, creditus	to believe	credible, credit
curro, cursus	to run	current, cursory
dico, dictus	to say	diction, predict
do, datus	to give	donate, data
doceo, doctus	to teach	docile, doctrine
duco, ductus	to lead, draw	conductor, ductile
facio, feci, factus	to make, do	fact, manufacture
fero, latus	to bear	transfer, translate
flecto, flexus	to bend, turn	deflect, flexible
fluo, fluxus	to flow	fluent, influx
jacio, jeci, jactus	to throw	ejaculate, projectile
lego, lectus	to read	legible, lecture
loquor, locutus	to speak	loquacious, elocution
mitto, missus	to send	transmit, missionary
moneo, monitus	to warn, remind	admonish, monitor
moveo, motus	to move	move, motion
pello, pulsus	to drive	propel, repulsive
pendo, pensus	to hang	pendant, suspense
pono, positus	to put, place	postpone, position
porto, portatus	to carry	porter, import
scribo, scriptus	to write, draw	inscribe, scripture
sequor. secutus	to follow	sequence, consecutive

ROOT	MEANING	EXAMPLES
specto, spectatus	to look at	inspect, spectator
spiro, spiratus	to breathe	transpire, spirit
sto, steti, status	to stand	state, station
traho, tractus	to draw	tractor, subtract
venio, ventus	to come	convene, advent
verto, versus	to turn	revert, reverse
video, visus	to see	provident, vision
voco, vocatus	to call	convoke, vocation

Adjectives and Nouns. The first word in a group is the nominative case form; the second, the genitive case.

ROOT	MEANING	EXAMPLES
anima	breath, spirit	animated, inanimate
annus	year	annual, annuity
aqua	water	aquatic, aquarium
brevis	short	brevity, abbreviate
caput, capitis	head	capital, decapitate
cor, cordis	heart	cordial, concord
corpus, corporis	body	corpse, corporation
cura	care, attention	cure, curator
dens, dentis	tooth	dentist, indent
fides	faith, trust	fidelity, confidence
frater	brother	fraternal
lex, legis	law	legal, legislation
liber	book	library
liber	free	liberal, liberty
locus	place	location, locomotion
lumen, luminis	light	luminous, illuminate
lux, lucis	light	lucid, translucent
manus	hand	manual, manufacture
mater	mother	maternal
mens, mentis	mind, intellect	mental, demented
novus	new	novelty, renovate
nox, noctis	night	nocturnal
pater	father	paternal
pes, pedis	foot	pedal, pedestrian
terra	earth	terrestrial, territory
urbs, urbis	city	suburb, urban
velox, velocis	swift	velocity
verus	true	verify, verity

COMMON GREEK ROOTS AND PREFIXES

ROOT OR PREFIX	MEANING	EXAMPLES
anti	against	antidote, anti-slavery
aster	star	astronomy, astral
auto	self	automobile, autograph
chrono	time	chronometer, chronology
cyclo	circle	bicycle, cyclone
dynam	force, power	dynamo, dynamite
eu	well, good	eulogy, euphony
graph	write	graphic, telegraphy
logos	word, discourse	chronology, astrology
metro	measure	meter, chronometer
mono	one, alone	monologue, monoplane
pan	all	pan-American, panacea
phone	sound	phonograph, telephone
syn, sym	together, with	synthesis, sympathy
tele	afar	telephone, telegraph

Exercises

A. Without consulting a dictionary, point out the prefixes (if any) and roots. Give the meaning of each prefix and root. What is the relation between the original and the present meaning of the word? After you have made the analysis, check your results with the dictionary.

repel	illegal	animated	introvert
dependent	aqueduct	retract	nonsubscriber
inject	discredit	aversion	inspiration
infidel	transport	biped	supervisor
conversion	provide	innovation	recurrence
evoke	confide	irrevocable	indention
circumvent	chronic	precedent	concession
audition	dictating	discord	injection
precursor	monograph	premonition	circumlocution
intercede	sequel	confluence	localism
revise	reflect	subjection	colloquialism
composition	adjacent	excursion	velocipede

B. Give as many English words as you can find which contain the roots in the list below. For example, the following words belong to the family of the root *dicere*, "to say":

diction	contradict	indicate	dedicate
dictionary	predict	addict	abdicate
dictate	benediction	edict	predicate

Make a similar list for each of the following roots:

credo, creditus	fluo, fluxus	caput, capitis
mitto, missus	porto, portatus	cura
scribo, scriptus	venio, ventus	manus
video, visus	loquor, locutus	terra
moveo, motus	verto, versus	pater
amo, amatus	doceo, doctus	aster
jacio, jectus	do, datus	phone
cor, cordis	spiro, spiratus	

In the course of its development a word may change its form somewhat. Letters may change or may be omitted. The skeleton, or basic form, however, is usually recognizable. Thus English *flow* is from the Latin root *fluo;* the words *capture, reception, receive,* and *receipt* are all from the Latin *capio, cepi.*

Changes in Meaning

The original meaning of a word, as shown by its etymology, is frequently retained in its present use: for example, *dejected* (Latin, *de-*, down, and *jacio, jectus*, cast, throw) still carries the idea of being "cast down" in spirit.

In other instances, however, the meaning may change —sometimes slightly, sometimes considerably. Thus, *prevent* originally meant "to come before" (Latin, *pre-*, before, and *venio*, come). The present use has developed from the idea of coming to a place before someone arrived in order to keep him from doing something.

In tracing the family history of a word, the student

begins with its etymology as given in the dictionary. The original meaning is that noted under the etymological entry.

The dictionary may then cite some early definitions—perhaps marked *Obsolete* or *Archaic*. These are followed by the present uses of the word. From the successive entries, the student can sometimes obtain a clear picture of the development.

Often, however, the successive stages are not shown; only the original and the present meaning are given. In such instances the student must use his ingenuity. For example, the word *focus* originally meant a "fireplace," the ordinary source of heat in a Roman home. At present it designates a point where lines, rays of light, heat, etc., meet. What is the relation? A moment's thought brings a picture of the fireplace as the place about which the life of the household centered. It was the focal point. The transition from this picture to the present idea of a focal point for lines and rays of light is an easy step.

Valuable and interesting works on changes in meaning are Greenough and Kittredge, *Words and Their Ways in English Speech*, and George McKnight, *English Words and Their Background*. These should not be consulted for any particular word until the student has made his own analysis.

Exercise in Changes in Meaning

The following words have undergone interesting changes in meaning. Not all the prefixes and roots are included in the lists on p. 281 f. Look up the words in the dictionary; note the original and the present meaning. Then ask yourself, "How and why did this change occur?" To answer the question, you will need to draw upon your knowledge of various fields—history, earlier manners of living, earlier customs, astrology, etc. Words take on new meanings because of changes in the environment in which they are used. It is advisable to consult an unabridged dictionary in this exercise.

umbrella	ballot	manufacture	dandelion
cynic	lunatic	September	dexterous
paper	hussy	amateur	sinister
pen	boor	impediment	palace
homely	insect	astonish	derrick
boudoir	volume	discourse	orient
quell	gospel	disaster	occident
infant	petroleum	quarantine	sombrero
thimble	academy	cunning	carouse
clove	salary	iconoclast	retail
fanatic	finance	diamond	bedlam
curfew	bombast	sullen	alphabet
crazy	miser	amethyst	candidate
hypocrite	dilapidated	equinox	symposium
barter	pecuniary	transpire	porcupine

B. SYNONYMS AND NEAR–SYNONYMS

Synonyms are words which have the same, or practically the same, meaning. They can be used interchangeably.

Near-synonyms have the same basic meaning, but express varying degrees or shades of that idea.

For many words the dictionary gives a list of synonyms and makes a careful distinction in the use of the different members of the group. The list is generally found under only one of the members, the reader being referred to the proper place by some notation like "See ——" under the other words.

The regular definitions in the dictionary are usually too general to be of much assistance in distinguishing the finer shades of meaning.

Special books on synonyms are *Allen's Synonyms and Antonyms, Crabb's English Synonyms,* Fernald's *English*

Synonyms and Antonyms, Roget's *Thesaurus of English Words and Phrases,* and *Webster's Dictionary of Synonyms* (1942).

Exercises in Synonyms and Near-synonyms

A. Each group in the following list consists of words which express various shades of the same meaning. In some instances the variation is so slight that the words are practically interchangeable. Generally, however, there is an appreciable difference. Point out the differences; then use the words in sentences.

Add other related words when you are able to do so.

ignorant, illiterate
genial, cordial
leave, abandon
regret, remorse
legal, legitimate
follow, pursue
praise, flatter
unique, unusual
probable, possible
new, novel
damp, dank
pessimistic, cynical
approaching, impending
early, primitive
skeptic, agnostic
less, fewer
much, many
heal, cure
envy, jealousy

obsolete, obsolescent
politician, statesman
allow, tolerate
copy, facsimile
nightly, nocturnal
knowledge, wisdom
intercede, intervene
convince, persuade
commercial, industrial
attain, obtain
fatherly, paternal
charity, alms
imperious, imperial
ambiguous, equivocal
inability, disability
call, summon
wages, salary
deceitful, deceptive
temperance, abstinence

civil, polite, courteous
pride, vanity, arrogance
abundant, adequate, lavish
frugal, thrifty, stingy
work, toil, drudgery

boyish, juvenile, puerile
respect, esteem, honor
circle, coterie, clique
pity, sympathy, compassion
bravery, courage, fortitude

shy, bashful, modest, demure
brief, concise, curt, terse
wages, salary, stipend, hon-
  orarium
alike, akin, similar, identical
gaudy, garish, tawdry
fear, alarm, fright
old, aged, venerable, senile, decrepit
affection, love, infatuation, devotion
proud, vain, haughty, supercilious
present, gift, fee, gratuity, bequest, bribe

B. Give synonyms and near-synonyms for the following words. Explain the different shades of meaning.
Make the list for each word as complete as possible without consulting a dictionary. Then refer to a dictionary or
a book of synonyms for additional words.

grief	lively	shy (adjective)	happy
fat	disease	say	opponent
inquisitive	big	hate	poverty
real	small	rich	herd
brave	mistake (noun)	throw	lazy
break (verb)	ugly	beg	irritate
calm	event	ask	journey
govern	stop	liberty	noisy

C. WORDS FROM READING

Once each week select a page or two from a good book
or magazine. Make three lists of words that you find
there.

1. Words which you recognize, but which you yourself
do not use.

2. Words which you do not know (look them up in the
dictionary).

3. Words which you think are particularly apt, well-
chosen, and effectively used.

Be ready to submit the lists to the instructor.

D. BROWSING IN THE
DICTIONARY

Open the dictionary at random. Look at all the words on one page. Report in class anything of interest that you find there: some interesting etymology, any word that you have been misspelling or mispronouncing, and words that might profitably be added to your own working vocabulary.

Chapter Ten

PUNCTUATION, SPELL-ING, AND MECHANICS

PUNCTUATION

Punctuation is a means of helping the reader to see the points of division and the relation in thought between groups in the sentence. Punctuation in places where it does not belong—or the use of the wrong mark—makes a false division into groups or indicates the wrong relationship. Lack of proper punctuation puts upon the reader the extra task of recognizing connections unaided.

General Principles of Punctuation

The three chief factors governing punctuation are:

1. The logical relation between the parts of a sentence: for example, closeness or remoteness in thought, a sudden break, an explanation or an enumeration, a "bridging" of the thought from one part to another over an intervening expression, and so on.

2. The length and importance—that is, the "weight"— of the groups. Thus, a long phrase or clause sometimes requires stronger punctuation than that used with a smaller group having the same logical and grammatical relation with the context, the reason being that the reader does not readily see the longer group in its entirety and immediately recognize its relation as he would do in the case of the smaller one.

3. The position of a group in the sentence—this will be discussed later (see Straight-line Sequence and Delayed or Interrupted Sequence, pages 296–299).

Marks of Punctuation. For purposes of punctuation, the writer has his choice of various marks:

Period (.)	Parentheses ( )
Semicolon (;)	Brackets [ ]
Comma (,)	Interrogation Point (?)
Colon (:)	Exclamation Point (!)
Dash (—)	Quotation Marks (" ")

Characteristics and Uses of These Marks. These marks have the following characteristics and uses (only the five in the first column are considered here):

1. The period, semicolon, and comma form a series in which the distinguishing characteristic of the members is their relative strength. In accordance with the two factors given above—the relation between groups and the length of groups—the general principle governing the use of these three marks is as follows:

a. The *period* is the strongest mark. It therefore points out the longest and most important division of thought—the sentence; and also indicates the greatest remoteness in thought.

b. The *semicolon* ranks next in strength. It is suitable for use between the longer and more important co-ordinate elements *within the sentence,* or between those which have a comparatively remote connection in thought.

c. The *comma* is the weakest. It separates the shorter groups, and indicates a comparatively close connection.

Sometimes, however, two long groups may be so closely related in thought that a comma is preferable to the semicolon; and, on the other hand, short groups may be so remotely connected that a semicolon is needed. Nevertheless, the chances are more in favor of a semicolon with a long group than with a short one; and when there is a combination of length and remoteness, the semicolon will almost always be used.

2. The colon and the dash fall outside the preceding series. With them the question is not of relative strength; they have special functions:

a. A *colon* indicates explanation or anticipation; it warns the reader to be on the watch for additional explanatory matter.

b. A *dash* indicates a sudden break or unexpected change in thought; sometimes gives emphasis to the statement that it introduces; and frequently sets off an expression over which the thought is "bridged" from one part of the sentence to another part. It is a valuable means for securing variety and special effects in punctuation.

Conclusion. The writer who would punctuate effectively must first know the relation in thought that he wishes to show, and then select the mark that most clearly indicates it. The study of rules, such as are given in the following pages, will help him to do this; but in applying these rules, he must remember that they are only statements of general practice. In actual writing there are many nice distinctions which must be indicated by the punctuation, and these distinctions are so numerous that it is impracticable to make the rules broad enough to cover all of them. The writer, therefore, must use the rules intelligently, and be ready to vary the punctuation to suit different conditions. For example, parenthetical expressions may be set off with commas, dashes, or parentheses, the choice depending upon the closeness of relation. Similar variations will also be found in other rules.

COMMA

The comma is the weakest of the punctuation marks. It is used to indicate comparatively close connection between parts of a sentence, or comparatively slight interruptions in the run of the thought.

K1. Observe the following standard uses of the comma.

A. Main Clauses

For purposes of punctuation, main clauses are divided into two classes: (1) those connected by the chief coordinating conjunctions, *and, but, or,* and *nor;* (2) those which are not connected by these four conjunctions.

Main Clauses Connected by And, But, Or, *or* Nor

A comma is regularly used to separate main clauses of medium length when they are connected by *and, but, or,* or *nor.*

The copy is almost ready for the printer, *and* you should get the proofs early next week.
The library is usually closed in the evening, *but* it will be open until nine o'clock tonight.
We must have a good rain within a week, *or* the lawns and gardens will be ruined.

Very short main clauses connected by *and, but, or,* or *nor* are sometimes not punctuated.

My watch was slow and I was late.

Semicolon. Long main clauses are generally separated by a semicolon, especially if they contain elements set off by commas (see Sec. **K 2**). The semicolon is valuable here because it clearly marks the main point of division in the sentence.

Benjamin Franklin, who was a leader in the Revolutionary War, began life as a printer's apprentice, as he himself tells us in his autobiography; but by hard work, combined with shrewd common sense, he rose to a position of honor, and became the American ambassador to France.

Main Clauses Without And, But, Or, *or* Nor

Main clauses which are not connected by *and, but, or,* **or** *nor* **are separated by semicolons (see Secs. D 11 and K 2).**

This rule applies to both long and short clauses.

> John is a freshman at Princeton; his brother is a senior in the business school at Harvard.
>
> The Toledo Bears are a powerful team; *nevertheless,* they can be beaten.
>
> Many unexpected difficulties arose in the digging of the canal; *therefore* it was not finished until after the specified time.

This group may have no conjunction between the clauses, or may have any co-ordinate conjunction other than the four specified above: as, *therefore, nevertheless, however, consequently, thus, as a result,* etc.

Colon. For the use of a colon between two main clauses when the second one is explanatory of the first, see Sec. **K 3**.

Exercises in Main Clauses

A. Punctuate the main clauses that need punctuation, and give the reason. If punctuation is not needed, give the reason.

1. The coast guard arrived soon after the signal for help was broadcast and the passengers in the disabled ship were taken safely to shore.

2. The night had been clear and cold and a slight frost had nipped the leaves and flowers.

3. He was, of course, familiar with French, German, and Italian, as well as some of the Asiatic languages but he was out of favor with the party in power and could not get a position in the diplomatic corps.

4. I tried once for the prize and failed the next time I won second place in the contest.

5. He had found the pot of gold at the end of the rainbow but now he was too old to enjoy it.

6. He could not do the work alone therefore he had to hire an assistant.

7. John sang and I played the piano.

8. We spent ten days at the fair in New York and then we went for a week's cruise to Bermuda.

9. He wore a ragged coat, down-at-the-heel shoes, and a shapeless, dilapidated hat but, in spite of his shabbiness, he was obviously a man of some refinement.

10. An immense stone fireplace almost filled one end of the room and over the mantel was hung a portrait of Mr. Grange painted by an English artist.

B. Bring to class ten sentences—from a book or a magazine—showing the punctuation of main clauses.

B. Phrases and Subordinate Clauses

The punctuation of phrases and subordinate clauses depends partly upon their position in the sentence and partly upon the nature of their relation to the context.

According to their position, these elements either carry on the main thought of the sentence in a straight-line sequence, or delay or interrupt the line of thought.

Straight-line Sequence. The natural or straight-line arrangement is as follows:

> Subject / adjective phrases and clauses modifying the subject / verb / object / adverbial phrases and clauses modifying the verb.

> The child / who was lost / was wearing / a blue dress / when she left home.

In sentences of this type, the flow of the thought is direct from subject—to verb—to object: the three essential elements which the reader must recognize in order to comprehend the meaning.

Phrases and clauses in straight-line sequence are not usually punctuated.

Subject of a verb:

That he will be here is certain.
To do the work well would require a month.

Predicate noun:

The fact is *that no one is responsible*.
The plan was *to import laborers from the city*.

Object of a verb:

The employers have said *that they are willing to accept
the proposal*.

Adverbial element following the verb:

He will be satisfied *if he receives the appointment*.
She entered the room *as the clock was striking ten*.
The target is painted white *so that it may be easily seen*.

Since these elements are in their normal positions, the
reader easily sees their relation to the context, and does
not need the aid of punctuation.

Exceptions. The following phrases and subordinate
clauses in straight-line sequence are generally set off
with commas:

1. A noun clause or phrase used as the subject, if it is
long or if it ends with a verb that makes an awkward
combination with the main verb.

*That he fully intended to follow his own judgment in
the hiring of employees,* was evident from the beginning.
Whoever speaks, does so at his own peril.

2. Adverbial clauses of concession introduced by *although* or an equivalent word, and adverbial clauses of
reason introduced by *as* or *for*.

He will be there, *although he was not invited*.
We came early, *as we did not want to interrupt the
meeting*.
He is sure to succeed, *for his plans have been carefully
made*.

3. A phrase or clause which is separated from the word that it modifies. (Punctuation is used here if it makes the relation between the parts clearer to the reader.)

> *They* walked down the street, *laughing and talking gaily.*
> After dinner *we* lay down to rest, *contented with the world.*
> He *arrived* in Naples early on a Sunday morning, *long before the city was astir.*
> (Compare: "He *arrived long before the clock struck eight*"—close connection, not punctuated.)

4. Non-restrictive adjective clauses and phrases. Although these are in straight-line sequence, they are always punctuated (see Sec. **K 1c**).

Delayed or Interrupted Sequence. This type of sequence occurs when phrases or subordinate clauses are placed in the following positions:

1. An introductory adverbial phrase or clause preceding the main clause.

2. A noun phrase or clause used as the object of the verb, but placed before the subject.

3. An adverbial phrase or clause between the subject and the verb.

4. An adverbial phrase or clause between the verb and the object.

The groups in (1) and (2) delay the beginning of the main statement. Those in (3) and (4) interrupt the natural flow of the thought from subject—to verb—to object. In these cases, punctuation makes it easier for the reader to see the grouping and relation of the parts.

A comma is regularly used to set off phrases and clauses which delay or interrupt the main line of thought.

Adverbial group before the subject:

> *After the general plan has been approved,* there will be time enough to discuss the details.

Hearing a shot in the street, we rushed to the window.
To reach the village in the mountains, he had to ride
forty miles on horseback.

Noun group—object of the verb—placed before the
subject:

What the argument was, he did not say.
That he was guilty of any misdoing, the prisoner vehe-
mently denied.

Adverbial group between the subject and the verb:

This leader, *when he was at the height of his power,*
had only two thousand followers.
A man, *to do the work well,* must have experience.
The company, *after a short rest,* proceeded on its way.
The captain, *fearing a night attack,* doubled the guard.

Adverbial group between the verb and the object:

He decided, *after he heard the offer,* that he could not
afford to accept it.
He refused, *on the advice of his attorney,* to testify at
the trial.

Exception. Elements that are short and closely connected with the context are not usually punctuated.
They do not appreciably delay or interrupt the run of
the thought.

If you wish you may go.
I knew *from his appearance* that he had been fighting.

Note. The rules for delayed or interrupted sequence apply
to groups belonging to a clause within a sentence as well as to
groups belonging to the main clause at the beginning of the
sentence.

Every seat was filled long before the appointed hour;
but *when the time came to begin the program,* the
speaker had not arrived. (Before the subject of the
second main clause.)
He will succeed if, *after he has planned his campaign,*
he selects the right man to direct it. (Before the subject of the *if*-clause.)

Exercises in Straight-line, Delayed, and Interrupted Sequence

A. Punctuate the phrases and clauses that need punctuation, and give the reason.

1. While we were visiting in London we spent several days in the British Museum and in the National Gallery.

2. He knew as soon as he looked at the letter that someone had tampered with it.

3. Before leaving the house we hid the money where we could easily find it.

4. The street vendors forced their way through the crowd pushing their heavy carts before them.

5. This physical work though it was tiring at first kept me in shape for fall football practice.

6. He knew that the boat would be swamped if he stopped rowing even for a minute.

7. The trunk being much too heavy to carry we left it behind in the burning house.

8. The book being written in a strange dialect was not easy to read.

9. When he finished school early in June he had considerable difficulty in finding a position for there were many experienced accountants looking for work.

10. Several days before we had read an account of his adventures in the *Tribune*.

11. To get the most benefit from the course a student should prepare each day's assignment carefully.

12. A student in order to get the most benefit from the course should prepare each day's assignment carefully.

13. A student should carefully prepare each day's assignment in order to get the most benefit from the course.

14. At midnight the watchers went home for the worst part of the flood had passed.

15. For a full moment he looked at us smiling at our embarrassment.

16. What the results will be no one will know until all the returns have been tabulated.

17. They knew that someone had been in the house dur-

ing their absence although nothing seemed to have been disturbed.

18. John Hamlin though he was only a freshman was given the leading part in the school play.

19. Brooklyn and New York were to play a double header that afternoon, and because of the intense rivalry between the teams there was not a vacant seat in the stadium when the first game was called.

20. When the first game of the double header was called there was not a vacant seat in the great stadium for the rivalry between the teams was intense.

B. Select a page or two from a good book or magazine. Bring to class at least ten sentences that you found there, showing punctuation of phrases and subordinate clauses in delayed or interrupted sequence.

C. Restrictive and Non-restrictive Elements

Adjective clauses and phrases are practically always in straight-line sequence, since they follow the words that they modify. Their position, however, has nothing to do with their punctuation; that depends upon whether they are restrictive or non-restrictive in nature.

A *restrictive* clause or phrase is one that is needed to show which person or thing—which member of a class of objects—is meant.

The general *who commanded the third division* was captured. (Which general was captured?)

A *non-restrictive* clause or phrase is one that is merely explanatory or descriptive. In other words, it is not needed to point out which person or thing is meant, for that is already known.

General Frank Young, *who commanded the third division,* was captured. (Presumably there would be only one General Frank Young in the army.)

Non-restrictive Elements

A non-restrictive adjective clause or phrase is set off by commas.

I then met my father, *who had just returned from a business trip.*

History, *which is a record of what man has done,* is a fascinating study.

The *Oregon, flying the admiral's flag,* steamed into the harbor.

This report, *printed on hand-made paper,* will be sent free of charge.

Mr. F. A. Price, *in the left foreground of the picture,* was the toastmaster.

Restrictive Elements

A restrictive clause or phrase is not punctuated.

A man *who pays his debts promptly* can always get credit.

He has sold the house *that stands on the corner.*

The boy *carrying the banner* was arrested.

Bring me the note *lying on the table.*

A letter *written by Robert Burns* is offered for sale.

Note. If a long restrictive clause or phrase is placed between the subject and the verb, a comma may be inserted *after* it (but *not before* it) in order to show the location of the verb.

The company *which furnishes the most satisfactory proof of its ability to finish the work within the specified time,* will be awarded the contract.

Exercises in Non-restrictive and Restrictive Elements

A. Punctuate the phrases and clauses that require punctuation.

1. Among the suspects that were questioned was "Sparrow" Borlin who was paroled last spring.

2. She has received a number of offers from Hollywood all of which she has refused.

3. All the typists who completed the course have been placed in good positions.

4. The novels which he has written thus far deal with pioneer life in New York.

5. The professional at the Club is Bobby Burke who was runner-up in the state tournament last fall.

6. On this short hole I took a No. 16 iron which my father still calls a niblick.

7. My mother who had been a librarian before her marriage objected to my reading so many detective stories.

8. He made an A in calculus which was his favorite study.

9. He makes good grades in the studies which he likes.

10. The bulbs planted in sandy soil have grown faster than the others.

11. General Grant mounted on a black horse rode at the head of the procession.

12. The crowd became silent as the chief justice wearing a wig and gown entered the courtroom.

13. People sitting in the gallery were unable to hear the speaker.

14. The president speaking informally gave the reporters a graphic account of the incident.

15. This is an account of the battle which was written by an American officer who had taken part in the attack.

16. Soldiers who are in the city on leave should register at the local headquarters of the Red Cross which are on the sixth floor of the Stevens building.

17. Jack Richards who plays left guard was praised by the coach who said that Jack's excellent blocking was largely responsible for the victory.

18. Only two copies of the first edition of the book printed in 1802 are known to exist.

19. The moon which was just rising laid a path of gold across the lake.

20. This is the house that Jack built.

B. Select a page or two from a good book or magazine. Bring to class ten sentences that you find there—five containing non-restrictive and five containing restrictive adjective phrases or clauses. Note the punctuation in each sentence.

D. *Addition and Repetition*

Under the heading, "Addition and Repetition," are included words, phrases, and clauses which carry forward a line of thought, or repeat a thought.

Observe the use of the comma in the following cases of Addition and Repetition:

Here the purpose of the punctuation is to indicate the points of division between the groups in the series.

1. Members of a Series. Co-ordinate members of a series of words, phrases, or clauses are separated by commas.

You will find *pen, ink, and paper* on the desk.
The *clear, dry, invigorating* air restored him to health.
He walked *into the house, through the hall, and up the stairs.*
The judge asked the prisoner *where he found the money, why he took it, and what he had done with it.*
There was *water, water* everywhere.

In a series of adjectives, only members of co-ordinate rank are separated by commas.

a *garish, dazzling* electric sign.
a *good, substantial* American dinner.

Note that in the first of these examples, *garish, dazzling,* and *electric* are not co-ordinate. *Electric* is closely associated with the noun *sign;* together they name a definite type of illumination. *Garish* and *dazzling* tell what kind of *electric sign* it is. They are co-ordinate and are separated by commas, but no punctuation is used between them and *electric.*

Note 1. Some writers omit the comma before the conjunction between the last two members of a series: "The committee is made up of lawyers, physicians and teachers." The form with a comma is preferable, since without punctuation there is sometimes danger of ambiguity.

Note 2. When all the members are connected by conjunctions, the punctuation is usually omitted: "Soldiers and sailors and marines took part in the attack."

Semicolon. Semicolons are generally used between the members of a series when they contain parts set off by commas. In this way the main divisions are clearly shown.

> The committee consists of *Mr. E. F. Meyers, a banker; Dr. J. B. Green, a physician; and Mr. C. E. Miner, a lawyer.*
>
> He carried a *faded, greenish-black umbrella; an oilcloth satchel, torn at the seams; and a small package wrapped in paper.*

2. Compound Predicates. The parts of a long compound predicate are separated by a comma.

> The company *was outnumbered* two to one by the attacking party, and *was forced* to retreat to the second line of trenches.

3. Words in Apposition. Words in apposition—together with their modifiers—are set off by commas.

> My dictionary, *an old edition,* did not contain the word.
> Mr. Atkins, *the manager,* is in the office.
> We then took the steamer for Bannister, *a beautiful city on Broad Lake.*

Note. The punctuation is omitted when the appositive is closely related to the preceding noun.

> My *brother Charles* will call tomorrow.
> The *word "viaduct"* is derived from the Latin.

4. Declarative Statement and Question. A declarative statement is separated by a comma from a question following it in the same sentence.

> This book is interesting, *isn't it?*

5. Titles, Addresses, Dates, etc. Commas are used to set off the items in the following groups:

a. A personal name followed by a title.

Mr. John R. Adams, Superintendent.
Professor F. R. Brown, A.B., Ph.D.

b. Addresses and geographical names.

His address is 248 Linden Street, Canton, Ohio.
He was born in Lexington, Kentucky, in 1869.

c. Dates.

The law was passed on May 1, 1920, without opposition.
In April, 1652, the first settlement was made.

d. Bibliographical entries.

W. Stubbs, *The Constitutional History of England,* Vol.
  I, p. 248. (Or, I, 248.)

Dash. For special emphasis, a dash, instead of a comma, may be used in some of the types of Addition and Repetition discussed in Sec. **K 1d.**

The captain was a brave, experienced—*but reckless* leader (series of words).
He was a kind father, a devout Christian—*and a stanch Republican* (used here for humorous effect).
He attributes his success to genius—*genius* for hard work.
The speaker—*a typical tourist in tweeds*—had arrived that morning (emphatic apposition).

Exercises in Addition and Repetition

A. Punctuate wherever punctuation is needed, and give the reason.

1. He disposed of his stocks bonds and mortgages and invested the money in government securities.
2. This is his most recent novel isn't it?

3. It is a light airy room on the twelfth floor of a modern apartment hotel.

4. He was born on July 14 1912 in Madison Wisconsin where his father was practicing law.

5. The toastmaster then introduced the principal speaker Senator Forbes the senior senator from Idaho.

6. We visited countless cathedrals museums and art galleries strolled through the noisy colorful Italian streets and gorged ourselves on spaghetti and cheap red wine.

7. She was tired tired of bridge parties and teas tired of all the social rigmarole.

8. Frank was an industrious conscientious young man with an undeveloped sense of humor and was the constant butt of office jokes.

9. He lived at 18 North Central Avenue Canton Indiana until July 1940 when he moved to Boston Massachusetts.

10. The inspector asked me where I was living in Chicago what my business was and how much money I made.

11. They have never paid off the mortgage on the farm have they?

12. The scout master a retired army officer was strict with the boys when they were in camp and expected them to observe every rule.

13. The party consisted of the former president of the club Mrs. Kline the president-elect Mrs. Seager and the chairmen of the various committees.

14. At that time the three main streets Lake Hamilton and Jefferson were paved with cedar blocks.

15. The girl wore a light blue silk dress and a small brimless hat.

16. For a detailed account of this incident see R. B. Sprague *American Pioneer Life* Vol II pp 364 ff.

17. It was in February 1941 that the branch factory at Plymouth Illinois was closed and dismantled.

18. On a warm bright June morning we started on a motor trip across the desert over the mountains and along the western coast.

19. A lone pine tree protected the house from the winter snows.

20. An authoritative article on Bees will be found in Vol III p 625 ff of the *Encyclopædia Britannica* eleventh edition.

B. Select one or two pages in a good book or magazine. Bring in ten sentences showing the punctuation of types of construction discussed under Addition and Repetition.

E. Independent Elements

Independent elements are words or groups of words which are outside the regular grammatical framework of a sentence. They are thrown in as "asides," as supplementary explanations, as connecting or transitional devices, etc.

Observe the use of the comma in the following types of Independent Elements:

1. Parenthetical Expressions. Mildly parenthetical expressions are regularly set off by commas.

> Most of you, *I feel sure,* will agree to this plan.
> This work, *it must be admitted,* is not essential.

Longer parenthetical expressions and those which conspicuously break the continuity of thought in the sentence, are set off by dashes (see Sec. **K 4b**).

> This so-called remedy—*any physician will confirm my statement*—is worse than useless.

(Some writers use parentheses instead of dashes in sentences like the preceding one—see Sec. **K 7a**.)

2. Transitional Devices. Conjunctive adverbs and transitional devices used independently are regularly set off by commas.

This group includes expressions such as, *however, therefore, moreover, finally, of course, on the other hand, to tell the truth.*

> The result, *however,* is not entirely satisfactory.
> It is evident, *therefore,* that the money was lost.
> *In short,* the expedition was a failure; but this, *of course,* was to be expected.

Well, what do you think is the trouble?
Frankly, I am opposed to the plan.

Sometimes an expression of this sort fits so smoothly into the sentence that punctuation is not required.

His work was *therefore* in vain.
He was *accordingly* elected to the office.

3. Direct Address. Words in direct address are set off by commas.

John, bring me the book.
Your remark, *sir,* is impertinent.
Yes, *Mary,* you ought to go.

Exercise in Independent Elements

Punctuate wherever punctuation is needed, and give the reason.

1. A defective flue it is thought was the cause of the fire.
2. It is still too early however to foretell what the result will be.
3. Frank may I have your pen please?
4. Profits on the other hand have steadily decreased.
5. Some of these principles in fact the majority of them have been tried and found practical in Great Britain.
6. Late in April it was just after the ice had gone out of the lake we began to drive the pilings for our new boathouse.
7. I want to tell you Mr. Brayton how much we have enjoyed your talk.
8. In some of the professions in medicine for example the period of training is long and arduous.
9. Naturally he will not want to pay more than the property is worth.
10. He too was one of the candidates.

F. General Rules for Commas

In general, commas should be used:

1. To indicate any appreciable interruption in the run of the sentence.

The carriage was *preceded,* as well as *followed, by* guards.

For years he was interested *in,* and intimately associated *with,* various charitable organizations.

2. To mark any appreciable change in the direction of the thought—for example, a definite contrast in thought.

I gave the book to him, *not to you.*

He was defeated, *not because he was over-confident,* but because he was over-trained. (Also illustrates 1 above.)

3. To prevent any confusion from the running together of parts of the sentence.

Because of *this, friendship* was impossible.

The exterior of the house was shabby; and *within, the rooms* were bare and cheerless.

To the *French, Canadian* provinces such as Quebec would seem much like home.

4. To separate groups which would make an awkward combination if not punctuated.

For *him, his* father had planned a surprise.

Whatever *is, is* right.

Note. These principles are the basis of many of the specific rules discussed in the preceding sections.

Superfluous Commas. Commas should not be used in the following instances:

1. Between the subject and the verb.

Incorrect: The man at the desk, gave me the key.
Correct: The man at the desk gave me the key.

Incorrect: All shops, stores, and offices, are closed on Saturday.
Correct: All shops, stores, and offices are closed on Saturday.

2. Between a verb and its object or predicate noun.

Incorrect: He said, that he would come tomorrow.
Correct: He said that he would come tomorrow.

Incorrect: I understand clearly, the reason for the delay.
Correct: I understand clearly the reason for the delay.

Incorrect: The chief products of the state are, wheat, corn, and oats.
Correct: The chief products of the state are wheat, corn, and oats.

3. Between an adjective and its following noun.

Incorrect: He wore a red, white, and blue, necktie.
Correct: He wore a red, white, and blue necktie.

4. After a co-ordinate conjunction.

Incorrect: He had many friends in the city but, he would not ask them for help.
Correct: He had many friends in the city, but he would not ask them for help.

5. With restrictive adjective clauses and phrases (see Sec. **K 1c**).

Exceptions to the general rules in 1 and 2 occur when there are long interrupting clauses and phrases between the subject and the verb or between the verb and its object (see Sec. **K 1b**); or when there are parenthetical elements in these positions (see Sec. **K 1e**).

Exercises in Section K 1

A. Punctuate wherever punctuation is needed, and give the reason.

1. This rumor unfortunately cannot be verified for the witnesses have all disappeared.
2. In front of the cottage there was a clean sandy beach but the water was too cold for swimming.
3. This too is a product of the Chapman Radio Corporation which was a pioneer in television.
4. The first attempt having failed we laid our plans carefully before we tried again.
5. One of the brothers I understand is practicing law in Seattle the other is an engineer in Laramie Wyoming.

6. The heaviest sentence thirty days for driving while intoxicated was given to Byron Johnson who is the foreman of a local machine shop.

7. We were ushered into a stuffy old-fashioned reception room and had to wait an hour before we could see the proprietor.

8. Yes Mr. Bronson it was in May 1938 that I first met your son John.

9. The faculty dressed in cap and gown were seated on the platform waiting for the convocation speaker to begin.

10. The girls dressed like Swiss peasants are members of the ballet.

11. If that story had been true Mr. Wallace would not be a confirmed adventurer now.

12. His proposal although it looks reasonable on the surface is impractical and it will undoubtedly be rejected by the governor.

13. They live anxiously from day to day fearful of what the future will bring.

14. When there is a strong wind from the north it is impossible for a ship to enter the little harbor which is reached through a narrow rocky channel.

15. Unfortunately however he lost most of his money during the depression although it was supposedly invested in sound securities.

16. His reasoning of course was false but it seemed sound to most of his readers.

17. Addison our fullback had failed in both Latin and mathematics and was required to repeat the courses in summer school.

18. Three members of the committee Senators Brown of Ohio Franklin of Delaware and Billings of Arizona were Republicans.

19. In my freshman year chemistry was my most difficult subject this year however it is much easier.

20. In our hurried flight we had lost our friend the scientist and although we searched for him the rest of the afternoon we could find no trace of him.

21. For lighter reading I had brought with me a thrilling detective story The Black Pearl an anthology of modern poetry essays and plays and a collection of short stories.

22. Wherever he was was home to him.

23. Frankly I am more than satisfied with the new arrangement which the council has proposed.

24. The letter should be addressed to Professor A C Palmer Ph D 628 College Avenue Prentice Ohio.

25. He asked for five gallons of petrol which I did not recognize as another name for gasoline.

B. Tell what each sentence says as it stands. Then punctuate it to make it say something very different. For instance, compare "Far below the street was a seething mass of people" and "Far below, the street was a seething mass of people." What is the difference in meaning?

1. The leader stopped thinking that the rest of the party were lost.

2. We are ready to eat Harry as soon as the bell rings.

3. The captain told me to call you sergeant.

4. The defendant said the plaintiff was clearly at fault.

5. Well children don't fuss and whine.

6. In the first carriage rode Mrs. Stanton, the wife of the commanding officer and two captains from Fort Pierce.

7. The story he told us was an old folk tale.

8. Our failure to be perfectly frank was due to our own carelessness.

9. Some of the men we knew had already enlisted.

10. You should have stopped John when the traffic light turned red.

11. George, the porter is waiting outside.

12. What did you say you were waiting for, Mary?

13. Why did you ever marry mother?

14. The husband who was drunk was at home.

15. What did you say to her father?

SEMICOLON

The semicolon is the strongest mark of punctuation in a sentence. It is used to separate long co-ordinate groups and to emphasize important points of division.

K2. The semicolon has three uses:

1. To separate two main clauses which are not connected by *and, but, or,* or *nor* (see page 295).

> Fifty laborers are needed at once; without them the work cannot be completed on time.
> No word had been received from headquarters; nevertheless, the colonel ordered the regiment to advance.

2. To separate two long or remotely connected main clauses, even though they are connected by *and, but, or,* or *nor*—especially if they contain commas (see page 294).

> According to the latest reports, he has spent the last ten years in India, China, and Japan; and he is now preparing to make an extended trip through South America and the islands of the South Pacific.

3. To separate the members in a series of long subordinate clauses or phrases—and even in a series of short phrases or clauses if they contain commas.

> *If you find any defect due to faulty material or workmanship in this machine; if it does not fulfill our claims for efficiency and economy in operation; if you do not find it satisfactory in every respect*—then you may return it at our expense and your initial payment will be refunded.
> The company consists of *Miss Adams, pianist; Miss Brown, vocalist; and Miss Phelps, reader.*

The semicolon is used only between elements of equal rank. It is not to be employed between a main clause and a subordinate element which belongs to that clause.

Exercises in Section K 2

A. Punctuate the following sentences. Give your reason for each mark that you use.

1. They were afraid that the ship would sink nevertheless they would not take to the lifeboats.

2. In our first year we studied English, French, and algebra in the second, we had English, German, and geometry.

3. The journey back to the base would be difficult, perhaps impossible but, with a little luck, he might be able to make it.

4. The hardier members of the party had gone out fishing the others were lounging about the camp, waiting for the rain to stop.

5. The framework of the machine is made of aluminum therefore it is very light and sturdy.

6. He was not lazy on the contrary, he was alert and interested in his work.

7. During the previous war he had fought in the English, Canadian, and American armies and now, in spite of his age, he was trying to enlist again.

8. These notes are payable in April 1944 October 1944 and April 1945.

9. The committee consists of A. R. Price professor of history C. L. Gregory instructor in sociology and R. F. Gray dean of men.

10. He has not had the elementary courses in physiology consequently he finds his pre-medical work rather difficult.

B. Bring to class five sentences—from a book or a magazine—showing the use of the semicolon.

COLON

K3. The colon is used:

1. To indicate explanation or enumeration. (The explanation or enumeration may be introduced by a connective, such as *for example, for instance, that is, as follows, the following;* or there may be no connective.)

The boy was weary: *he had been tramping all day.*

He had one serious fault: *namely, he could not write legibly.*

They invited only two men: *the manager and his assistant.*

He has a number of annoying habits: *for instance, he is constantly gnawing his finger nails.*

They were late: *that is, they did not arrive until an hour after the time set for the dinner.*

We agreed on *the following* arrangement: *the first car was to leave at ten o'clock, and the others were to start at twenty-minute intervals.*

2. To introduce a long, formal direct quotation. (Before a less formal quotation, a comma is used.)

Concerning this matter, Mr. Bryce says: *"A further consequence of this habit is pointed out by one of the most thoughtful among American constitutional writers,"* etc.

He replied, *"This house was the former home of Sir Henry Graham, the English ambassador."*

3. To separate numbers indicating the time of day, or the parts in a biblical reference.

12:46 P.M.   Genesis 9:8–12

4. To mark the salutation in a letter.

Dear Sir: Dear Mr. Adams:
Gentlemen: Dear Mrs. Lane:

In social correspondence a comma is regularly used, because it seems less formal.

Dear John,   Dear Mr. Crewe,

Exercises in Section K 3

A. Supply punctuation where it is needed.

1. You should learn to spell these two words *separate* and *mischievous.*

2. The following equipment has been ordered a two-ton truck, a light delivery wagon, and a service car.

3. There is only one explanation for his failure namely his inability to express himself clearly.

4. His itinerary was as follows from Chicago to New York by train, then to London by steamer.

5. These are your instructions go to Albany at once and report to headquarters.

6. Dear Mr. Adams

The members of the club will meet tomorrow at 3 45 to discuss dues for next year that is the question of whether they should be increased.

7. The repairs will be expensive for example the cost of replacing the glass alone will amount to about eighty dollars.

8. On Monday we sent the following telegram "Out of money. Check for $100 would help."

9. Services will begin at 10 30 A.M. The sermon will be on the text found in *Proverbs* 5 8–9.

10. It is a simple remedy for which only two ingredients are needed a spoonful of salt and a quart of water.

B. Bring to class five sentences—taken from a book or a magazine—showing the use of the colon.

DASH

K4. The dash is used:

1. To indicate a break or unexpected change in thought.

He is selfish, unscrupulous, unprincipled—*but why say more?*

He began his professional career with bright hopes and brilliant prospects; and at the age of fifty he retired— *to the poorhouse.*

2. To indicate an unfinished statement or halting speech.

"You surely don't think—," I began.

"I—I called to speak with you—about a matter," he replied.

Note. For the use of a series of periods instead of a dash in 2, see Sec. **K 5** (3).

3. To set off a long introductory series of phrases or subordinate clauses, or even a short series when it is intended to be emphatic.

> *That he has been negligent in attending to his duties; that he is lacking in the qualities necessary for an executive; that he has willfully disregarded instructions*—all these charges have been brought against the manager.
> *Wealth, power, position*—these are the things he sought.

a. Special Emphasis. A dash is used to give special emphasis to various expressions that ordinarily would be set off by a comma (see page 306).

Because it is a more conspicuous and attention-arresting mark than a comma, the dash is especially adapted for calling attention to a particular element in the sentence.

> The captain was a brave, experienced—*but reckless* leader (member of a series of adjectives).
> The speaker—*a typical tourist in tweeds*—had arrived that morning (in apposition).
> The manager—*anxious, white-faced, and thin-lipped*—waited for the foreman to appear.

b. Bridged Constructions. The dash is used before and after constructions which definitely interrupt the sequence of a sentence.

This situation occurs when the words that follow the interrupting element are in close grammatical relation with the words that precede it. The grammatical structure then has to be "bridged" across the intervening element. Because the dashes are conspicuous, the eye of the reader easily sees where the interruption stops and the regular run of the sentence is resumed.

> One important factor—*that is, his ability to win the loyal support of his followers*—has been overlooked by his enemies.

This statement—*I know you will agree with me*—is unfair to the employees.

The quotation from Mr. Bryce—"*A further consequence of this habit is pointed out by one of the most thoughtful among American constitutional writers*"—is in the first chapter.

The following employees—*Frank Smith, James Kline, and George Fargo*—will report at once to the manager.

The three principal causes of crime—*intemperance, poverty, and ignorance*—must be removed.

Exercises in Section K 4

A. Use a dash wherever it is required, or will make a statement clearer or more emphatic.

1. Three students and only three were able to pass the physical tests.

2. He was driving at ninety miles an hour, and well, you can guess what happened.

3. "You you mean that that you won't go unless" he said.

4. The mayor's threat for that was what it amounted to brought no response from the voters.

5. Some members of the party that is, the more radical element have tried to make this a major issue in the campaign.

6. Someone presumably an enemy agent had spread the rumor among the workers in the steel mills.

7. The meeting is on Tuesday not Thursday.

8. Students, alumni, and faculty all are asked to contribute to this fund.

9. The faculty and the alumni but not the student body you will notice are represented on this committee.

10. We had the time and the desire to travel but no money.

B. Select one or two pages in a good book or magazine. Bring to class five sentences from that source, illustrating the use of the dash. Explain the reason. Also select two sentences showing the use of a series of periods instead of a dash.

PERIOD

K5. The period is used:

1. At the end of a declarative or an imperative sentence.

They will come tomorrow.
Bring me the package.

2. After an abbreviation.

He was born in Brooklyn, N. Y., in 1845.
What is the meaning of *etc.*?

Notice that the period after an abbreviation is followed by any other mark that is needed in the sentence.

3. A series of three or four periods may be used to indicate a break or hesitation in dialogue (see Sec. **K 4**), or the omission of part of a quotation.

I'm sorry . . . tremendously sorry . . . but you surely
realize. . . .
"Oh, don't think . . ." he began.
"We hold these truths to be self-evident . . . that
they [all men] are endowed by their creator with
certain inalienable rights."

QUESTION MARK AND EXCLAMATION POINT

K6a. The question mark, or interrogation point, is used:

1. After an interrogative sentence or a question of any sort.

Did you find the book?
What? You surely don't mean that.
"Will you come at once?" he asked.

2. After a doubtful statement—to indicate uncertainty as to its correctness. In this case the mark is enclosed in parentheses.

> He was born in Ohio in 1864 (?). (The date is uncertain.)

K6b. The exclamation point is used after an exclamatory word or sentence.

Look! See how they run!

PARENTHESES AND BRACKETS

K7a. Parentheses are used:

1. To enclose a parenthetical expression that is remotely related to the context.

> This matter (*I hope you will pardon my referring to it again*) must be settled now.

In this construction, many writers prefer dashes.

2. To enclose a parenthetical statement included in another parenthetical statement set off by dashes.

> This play—it was written by my friend Ayton (*you will remember him*)—has had a long run.

3. To enclose various explanations, references, directions to the reader, and the like.

> In the next year (1905) two changes were made.
> The intake valve (Fig. 3, b) is at the bottom of the cylinder.
> The subject of taxes (see Chapter V) should be carefully reviewed.
> The book was published in New York (?) in 1885. (The place of publication is uncertain. See **K 6a**.)

K7b. Brackets are used to enclose anything added to a direct quotation—anything that was not in the original statement.

"He [Napoleon] was not accustomed to defeat," said the historian.

Punctuation Before and After Parentheses and Brackets. When an expression is enclosed in parentheses, do not use other marks of punctuation unless they would be required if the parenthetical expression were not present.

Wrong: This criminal, (*I feel justified in calling him that*), is a menace to society.

Right: This criminal (*I feel justified in calling him that*) is a menace to society.

Right: When we discussed this theory in a preceding chapter (*see p. 37*), we saw the fallacy in it. (If the parenthetical expression were absent, a comma would be placed after *chapter* to set off the adverbial clause before the subject. See Sec. **K 1B.**)

A mark of punctuation which refers only to the parenthetical matter is placed inside the last parenthesis; one which refers to the rest of the sentence is placed outside the parenthesis. This rule applies also to brackets.

This system is now obsolete. (*It came into use in 1860.*)
Security of principal is also important (*see Chapter XV*).

QUOTATION MARKS

K8. Quotation marks are used as follows:

1. To enclose direct quotations.

"I can come at once," he replied.

Note. With indirect quotations the marks are not used.

He replied that he could come at once.

2. To enclose: (a) words used in a "different" sense; (b) slang; (c) technical words when used in general writing.

(a) An army "eagle" must undergo rigorous training.
(b) This reporter's "stuff" was always in demand.
(c) For "justifying" a line of type an "en-quad" may be used.

3. To enclose the title of a chapter or article in a book or magazine when the names of both the larger and the smaller unit occur in the same passage. The title of the complete work is in italics.

You will be interested in an article on "Folk Customs" in *Harper's Magazine* for July.
See W. F. Jacobs, "A Week in Tahiti," in *Journeys in the South Seas*.

Note. Quotation marks are sometimes used to enclose words spoken of as words; names of ships; and titles of books, plays, and the like.

The word "affect" is often misused.
The steamer "Empress of India" is in port.
Bryant's "Thanatopsis" was studied next.

Most writers, however, prefer italics in these cases—see Sec. **K 11**.

a. "Broken" Quotations. When a quotation is divided by an expression like *they replied, she said,* etc., each of the parts is enclosed by a separate set of quotation marks.

"This time," he replied, "you must not fail."
"The car is waiting," he said. "Are you ready?"
"Where are they?" he inquired. "They promised to be here."
"Never!" he shouted. "That can't happen here."
"You do not know," the boy answered; "our plans have been kept secret."

Study carefully the punctuation in the preceding examples. Note that:

A comma follows the first part unless a question mark or an exclamation point is required by the sense.

A comma, a period, or a semicolon follows the interpolated expression, the choice depending on the closeness of relation between the two parts of the quotation. A period is almost always used when the first part ends with a mark other than a comma.

Note also that the second part of the quotation begins with a capital letter after a period; with a small letter after a comma or a semicolon.

b. Quotation Within a Quotation. A quotation within a quotation is enclosed in single quotation marks.

She replied, "You should not say 'I ain't' at any time."

c. Quotation Covering More Than One Paragraph. When a quotation covers more than one paragraph, quotation marks are placed at the beginning of each paragraph, but at the end of only the last one.

d. Position of Quotation Marks with Reference to Other Marks. 1. The period and the comma should be placed inside the quotation marks.

The boy replied, "You know the answer."
"This work," he continued, "is too difficult."

2. Every other mark is placed inside the quotation marks when it belongs only to the quoted matter; outside, when it belongs to the whole sentence, part of which is not included in the quotation.

He called, "Come here!"
She couldn't spell a simple word like "their"!
"Did you hear the explosion?" they asked.
What is meant by the "survival of the fittest"?
He said "dizzy dean"; he meant "busy dean."
This is how he made the "boner": he tried to get, etc.

Exercises in Section K 8

A. Supply capitals, quotation marks, and other punctuation marks where they are needed.

1. The officer asked did you bring your registration card
2. In this struggle the old phrase liberty and equality seemed to be forgotten
3. If this is true she declared the entire program will have to be changed
4. Stop he shouted the rest of the party have gone the other way
5. I will come tomorrow he said we can then go over the paper together
6. The agent replied the telegram reads come at once and is signed by your father
7. When can I see him the stranger asked my time is limited and I must talk with him
8. We realized that it was probably a bum hunch but we decided to try it
9. I had been reading an article entitled the Last is Best in the June issue of Time.
10. The attorney remarked when a witness says I don't know he usually means that he won't tell.

B. From a good book or magazine select a passage containing several paragraphs of dialogue. Explain the use of capitals, quotation marks, and other marks of punctuation.

APOSTROPHE

K9. **The apostrophe is used:**

1. To indicate the possessive case of a noun.

boy's	child's	Frank's
boys'	children's	James'

The apostrophe is not used in the possessive case of any pronoun except the indefinite pronouns, like *one*, *somebody*, etc.

Wrong: The dog had hurt *it's* foot.
Right: The dog had hurt *its* foot.

Right: They said that the books were *theirs*.
Right: This might be *anyone's* game.
Right: I heard *somebody's* footsteps.

It's is an abbreviation of *it is*: as, "*It's* too early to go now."

Do not forget the apostrophe in expressions like *a day's journey, a dollar's worth, for old time's sake.*

2. To indicate the omission of a letter or letters in a word, or of figures in a number.

isn't	can't	won't	I'll	o'clock (of the clock)
aren't	hasn't	he's	we'll	'40 (1940)

3. To indicate the plural of letters, figures, symbols, and words regarded merely as words.

There should be three *f's* in the word.
He uses too many *and's*.
Two *6's* are equal to 12.
There are a number of *Ph.D.'s* on the staff.

Exercise in Section K 9

Supply apostrophes wherever they are needed.

1. We havent seen them since two oclock this afternoon.
2. There are two ms and two cs in *accommodation*.
3. They wont tell us when theyll be here.
4. It must have been somebodys mistake, but it wasnt ours.
5. Cant you find out whos responsible?
6. You should read todays *Tribune* and get its comments on the election.
7. They think its too late to go to the presidents reception.
8. Couldnt they find out whose watch it was?
9. It will cost him a months pay to have the car repaired, and when thats done hell not be satisfied.
10. Johns bicycle is larger than hers.

HYPHEN

Good writers and even the dictionaries do not always agree on what words should be hyphenated. A given combination may be treated by one writer as a single word, by another as two words, and by a third as a hyphenated compound. The general principle to be kept in mind is that a hyphen should always be used in any compound element which otherwise would be awkward or ambiguous.

The principal constructions in which standard usage calls for a hyphen are given below.

K10. The hyphen is regularly used:

1. To indicate the division of a word at the end of a line of written or printed matter. (This practice is universal.)

2. To separate the parts of a compound adjective placed before a noun.

a *five-mile* walk	a *well-to-do* person
a *so-called* poem	a *hand-to-mouth* existence
a *weak-kneed* policy	a *hit-and-run* driver
a *low-test* gasoline	*up-to-date* styles

3. To separate the parts of a compound noun.

father-in-law	German-American
soldier-poet	actor-manager

4. To separate parts of various words compounded with prefixes, suffixes, and prepositions which are not thoroughly assimilated into the word.

a by-line	passers-by
a by-pass	a tie-up
ex-president	make-up

The hyphen is required in some compounds to prevent an awkward combination of letters in the main word and the prefix or suffix, or in a prefix and a word beginning with a capital.

re-enlist	ante-Christian
anti-imperialistic	anti-Ally
semi-invalid	pro-British
pre-election	pre-Raphaelite

Note. When the prefix has become thoroughly assimilated, the hyphen is omitted: *premature, refrain, antiseptic, semi-circle.*

In the following sentences the hyphen serves to distinguish one word from another which has a different meaning.

The judge *released* the prisoner.
I have *re-leased* my apartment for another year.

5. To separate the parts of cardinal and ordinal numbers from twenty to one hundred.

twenty-five   twenty-fifth
forty-eight   forty-eighth

He is *twenty-five* years old today.
The last number is *forty-eight.*
He was *twenty-fourth* in a list of *sixty-nine.*
There were one hundred and *thirty-six* members. (Note
    that only the *thirty-six* is hyphenated.)

6. To separate the parts of fractions when they are used as adjectives before nouns (see 2 above).

one-fourth ounce
two-thirds interest
five-eighths-inch bolt

When they are not used as adjectives before nouns, fractions are not generally hyphenated.

One half of the population has gone.
It weighs *one fourth* of an ounce.

Exercise in Section K 10

Use hyphens where they are needed. If in doubt, consult the dictionary.

1. We drove the ninety eight miles in an hour and forty five minutes.

2. I bought a beautiful two piece suit at a shop on Fifty fifth Street.

3. In preRoman times this plain was a vast swamp.

4. He reentered the room while his fatherinlaw was examining the exconvict.

5. In the afternoon we played a three ball match at the golf club.

6. Two thirds of the house had been destroyed and only the one story kitchen was left standing.

7. The commander in chief had a heart to heart talk with his subordinates.

8. County Judge Roth was reelected by a two thirds majority.

9. The poster was printed on a standard eight by eleven sheet.

10. The contingent of French Canadian volunteers was convoyed by an American man of war.

ITALICS

K11. Italics are used in the following cases:

1. To indicate the title of a book, magazine, poem, musical composition, and the like.

He was reading Smith's *Principles of Forestry* when we arrived.

2. To indicate the names of ships.

The *Adriatic* will sail on Tuesday.

3. To indicate a word, letter, or number when it is spoken of as such.

You should insert *and* before the second *which*.
He writes an *n* like a *u*.

Note. For the use of quotation marks instead of italics in (1), (2), and (3) above, and for the combination of italics and quotation marks when the title of a chapter or article accompanies the name of the book or magazine in which it is contained, see Sec. **K 8.**

4. To indicate foreign words or phrases.

This is an *annus mirabilis*.
This confession is strictly *entre nous*, you understand.

But foreign words that have become naturalized are not italicized, even though they retain their foreign spelling and pronunciation: debris, menu, a priori, per annum, via.

5. To indicate an emphatic word or phrase.

This is *not* the truth.

In handwritten or typewritten manuscript, italicized words are designated by underscoring: the steamship Prince George.

Exercise in Section K 11

In the following sentences, underscore the words that should be in italics.

1. It was in Hardy's Return of the Native that I first saw the word reddleman.

2. Etymologically, recur is made up of the Latin prefix re- and the root curro.

3. The, an, and a are called articles, and are used as adjectives.

4. We took passage for London on the American liner, the President Grant.

5. Last evening we went to see a performance of Sheridan's Rivals at the Garrick Theater.

6. An interesting story of the old method of keeping accounts is told in the article entitled Tally in the Encyclopaedia Britannica.

7. He wasted no time in an introduction, but began his story in medias res.

8. The flagship Santiago led the way into port.

9. He made his reputation as an actor in playing Macbeth in Shakespeare's Macbeth.

10. The sound of l is sometimes omitted in the pronunciation of golf.

SPELLING

K12. Learn to apply the rules of spelling given below. Guard against repeatedly misspelling the same words. In case of doubt consult the dictionary.

a. Keep a List of Misspelled Words. Even the poor speller makes the greater part of his mistakes in a comparatively few words which he misspells again and again. He should keep a list of these words and go over them repeatedly until he has mastered them. A little extra care and attention should bring about a decided improvement.

b. Pronounce Words Correctly. Misspelling is often caused by failure to pronounce a word correctly. If a letter or syllable is omitted or added or transposed in pronunciation, it is likely to be omitted, added, or transposed in the spelling.

Parts Omitted

WRONG	RIGHT	WRONG	RIGHT
artic	arctic	occasionly	occasionally
boundry	boundary	practicly	practically
canidate	candidate	quanity	quantity
convient	convenient	reconize	recognize
Febuary	February	sophmore	sophomore
generly	generally	supprise	surprise
goverment	government	temperment	temperament
labratory	laboratory		

Parts Added

WRONG	RIGHT	WRONG	RIGHT
athelete	athlete	enterance	entrance
atheletics	athletics	hinderance	hindrance
disasterous	disastrous	lightening	lightning
drownded	drowned	mischievious	mischievous
evidentally	evidently	similiar	similar

Parts Transposed

WRONG	RIGHT	WRONG	RIGHT
cal*v*ary	cavalry	pe*r*fer	prefer
child*er*n	children	predu*j*ice	prejudice
hund*er*d	hundred	p*r*eform	perform
io*r*ny	irony	p*r*espiration	perspiration
irre*vel*ant	irrelevant		

c. Do not confuse words that are similar in sound.

advise, advice

allowed, aloud

all ready, already

all together, altogether

altar, alter

ascent, assent

bare, bear

berth, birth

born, borne

break, brake

breath, breathe

cannon, canon, canyon

canvas, canvass

capital, capitol

cloths, clothes

coarse, course

compliment, complement

corps (not corp), corpse

council, counsel, consul

dairy, diary

decent, descent

desert, dessert

dining, dinning

duel, dual

formerly, formally

fourth, forth

hear, here

later, latter

lead (metal), led

lesson, lessen

lose, loose

past, passed

peace, piece

plain, plane

pore, pour

precede, proceed

principle, principal

quiet, quite

right, rite, write

shown, shone

stake, steak

stationary, stationery

statue, statute, stature

straight, strait

than, then

there, their, they're

to, too

your, you're

Doubling a Consonant Before a Suffix

A. When a suffix *beginning with a vowel* is added to a word, the rules for doubling or not doubling the final consonant are as follows:

1. Consonant Doubled. The final consonant is doubled only when it is preceded by a *single vowel* in a one-syllable word or in a word of more than one syllable having the accent on the last syllable.

sit, sitting	pro-pel', propeller
stop, stopped	con-fer', conferring
dip, dipper	oc-cur', occurred
bid, biddable	re-mit', remittance

2. Consonant not Doubled. In all other instances, the final consonant regularly is not doubled before the suffix.

a. Consonant preceded by two vowels:

beat, beaten (one-syllable word)
read, readable
sweep, sweeping
clear, clearance
re-peal', repealed (last syllable accented)
con-tain', container
ap-pear', appearance
pre-vail', prevailing

b. Final syllable unaccented (regardless of the number of vowels):

trav'el, traveling	dif'fer, difference
of'fer, offered	cal'lous, calloused

Compare the following two forms made from *prefer'*:

pre-ferred' (accent on the last syllable—double consonant)
pref'erence (accent shifted to the first syllable—single consonant)

Note. For some words with an unaccented final syllable, especially those ending in *-el,* the dictionary gives optional forms: as *traveled, travelled, traveling, travelling.* The forms with the single consonant, however, are cited as preferable.

When a suffix is added to a word ending in a vowel, the last consonant is not doubled.

dine, dining (not dinning)
file, filing (not filling)

The consonant is doubled, however, when a long vowel in the original word becomes a short vowel in the new form.

rīde, rīding, rĭdden
bīte, bīting, bĭtten

B. Before a suffix *beginning with a consonant,* the final consonant of a word is not doubled.

commit, commitment   sap, sapless
fat, fatness   regret, regretful

Final E *Before a Suffix*

A final *e* is generally dropped before a suffix beginning with a vowel.

force, forcing, forcible
believe, believing, believable
guide, guiding, guidance

Exceptions. The *e* is retained in some instances.
1. After the soft sound of *c* and *g* when a suffix beginning with *a* or *o* is added. (*C* and *g* have a hard sound before these vowels.)

notice, noticeable (but *noticing*—soft *c* before *i*)
change, changeable (but *changing*—soft *g* before *i*)
courage, courageous

Compare also:

notice, noticeable (soft *c*—the *e* is retained before *a*)
practice, practicable (hard *c* before *a*—the *e* is dropped)

2. In certain words where *e* is needed to prevent awkward combinations or confusion with other words.

dye, dyeing (cf. die, dying)
singe, singeing (cf. sing, singing)
shoe, shoeing

Ie *and* Ei

When Sounded as *e*. When *ie* or *ei* is sounded as *e*, the following rules generally apply:

1. *Ie* is used after all letters except *c*.

believe	chief	piece	friend (short *e*)
relieve	grief	pierce	priest
lien	field	siege	chieftain
reprieve	wield	fiend	yield
niece	brief	shriek	thief

2. *Ei* is used after *c*.

receive	deceive	conceive	perceive
receipt	deceit	conceit	ceiling

Exceptions:

leisure   heifer   seize   foreign   neither

When not Sounded as *e*. When the sound is other than that of *e*, the form *ei* is generally used.

weigh	deign	heinous	sleight
weight	veil	neighbor	forfeit
their	counterfeit		

Words Ending in Y

1. Words ending in *y* preceded by a consonant usually change the *y* to *i* before a suffix.

busy, business	study, studies, studied
hearty, heartiest, heartiness	try, tries
duty, dutiful, duties	hurry, hurries

The *y* is retained before *-ing*.

bury, burying (cf. buried)
study, studying

Other variations are also found: as

sly, slyness, sliest or slyest, slier or slyer

2. Words ending in *y* preceded by a vowel retain the *y*.

valley, valleys
convoy, convoys, convoying
play, playing, playful

monkey, monkeys
delay, delayed
employ, employment

The past tenses of verbs like *say, lay* change the *y* to *i* before *d*.

say, says, said
pay, pays, paid
lay, lays, laid

Miscellaneous Rules

1. Words ending in *ie* change the *ie* to *y* before *-ing*

lie, lying   die, dying

2. Words ending in *l* retain that letter before a suffix beginning with *l*.

final, finally   occasional, occasionally

3. Words ending in *n* retain that letter before the suffix *-ness*.

greenness   openness

Commonly Misspelled Words

absence	accessible	accumulate	across
absorb	accidentally	accustom	address
absorption	accommodate	acquaintance	advice (noun)
accept	account	acquitted	advise (verb)

aeroplane
affects
(effects)
aggravate
aghast
aisle
(isle)
alley, alleys
ally, allies
all ready
already
all right
altar
alter
although
altogether
always
among
analysis
analyze
angel
angle
apartment
apparatus
apparent
arctic
arrangement
article
ascend
assistance
assistants
athlete
athletics
auxiliary
bachelor
balance
balloon
banana
baring
barring
becoming
beggar

believe
benefited
berth
(birth)
bicycle
boarder
border
born
borne
boundary
brake
break
breath
breathe
bridal
bridle
Britain
Briton
buoy
buoyant
business
calendar
Calvary
cavalry
candidate
can't
canvas
canvass
capital
capitol
career
carriage
casualty
cemetery
changeable
changing
chauffeur
choose
chose
chosen
cite
clothes

cloths
coarse
course
column
coming
commission
committee
comparative
comparison
complement
compliment
concede
conceive
conference
conferred
confidant (e)
confident
connoisseur
conscience
conscious
convenience
convenient
corps
corpse
costume
(custom)
council
counsel
courteous
criticism
criticize
crowd
dairy
(diary)
dealt
deceased
(diseased)
depth
descent
(decent)
describe
description

desert
dessert
despair
desperate
device
devise
die, dying
dye, dyeing
dining room
disappear
disappoint
disastrous
discipline
dissatisfied
divide
dual
duel
duly
ecstasy
eighth
embarrass
equipped
especially
etc.
exaggerated
exceed
excellent
exercise
exhaust
exhibit
explanation
extraordinary
fascinate
February
fiery
finally
forbear
forebear
forehead
foresee
foretell
formally

formerly
forth
(fourth)
forty
fourteen
friend
fulfill
gases
gauge
generally
government
governor
grammar
grievous
guard
harass
haven't
having
height
hindrance
hoping
hopping
huge
Hugh
human
humane
hundredths
hurriedly
hypocrisy
imaginary
immediately
incidentally
independent
indictment
indispensable
ingenious
ingenuous
instance
instants
intercede
irresistible

its
it's
itself
judgment
knowledge
laboratory
laid
later
latter
lead (verb)
lead (metal)
led (verb)
leisure
lessen
lesson
library
license
lightning
likely
literature
liveliness
lonely
loose
lose
lying
maintain
maintenance
maneuver
mantel
mantle
manual
marriage
mathematics
meant
miniature
minute
(minuet)
mischievous
misspelled
mistake
momentous

morale
murmur
muscle
mysterious
necessary
neither
nickel
niece
nineteen
ninety
ninth
noticeable
oblige
occasionally
occurred
occurrence
o'clock
officer
omission
omitted
oneself
opportunity
outrageous
paid
pamphlet
parallel
parliament
participle
partner
passed
past
pastime
peace
(piece)
peaceable
perceive
perform
perhaps
permissible
personnel
perspiration

physician
picnic
picnicking
plain
plane
possess
pour
(pore)
practically
prairie
precede
precedence
precedents
preference
preferred
prejudice
preparation
presence
principal
principle
privilege
probably
procedure
proceed
professor
pronunciation
psychology
pursue
quantity
quiet
quite
ready
really
receive
recognize
recommend
reference
referred
regard
relief
religious

restaurant	sincerely	supersede	undoubtedly
rhetoric	site	surprise	until
rhyme	sight	syllable	usually
rhythm	(cite)	temperament	villain
ridiculous	sophomore	temperature	weak
safety	specimen	therefor	week
scene	speak	therefore	Wednesday
scent	speech	they're	weird
schedule	stationary	(there)	welcome
seize	stationery	(their)	welfare
separate	strength	to, too, two	wherever
shining	studying	together	whether
shone	succeed	track	wholly
shown	successful	tract	writing
shriek	suit	tragedy	written
siege	suite	truly	your
similar	superintendent	Tuesday	you're

DIVISION INTO SYLLABLES

K13. In dividing a word at the end of a line, observe the following rules:

1. The hyphen is placed at the end of a line, never at the beginning of the following line.

2. Words are divided only between syllables. The proper points of division can usually be determined from the pronunciation.

Right: cap-tain (not capt-ain).
Right: pre-tend (not pret-end).
Right: contra-dict (not contrad-ict).

3. Prefixes and suffixes are usually kept distinct from the root.

ex-pand-ing   ap-pear-ance   re-spect-able
in-clud-ed   ap-pease-ment   con-tend-er

Note that the suffixes *-tion* and *-sion* retain the *t* and *s* even though these letters are also a part of the root.

sugges-tion (from *suggest*). (Compare *suggest-ing* and *suggest-ible*.)

preci-sion (from *precise*).

There are also other exceptions to the general rule. In case of doubt, the dictionary should be consulted.

When a single consonant at the end of a word is doubled before an added suffix, the second consonant goes with the suffix.

> ex-pel, ex-pel-ling   fit, fit-ted
> hem, hem-ming   rot, rot-ten

With these compare *tell, tell-ing; add, add-ing,* which have the double consonant in the original word.

The suffix *-ed* is not divided unless it is pronounced as a separate syllable. Compare *de-fined* and *com-plet-ed* (here *-ed* is a separate syllable).

4. A single consonant after a long vowel goes with the following syllable; after a short vowel it goes with the vowel.

> pro-duce, prod-uct   pre-sid-ing, pres-i-dent
> va-por, vap-id   po-lice, pol-icy

5. Words of one syllable are not divided.

Wrong: sta-nd, thro-ugh

Exercise in Section K 13

Indicate with hyphens the division into syllables: as *con-sum-ing*. If in doubt, consult the dictionary.

occasion	reconstruction	provident	conspired
syllable	recommendation	gentlemen	conspiring
pleasant	profundity	marriage	recurring
radiant	heaviness	although	filling
throughout	provision	depleted	controlling
panorama			

CAPITALS

K14. Use a capital letter in the following cases:

1. To begin a sentence.
2. To begin each line of poetry.

The boast of heraldry, the pomp of power,
  And all that beauty, all that wealth e'er gave,
Awaits alike the inevitable hour.
  The paths of glory lead but to the grave.

3. To begin a formal direct quotation.

He replied, "This is only the beginning."

4. To begin a proper noun or a word derived from a proper noun.

England	Twelfth Street	Wednesday	Baptist
Great Britain	Euclid Avenue	French	Society of
Illinois	Ohio River	Russian	Friends
Adams County	Lake Huron	Christmas	Bible
Lake Michigan	December	Fourth of July	God

Right: I study *English* and *French*. (Compare, "I study *chemistry* and *mathematics*.")

Note. In writing of an informal nature, words like *street, county*, etc., are often not capitalized after a specific name: as *Grand avenue, Fourth street, Adams county*.

5. To begin each important word in the title of a book, musical composition, and the like.

Prepositions, conjunctions, and *a, an,* and *the* are not usually capitalized except at the beginning of the title.

Studies in History and Economics
The Business Outlook for the Year

6. To begin the names of points of the compass when used for parts of a country, not for directions.

Right: He lives in the *East*.
Right: He went *east* on Madison Street.

Exercise in Section K 14

Supply capitals wherever they are needed.

1. They live a little west of the burlington tracks on locust street.

2. His first book, the dawn of a new era, is a discussion of the conditions in the south before the war.

3. She made A's in economics, french, and chemistry, but the instructor in spanish gave her a C.

4. On sunday morning we went to the first baptist church and heard dr. brown preach on a text from genesis 3:21.

5. He replied in english, yes, this picture by rembrandt is now in the louvre.

NUMBERS

K15. As a rule, in general writing, spell out numbers up to one hundred, and round numbers over one hundred; use figures for numbers above one hundred (except the round numbers).

Right: Six; eighty-seven; three hundred; six thousand.
Right: 101; 385; 7479; 6,500,000.
Right: He is twenty-three years old, and has four brothers.
Right: There are 365 days in the year.
Right: They left the car at Fourteenth Street.

Exceptions. In the following cases figures are generally used even for numbers under one hundred:

1. Dates, street numbers, numbered objects, numbers containing decimals, and the like.

June 18, 1940; 89 Cedar Street; Room 4; Track 9; page 6; 8.17.
Right: You will find him in Room 18.
Right: The book cost $2.75.

2. Groups of numbers in the same passage, as in dimensions, statistics, and the like.

Right: The specifications are as follows: length, 2 feet; width, 19 inches; depth, 4 inches; weight, 4 pounds.

3. It is to be noted also that in business, scientific, and technical writing figures are used much more freely than in general writing.

Note 1. In formal invitations dates are regularly spelled out.
May the fourth, nineteen hundred and forty.

Note 2. A number at the beginning of a sentence should be spelled out.
Right: Eight hundred and forty men were lost in the attack. (Compare: In the attack, 840 men were lost.)

Exercise in Section K 15

In the following sentences indicate which numbers should be written out.

1. Roger was born on March 8, 1906, and was graduated from college when he was 19 years old.
2. A herd of 60 cows was grazing in the 20-acre field.
3. The fur coat cost $275 and she has worn it for 3 seasons.
4. 132 men are now employed in the factory, but 24 of them are working only half time.
5. Services begin at 9:45 A.M. and will continue for 2 hours.

ABBREVIATIONS

K16. In general writing abbreviations should be used sparingly.

Not Good: He will arrive tomorrow *A.M.*
Correct: He will arrive tomorrow *morning*.
Correct: He will arrive at *10:35 A.M.* (after a designation of a specific hour).

Not Good: They immediately sent for a *Dr.*
Correct: They immediately sent for a *doctor*.

Not Good: The fish weighed five *lbs.*
Correct: The fish weighed five *pounds*.

Not Good: I met *Geo.* Allen today.
Correct: I met *George* Allen today.

Not Good: I saw it in the *chem. lab.*
Correct: I saw it in the *chemistry laboratory.*

Titles like *General, Professor, Superintendent,* etc.; names of states; and words like *street, avenue, boulevard,* etc., are written out in full (see 1 below):

Right: *General* U. S. Grant (not *Gen.* U. S. Grant).
Right: Brooklyn, *New York* (not Brooklyn, *N. Y.*).
Right: Michigan *Avenue* (not Michigan *Ave.*).

The symbol *&* should not be used for *and* in an ordinary sentence.

Allowable Abbreviations. Certain abbreviations are in good form.

1. *Mr., Mrs., Dr., A.B., Ph.D., Jr., Sr.,* etc., when they accompany a name.

Dr. E. F. Cook, A.B., Ph.D.

2. *Vol., p., ch.* or *chap., sec.,* etc., when they are followed by a number in a bibliographical reference.

E. G. Crane, *Economic Values,* vol. I, p. 224.

Exercise in Section K 16

In the following sentences correct the errors in the use of abbreviations.

1. Gen. A. F. Drake is visiting at the home of Dr. C. O. Linton at 62 W. Grove Ave., Arcola, Ind.

2. I met my math prof on the street and he told me there would be an exam tomorrow at 9 A.M.

3. We left for home Sat. A.M. in order to be there for Xmas.

4. Chas. Atwater is a student at Wisconsin U, which is located at Madison, Wis.

5. On Dec. 10 we listened to a debate between Mr. L. C. Mann, Sr., and Prof. Chas. K. White, on the local tax situation.

Chapter Eleven

THE LIBRARY, THE
TERM PAPER, AND
LETTERS

THE LIBRARY

Since the student spends much of his time in the library, where he obtains a very important part of his education, he should acquire skill in handling its facilities. The present discussion is intended as a general guide to help him find and use such resources.

To make books, periodicals, and other materials readily available, librarians arrange them according to a well-organized plan, and provide an index to their location. Most large libraries, for example, contain the following departments:

1. Card Catalogue. This indispensable index is explained on pages 346–350.

2. Reference Room. In this department, books that are most frequently consulted are arranged in related groups, such as atlases, yearbooks, encyclopedias, and bibliographies. Most of these volumes are placed on open shelves and are to be used only in this room. A chart showing the location of the various groups is usually displayed near the Reference Desk.

3. Reserve Reading Room. Books assigned by the faculty for supplementary reading in various courses are grouped in this room. Sometimes several reserve rooms are set aside for the convenience of students specializing in certain subjects. For instance, a library may have a Commerce Reserve, a History Reserve, and an English Reserve.

4. Periodical Room. As its name indicates, this part of the library contains current issues of magazines and newspapers. Bound volumes of magazines may also be kept here; or they may be filed in the Reference Room and in the stacks.

5. Newspaper Room. Bound files of newspapers are available in this department.

To use the Newspaper Room, as well as the Treasure Room and the Document Room (6 and 7 below), the student usually must obtain permission from the head librarian.

6. Treasure Room. In this division, often called the Rare Book Room, are preserved old books and manuscripts, limited editions, and other valuable pieces which would be difficult to replace.

7. Document Room. Official publications of federal, state, and city governments are stored here.

8. Browsing Room. Designed for leisure-time and recreational reading, this room is usually furnished with convenient tables, reading lamps, and comfortable chairs. Students may make themselves at home as they read fiction, poetry, biography, and other subjects of interest to them. Sometimes books may be taken out for a day or two at the discretion of the librarian.

9. Stacks. All library resources which are not stored in separate departments, such as those already mentioned, are systematically filed in the stacks. To obtain such materials, students are required to present call slips to attendants at the Loan Desk.

The Card Catalogue

The distribution of resources among the various divisions outlined in the preceding section is indicated in the card catalogue. Obviously, then, this index represents an inventory of all sources of information available in the library, and designates the place where they may be found.

Arrangement. All cards in the catalogue are filed alphabetically according to the first important word on each one. *A, an,* and *the* are disregarded in the alphabetical arrangement.

Index Cards. For each book in the library, the catalogue contains the following cards:

1. *Author Card.* The author's surname, followed by his given name, appears as the first printed line.

```
810.9
L677  Lewisohn, Ludwig, 1882–
```

The author card is the quickest and most convenient means of locating a book when the author's name is known.

2. *Title Card.* The title of the book is typed, above the author's name, at the top of the card.

```
810.9  Expression in America
L677  Lewisohn, Ludwig, 1882–
```

If the student knows the title of the book but not the name of the author, he will look for the title card.

3. *Subject Card.* A word or phrase indicating the subject of the book is placed above the author's name.

```
810.9  American Literature
L677  Lewisohn, Ludwig, 1882–
```

Subject cards are most valuable when the student wants to know what books on a particular topic are available in the library. To find information on a certain subject, the investigator should look under specific, rather than under general, headings. If he is interested in the cultivation of flowers, for instance, he would locate subject cards headed *Floriculture,* rather than those labeled *Botany.*

Data on the Cards. The same information appears on the author card, the title card, and the subject card for any particular book. These data are shown on the following author card:

810.9
L677 Lewisohn, Ludwig, 1882–

    Expression in America, by Ludwig Lewisohn . . .
New York and London. Harper & Brothers, 1932
    xxxii, 642 p. 24½ cm.

    1. American literature—Hist. & crit. I. Title

                                           32–26245

Library of Congress   PS88.L45

—— ——— Copy 2

Copyright A 48895   32k5   810.9

---

1. In the upper left-hand corner, the call number
$\frac{810.9}{L677}$ indicates the classification of the book according to the Dewey Decimal system.[1]

[1] In the Dewey Decimal system, books are classified in the following order:

000	General Works	500	Pure Science
100	Philosophy	600	Useful Arts
200	Religion	700	Fine Arts
300	Sociology	800	Literature
400	Philology	900	History

These groups are further subdivided into various branches of knowledge under each of the main divisions. Books relating to medicine, for example, are classified under 610; books on engineering are listed under 620. The first digit of the number indicates

2. "Lewisohn, Ludwig, 1882–" gives the author's surname first and the date of his birth.

3. The complete title of the book, the name of the author, the place of publication, the publisher, and the date of publication are printed on the next section of the card.

4. The fourth line records that Lewisohn's work contains thirty-two pages numbered with Roman numerals and 642 pages numbered with Arabic numerals, and that it measures 24½ centimeters in height.

5. The first item on the next line shows that a subject card for the book is filed under the heading *American literature—history and criticism*. The second item, "I. Title," means that the work is also listed on a title card captioned *Expression in America*.

6. Information on the lower portion of the card is of minor importance to undergraduates. The items indicate:

    a. The number, "32–26245," by which duplicate cards may be ordered.

    b. The fact that the Library of Congress has two copies of the book filed under "PS88.L45."

---

the general classification; the second and following digits show the specific subdivisions. By the addition of a decimal point and one or more digits, the classification may be extended to minute parts of every field of knowledge.

Some libraries use the Library of Congress system, in which the main divisions of knowledge are designated by letters instead of numbers.

A	General Works	K	Law
B	Philosophy—Religion	L	Education
C	History—Auxiliary Sciences	M	Music
		P	Language—Literature
D	History—Topography (except American)	Q	Sciences
		R	Medicine
E–F	American History—Topography	S	Agriculture
		T	Technology
G	Geography—Anthropology	U	Military Science
		V	Naval Science
H	Social Sciences	Z	Bibliography—Library Science
J	Political Science		

Subdivisions are indicated by the addition of a second letter and whole numbers.

    c. The copyright number, "A 48895."

    d. The printer's key, "32k5."

    e. The classification number of the book in the Dewey decimal system, "810.9."

"See Also" Cards. In addition to the cards already discussed, the catalogue includes others which bear the title, "See also." A "See also" card usually follows a series pertaining to a particular subject. Its value is that it suggests other topics under which related material may be found. After a series on the subject of *Reciprocity*, for example, a "See also" card might give cross references to other headings, such as *Commercial Policy, Commercial Treaties, Economic Policy,* and *Tariff.* By following these leads, a student looking up material on the principle of reciprocity in international trade relations would find pertinent information that he might otherwise have overlooked.

The Call Slip

Most libraries provide forms to be used in securing books from the stacks. These forms, or call slips, have spaces for recording the call number, the author's name, the title, the volume and edition, and the identification of the borrower.

To obtain the right book, the student should fill in the required data—copied from the catalogue card—and present the call slip at the Loan Desk.

When a book is filed in one of the special departments, such as a reserve room or the Document Room, its location is noted on the catalogue card. A card for a book shelved in the Commerce Reserve Room, for example, would be labeled *Commerce.* In such cases, obviously, the student would go to the specified department rather than to the Loan Desk.

Reference Books

When the student consults a reference work for the first time, he should examine its prefatory section, which will generally give a detailed explanation of its scope, organization, special features, and limitations. Here also he will find directions for using the book. Unless he reads these instructions before he attempts to find the desired information, he will waste time in haphazard search and often will not locate the necessary data.

If the investigator does not know of any book that contains the particular facts which he wants, he can locate a source by consulting Isadore Mudge's *Guide to Reference Books* and its supplement. In this *Guide,* about four thousand titles are classified according to their special fields and types. Detailed information on the scope and uses of the reference works is also given.

The following list of books frequently consulted for ready reference is not intended to be complete, but it does suggest the variety of sources available in the Reference Room.

Dictionaries (Unabridged)

For the use of dictionaries, see pages 10–15 in this Handbook.

Webster's New International Dictionary. 2nd ed. 1934.

New Standard Dictionary. 1938.

New Century Dictionary. 1936. 2 vols.

Century Dictionary and Cyclopedia. 1911. 12 vols. Vol. XI, *Cyclopedia of Names,* is a pronouncing dictionary of proper names.

Oxford English Dictionary. 1933. 12 vols. and supplement.

Dictionary of American English. 1938– . Vols. I and II, and Parts XI, XII, and XIII have been published.

Dictionaries (Special)

For extended lists of synonymous words, for distinctions in their meanings, and for questions concerning idiom, the following books are helpful:

Allen's Synonyms and Antonyms. 1938.

Crabb's English Synonyms. 1934.

Fernald's *English Synonyms and Antonyms.* 1938.
Roget's International Thesaurus of English Words and Phrases. Rev. ed. by C. O. S. Mawson. 1938.
Webster's Dictionary of Synonyms. 1942.
Fowler's *Dictionary of Modern English Usage.* 1937.
Horwill's *Dictionary of Modern American Usage.* 1935.

Dictionaries (Biographical)

Biographical dictionaries may be classified into three main groups: (1) general, (2) national, (3) special classes.

General

Lippincott's Universal Pronouncing Dictionary of Biography and Mythology. 1930.
Chamber's Biographical Dictionary. 1929.
International Who's Who. 1936– . (Published annually.)

National

Dictionary of American Biography. 1928–37. 20 vols. and index volume.
National Cyclopedia of American Biography. 1892–1938. 29 vols. and supplements.
Who's Who in America. 1899– . (Published biennially.)
Dictionary of National Biography (British). 1921–1922. 22 vols. and supplements.
Who's Who (mainly Englishmen). 1848– . (Published annually.)

Special Classes

Kunitz's *Living Authors.* 1931.
Kunitz's *Authors Today and Yesterday.* 1934.
Kunitz's *British Authors of the Nineteenth Century.* 1936.

Kunitz's *American Authors:* 1600–1900. 1938.

Kunitz and Haycraft's *Twentieth Century Authors.* 1942.

American Men of Science. 6th ed. 1938.

Who's Who in the Theatre. 7th ed. 1933.

Who's Who in Art. 3rd ed. 1934.

Leaders in Education. 1937.

Composers of Today. 1934.

(For a more complete list of all types of biographical dictionaries, see Mudge's *Guide,* pages 281–314.)

Encyclopedias (General)

General encyclopedias contain authoritative articles in virtually all fields of knowledge. Bibliographies are appended to the more important articles.

Encyclopaedia Britannica. 14th ed. 1929. 24 vols.

Encyclopedia Americana. 1918–1920. 30 vols.

New International Encyclopaedia. 2nd ed. 1930. 25 vols.

Columbia Encyclopedia. 1935. One of the best one-volume comprehensive encyclopedias.

Encyclopedias (Special)

Special encyclopedias furnish information in limited fields of knowledge, as indicated in their titles. The longer articles usually include bibliographies.

Catholic Encyclopedia. 1907–1922. 17 vols.

Universal Jewish Encyclopedia. 1939– . 5 vols. published; the complete work will consist of 10 volumes. (Will probably supersede the older *Jewish Encyclopedia.* 1901–1906. 12 vols.)

Hastings' *Encyclopedia of Religion and Ethics.* 1908–1927. 12 vols. and index.

Harper's Encyclopedia of Art. 1937. 2 vols.

Harper's Encyclopaedia of United States History. 1912. 10 vols.

Hutchinson's Technical and Scientific Encyclopedia. 1936. 4 vols.

Encyclopaedia of the Social Sciences. 1930–1935. 15 vols.

Monroe's *Cyclopedia of Education.* 1911–1913. 5 vols.

Bailey's *Cyclopedia of American Agriculture.* 1908–1909. 4 vols.

Encyclopedia of Banking and Finance. Rev. ed. 1937.

Yearbooks

Yearbooks give information on current events and developments of the year in various fields, such as science, medicine, literature, business, industry, government, and sports. Some of them supplement encyclopedias; others specialize in statistical data.

Britannica Book of the Year. 1938– . Annual supplement to the *Encyclopaedia Britannica.*

Americana Annual. 1923– . Yearly supplement to the *Encyclopedia Americana.*

New International Yearbook. 1907– . Annual supplement to the *New International Encyclopaedia.*

World Almanac and Book of Facts. 1868– .

Statesman's Yearbook. 1864– .

The American Yearbook. 1910–1919; 1925– .

Statistical Abstract of the United States. 1878– .

Book Lists

For bibliographical information about books relating to various subjects, the student should refer to the following indexes. Most of these give the author, title, number of pages or volumes, publisher, and price. Except as indicated below, the entries are arranged alphabetically by author, title, and subject. To find books on finance, folklore, history, or travel, for instance, the student would look under those headings if he did not know the authors or titles of books in his field of interest.

United States Catalog. 4th ed. 1928. Lists books in print in the United States as of January 1, 1928. For books out of print, see the earlier editions. For later books, see the entry below.

Cumulative Book Index. 1898– . (Published monthly, except August; cumulated annually.) It supplements the *United States Catalog.*

A.L.A. (American Library Association) *Catalog.* 1926. (Supplemented at intervals.) Entries are arranged according to the main divisions in the Dewey Decimal system (see footnote 1, page 348, in this Handbook). Also contains an author, title, and subject index following the detailed entries. Annotations indicate the scope and value of the books listed.

A.L.A. Booklist. 1905– . (Published semi-monthly, except August.) Books are classified and annotated as in the *A.L.A. Catalog.*

Book Review Digest. 1905– . (Published monthly; cumulated annually.) Entries arranged alphabetically by author, with a subject and title index added. Includes, in addition to bibliographical data, a digest of contents, extracts from reviews, and exact references to the complete reviews.

Indexes to Periodicals and Newspapers

For references to articles on current topics, the student should consult indexes to periodicals and newspapers. Except as indicated below, the entries are arranged alphabetically by subjects, such as *Accidents, Actors, Agriculture, Aircraft,* and so on; by authors' surnames (for signed articles); and by titles. Cross references labeled *See* or *See also* generally are included.

Most indexes are published monthly in paper-bound issues, and at the end of the year are cumulated, in one alphabet, in permanent volumes.

The entries usually give the title, author, periodical,

volume, page reference, and date. The form commonly used is illustrated in the following item, listed under the subject heading, "Christmas," in the *Readers' Guide to Periodical Literature:*

> Christmas is made at home. A. Hagan. il House B
> 83:60–1 D'41.

This entry means that an illustrated article, "Christmas Is Made at Home," by A. Hagan, will be found in *House Beautiful,* volume 83, pages 60–61, of the December, 1941, number.

A list of the periodicals and a key to abbreviations are given in the forepart of every index.

General Indexes to Periodicals

Readers' Guide to Periodical Literature. 1900– . (Published monthly; cumulated quarterly, annually, and triennially.) The standard work for references to periodicals in general.

Poole's Index to Periodical Literature. 1802–1906. (No longer published.) Subject index to 470 periodicals of the nineteenth century.

International Index to Periodicals. 1907– . (Published monthly; cumulated annually.) Lists many scholarly journals not found in other guides.

Public Affairs Information Service. 1915– . (Published weekly; cumulated bimonthly and annually.) A subject index especially useful for articles on political science, commerce, finance, economics, and sociology. Lists publications of federal, state, and municipal governments.

Industrial Arts Index. 1913– . (Published monthly; cumulated annually.) Subject index. Lists articles chiefly from engineering, business, and trade periodicals.

Special Indexes to Periodicals

Agricultural Index. 1916– .
Annual Magazine Subject-Index. 1908– .

Dramatic Index. 1908– . (Bound with the *Annual Magazine Subject-Index*.)

Engineering Index. 1884– .

Index to Legal Periodicals. 1908– .

(For other special indexes, see Mudge's *Guide*.)

Index to Newspapers

New York Times Index. 1913– . (Issued monthly; cumulated annually.) Lists events and the dates when they were reported in the *Times*. Virtually an index to all newspapers because the events were reported in most papers on the same day.

Miscellaneous Reference Works

Rand-McNally Commercial Atlas. 1939.

Lippincott's New Gazetteer. 1931.

The Times [London] *Survey Atlas of the World*. 1924.

Putnam's Historical Atlas, Mediaeval and Modern. 1937.

Allibone's Poetical Quotations from Chaucer to Tennyson. 1891.

Bartlett's *Familiar Quotations*. 1937.

Brewer's *Dictionary of Phrase and Fable*. 1930.

Mencken's *New Dictionary of Quotations on Historical Principles*. 1942.

Strong's *Exhaustive Concordance to the Bible*. 1894.

Bartlett's *Concordance to Shakespeare*. 1894.

Cambridge History of English Literature. 1907–1916. 14 vols.

Cambridge History of American Literature. 1917–1921. 4 vols.

Harvey's *Oxford Companion to English Literature*. 2nd ed. 1937.

Thrall and Hibbard's *Handbook to Literature*. 1936.

Harper's Dictionary of Classical Literature and Antiquities. 1897.

Gayley's *Classic Myths in English Literature and in Art*. 1911.

Gray's *Mythology of All Races*. 1916–1932. 13 vols.

Walters' *Classical Dictionary of Greek and Roman Antiquities*. 1916.

Cambridge Ancient History. 1923– . Vols. 1–10.

Cambridge Mediaeval History. 1911– . Vols. 1–8.

Cambridge Modern History. 1902–1926. 14 vols.

Schmeckebier's *Government Publications and Their Use*. 2nd ed. 1939.

Swanton's *Guide to United States Government Publications*. 1918.

Ayer's *Directory of American Newspapers and Magazines*. 1880– .

Kelly's *Directory of Merchants, Manufacturers, and Shippers of the World*. 1937– .

Mudge's *Guide to Reference Books*. 6th ed. 1936. Supplements, 1939, 1941.

Shore's *Basic Reference Books*. 2nd ed. 1939.

Minto's *Reference Books*. 1929. Supplement, 1931.

Hutchins, Johnson, and Williams' *Guide to the Use of Libraries*. 5th ed. 1938.

Exercises

1. Cite one article—in a periodical published before 1900—on each of the following subjects:

        Immigration   Flying machines
        Baseball   College examinations

2. Find references to three articles—published within the past five years—on each of the following subjects:

        Education   Literature
        Airplanes   Health
        Architecture

3. In the *New York Times Index*, locate references to newspaper accounts of the Japanese attack on Pearl Harbor on December 7, 1941.

4. What did reviewers say about Benjamin Roland Lewis' *The Shakespeare Documents*, published in 1941?

5. Under each of the following headings in Mudge's *Guide,* find two reference books. Give full bibliographical details for each book, and briefly describe its contents and organization.

Essays	Games and Sports
Ships	Business Management
Costumes	Treaties and Foreign Relations
Aeronautics	
Debates	Popular Customs and Folklore
Bibliography	

6. Compare the articles on Sidney Lanier in the *Encyclopaedia Britannica,* in the *Encyclopedia Americana,* and in the *Cambridge History of American Literature.* Look up cross references in the index of each work.

7. Find the names and addresses of three companies that manufacture mining machinery in the United States.

8. List the names and the editors of newspapers published in Alaska.

9. Identify the sources of the following quotations:

"True nobility is exempt from fear."

"Hark! the numbers soft and clear
Gently steal upon the ear."

10. Give a brief account of David Livingstone's education.

11. Give a brief sketch of Thomas Paine's character.

12. Give the author, title, date, publisher, and the price of two books on American folk songs published in 1935. Give similar data on two books of poetry published within three months of the time of this assignment.

13. What were the average working hours and earnings of hotel employees in the United States in 1938?

14. What was the total number of automobiles in England in January, 1927?

15. Find the present age, address, and most recent book of the following:

>William Somerset Maugham
>Ruth Suckow
>George Fielding Eliot

16. Compare the discussion of the word *effective* in Fowler's *Dictionary of Modern English Usage* and in *Crabb's English Synonyms*.

THE TERM PAPER

The term paper, also called the investigative or research paper, usually is based on an investigation of a special subject. In some advanced courses, interviews and questionnaires, or laboratory experiments, are used to obtain facts for research papers. In most courses, however, students go to books and periodicals for their materials. The present discussion is, therefore, primarily concerned with the preparation of papers that require investigation in the library.

Selecting a Subject. The choice of a subject depends upon the student's interest, the availability of material, and the length of the paper. If he chooses a worth-while problem about which he is genuinely curious, his research will be interesting and valuable to him.

Since the investigation is usually carried on in the library, its resources must be considered. A student interested, for example, in a first-hand study of American magazines published before 1800 could not make the study if a sufficient number of these periodicals were not available. The library, however, probably would have books on the history of our early magazines.

Several volumes, of course, could be written about the history of these periodicals. Such a subject would be too broad for a term paper, which generally does not exceed thirty or forty pages. The subject, then, would have to be narrowed to one that could be treated adequately within the limits of the assignment.

The student, for instance, might write about the struggle of one publisher during the American Revolution. Another narrowed topic would be the influence of an editor upon some political issue. Within the limits of an investigative paper, it might be possible to treat the part that Benjamin Franklin played in developing the American magazine.

Subjects in other fields should be similarly restricted according to available sources and the number of pages required by the instructor. An undergraduate interested in chemistry might write about one contribution of a great scientist. A student of sociology could easily find data for a term paper on some phase of Jane Addams' efforts to establish Hull House in Chicago. A pre-legal student might investigate one of the new types of courts that have been set up to try violators of traffic ordinances.

The careful selection and the limitation of the subject are the first steps in the preparation of an adequate term paper.

Analyzing the Subject. Having chosen his subject, the student should analyze it carefully in order to find points that will require discussion in the paper. At this time he will not be able to list all of them, for presumably he is not thoroughly familiar with his problem. If he were, there would be no need for further investigation. This preliminary analysis is helpful, nevertheless, in suggesting possible leads to be followed in his search for data. As he gathers material on the topics, he will be constantly alert for other points which are uncovered in his reading. These he will add to the list until he has included all the elements essential to a thorough treatment of his limited subject.

Finding Sources. The next step is to find books and magazine articles that seem promising as sources of material for the paper. Each of these is to be listed on a separate card (see page 363). This record should include all the data necessary to identify the source when the student consults it for notes later in his research. The forms for listing these data are those used in the final bibliography (see pages 367–72).

In looking for sources, the student will make use of the available library facilities.

1. If he has no direct leads in the field, he will probably look up his subject first in a general reference work, such as the *Encyclopaedia Britannica* or the *Encyclopedia Americana*. At the end of the article which he consults, he will usually find a list of other sources. Any of these that appear to be promising should be recorded on individual bibliography cards.

2. If there are special reference works in his field, such as the *Cambridge History of English Literature,* the *Encyclopaedia of the Social Sciences,* Hastings' *Encyclopaedia of Religion and Ethics,* and similar compilations, he may begin his investigation by referring to articles in them. Most of these articles include bibliographies that will suggest other clues to information. Mudge's *Guide to Reference Books* contains the names of these special reference works, listed according to the fields which they cover: for example, *Philosophy, Religion, Science,* and *History.*

3. Indexes to magazines and newspapers should be consulted for articles relating to his subject. (See page 355 for a list of these indexes.)

4. The card catalogue of the library will supply the names of other sources. These the student will find by consulting pertinent subject cards in his field of investigation. For instance, to obtain information for a paper on a certain type of aircraft construction, he might look under such headings as: *Airplanes* (or *Aeroplanes*), *Aircraft, Aviation, Aeronautics, Flight,* and *Wings.*

When an author, a title, or a subject card that seems promising has been located, additional leads can be secured from the cross references which are given among the subject headings on the center portion of the card (see page 348). Clues worth following appear, too, on "See also" cards, explained on page 350 in this Handbook. The search should be continued until every possible lead has been noted.

When his search has been finished, the student has a series of cards, each of which lists a book or a magazine article. These entries represent an inventory of sources which he must now read to get material for his term paper.

Taking Notes. Each of the sources listed on the cards is to be examined. To save time, the student should first check the table of contents and the index for the parts of the text that seem pertinent to his subject. He can then turn to these parts and read them, without spending time on other sections that would be unfruitful. He should learn, also, to scan magazine articles as a preliminary step before reading them carefully. A little practice will enable him to tell whether an article is of value to him. If his first examination of a book or an article does not uncover suitable material, he eliminates that item from his bibliography cards, and proceeds to the next one.

From each source that contains useful information, he takes careful notes. For this purpose ruled index cards, $4'' \times 6''$ in size, are preferable.

Most of the notes should be paraphrases or summaries of the borrowed material. Items that the student expects to quote in his paper should be copied exactly as they appear in the source. Such notes must be enclosed in quotation marks to remind him when he writes his paper that he is using the original author's words.

Each note should be recorded on a separate card. Even though related to the same topic, notes from different parts of the same book or article should be kept separate. This method permits the student to file in one group all data pertaining to a single topic. Later, when he arranges his materials for the paper, he can easily shift his notes to their proper place in the discussion of the subject.

A simple method of identification will save the labor of copying the name of the source on each card referring to it. The first book or article from which notes are taken is indicated by writing the figure 1 on the bibliography card and also on each card containing a note from that source. This code number is placed on the first line, in the upper left-hand corner. As successive sources are used, they are identified by the figures 2, 3, and so on.

After the code number, a key word or phrase should be centered on the first line of the note card to indicate the topic to which the item relates. This key will help to simplify the organization of material when the writer makes his outline.

The number of the page on which the item appears in the source, together with the volume number if there is more than one volume, is placed at the beginning of the second line. The note proper then follows this page reference.

The following illustration shows the arrangement of data on a note card pertaining to a discussion of the paper industry.

12	Labor

P. 62. Women, employed chiefly as sorters, counters, and sheet cutters, constitute about 25 per cent of the workers in paper mills.

As previously explained, the figure 12 in the upper left-hand corner refers to the bibliography card identifying the source. "Labor" is the key indicating the topic to which the note belongs. "P. 62," the page reference in the source, is followed by the student's summary of the original passage.

Organizing the Material. After the student has collected sufficient data for the adequate treatment of his subject, he is ready to organize his material. For this purpose he will assemble his notes and prepare a logical outline (see pages 21–7).

The next step is to write on each note card the respective outline index number of the topic under which the notation will be used in developing the complete paper. The upper right-hand corner is a convenient place for this symbol.

12	Labor	II–A–3

"II–A–3" means that the item is to be used in discussing the third subordinate point under subdivision A of the second main heading in the outline.

After the cards are labeled, they should be arranged in sequence according to their outline index numbers. Each note will then automatically appear in its proper place when the material is needed in the writing of the paper.

The writer, of course, may work out some other system of correlating his notes with his outline; but unless he employs a definite method, he will overlook some notes and will lose time trying to find others that he recalls having taken. Indeed, without an orderly system of organization and identification, he will be almost hopelessly bewildered when he tries to use his materials.

Writing the First Draft. The outline and the notes serve as the foundation of the first draft. In preparing this preliminary copy, the student should follow the suggestions given on page 3 in this Handbook.

When he uses borrowed material in his own discussion

of the point to which the quoted, paraphrased, or summarized item relates, he should insert a footnote to acknowledge the specific source of his information. He will obtain the necessary identification from the bibliography card bearing the same code number as that which appears in the upper left-hand corner of the note card. (For the form of footnotes, see pages 373–5.)

Writing the Final Draft. After the first draft has been revised, with careful attention to the principles of effective writing, it should be copied in final form.

If the paper is typewritten, the main part of the text is double spaced, and quotations that extend beyond four lines are single spaced. Such quoted items are indented at least five spaces from the left margin of the text.

When centered captions and sideheads are used to indicate main divisions, a consistent form should be followed for the various parts.

Making the Final Bibliography. On a separate page at the end of the paper, the student will list all the sources from which he selected material. The form and arrangement to be used in this bibliography are explained on pages 367–72, 381.

Assembling the Parts of the Paper. The title of the paper, the name of the writer, the name and number of the course, and the date should be neatly arranged on a separate sheet. This title page precedes the first page of the text. The bibliography follows the last page of the text.

Instructors sometimes require a more complete form consisting of:

1. *Title Page* (as explained above).

2. *Table of Contents.* The titles of the various divisions and subdivisions, together with page references to them, are given in this part.

3. *Outline.* A detailed outline in the form given in Sec. **A 6** may be used instead of the Table of Contents.

4. *Text.*

5. *Appendix* or *Appendices.* Material of interest to the reader but not essential to the discussion of the subject may be presented in a special section or sections following the text.

6. *Bibliography.*

Bibliography

A list of sources that furnished data for the term paper is to be appended to it. This bibliography assists readers who might want to examine the extent and accuracy of the writer's investigation, or to secure additional information on the subject.

A bibliography may be organized in various ways. Whatever the arrangement, it is acceptable if it meets the writer's needs, if it gives accurately all the necessary data, and if it presents all similar entries in a consistent form.

Entries for Complete Works

The following sequence of data illustrates one of the forms that may be used for books:

> Name of the author (surname first)
> Title of the book (underlined to indicate italics)
> Edition (if other than the first)
> Place of publication
> Name of publisher
> Date of publication
> Number of volumes (if more than one)
> Number of pages (omitted when number of volumes is given)

The following examples show the order, spacing, and punctuation. In each entry all lines after the first are indented three or four spaces.

1. A book by one author:

Welby, T. Earle, *A Popular History of English Poetry,* New York, D. Appleton & Company, 1924, 284 pp.

2. A book by more than one author:

a. Scott, John Hubert, and Zilpha E. Chandler, *Phrasal Patterns in English Prose*, New York, The Ronald Press Company, 1932, 376 pp.

When there are more than two authors, the name of each may be given, or the name of the first one, followed by "and others," may be used.

b. Gough, Harry Bainbridge, and others, *Effective Speech*, New York, Harper & Brothers, 1937, 654 pp.

3. More than one book by the same author:

Jones, Robert Gomer, *Harmony and Its Contrapuntal Treatment*, New York, Harper & Brothers, 1939, 187 pp.
———, *Theory of Music*, New York, Harper & Brothers, 1936, 131 pp.

[After the first entry, a short line replaces the author's name.]

4. Editions other than the first:

Taussig, Frank William, *The Tariff History of the United States*, 7th ed. rev., New York, G. P. Putnam's Sons, 1923, 409 pp.

[Abbreviations which indicate the edition, such as *rev. ed.*, or *5th ed. rev.*, follow the title.]

Special Items

1. An edited or a translated text:

a. Franklin, Benjamin, *The Writings of Benjamin Franklin*, edited by Albert Henry Smith, New York, The Macmillan Company, 1905–1907, 10 vols.
b. Dekker, Maurits, *Beggars' Revolt*, translated from the Dutch by Irene Clephane and David Hallet, New York, Doubleday, Doran & Co., 1938, 399 pp.

[The name of the editor or of the translator follows the title.]

2. Books containing contributions from various sources.

These entries ordinarily begin with the title of the work:

a. *Dictionary of American Biography,* edited by Allen Johnson and Dumas Malone, New York, Charles Scribner's Sons, 1928–1936, 18 vols.

b. *Modern American and British Plays,* selected and edited by S. Marion Tucker, New York, Harper & Brothers, 1931, 950 pp.

Sometimes when the reader is likely to identify the work by the editor's name rather than by the title, the editor's name is placed first.

c. Burgum, Edwin Berry, editor, *The New Criticism,* New York, Prentice-Hall, Inc., 1930, 359 pp.

Entries for Parts of Larger Works

The same general principles that govern the order, spacing, and punctuation of entries for complete works apply to entries for parts of larger works. In addition, several special rules are observed:

A. Quotation marks are used to indicate the caption of the selection.

B. The title of the complete work is underscored; this indicates that in a printed book it would be in italic type.

C. The number of the specific volume that contains the selection is given if the complete work consists of more than one volume.

D. Only the page reference to the selection is given; the number of pages in the whole work need not be cited.

The following examples show how these principles are put into practice.

1. A selection from an anthology written by one author:

> Eliot, T. S., "Modern Education and the Classics," *Essays Ancient and Modern,* New York, Harcourt, Brace and Company, 1936, pp. 169–185.

2. An article in a collection compiled by an editor from various sources:

> Hoover, Herbert, "In Praise of Izaak Walton," *Readings in Present-Day Writers,* edited by Raymond Woodberry Pence, New York, The Macmillan Company, 1933, pp. 195–203.

3. Articles in reference books, magazines, and newspapers:

> a. Bonn, Moritz Julius, "Economic Policy," *Encyclopaedia of the Social Sciences,* V:333–344.
> b. "Hedonism," *The Encyclopaedia Britannica,* 14th ed., XI:377–378.

[Note that the caption of an unsigned article is in the place where the author's name would ordinarily appear.]

> c. Zenzinov, Vladimir M., "With an Exile in Arctic Siberia," *The National Geographic Magazine* (December, 1914), XLVI:695–718.

[Note that the place of publication and the name of the publisher are not given. Observe also the arrangement of the date, volume number, and pages.]

> d. "U. S. Power Capacity Far Above Needs," *The Chicago Daily News,* August 28, 1941, sec. 2, p. 25, col. 3.

Arrangement of a Bibliography

Items in a bibliography are usually listed in the alphabetical order of the authors' surnames. The title of an anonymous work is placed in its proper alphabetical position according to the first important word in the title.

The lines in each entry are single spaced, and successive entries are separated by double spaces.

Angoff, Charles, A *Literary History of the American People,* New York, Alfred A. Knopf, 1931, 2 vols.

Beers, Henry Augustus, *An Outline Sketch of American Literature,* New York, Chautauqua Press, 1887, 287 pp.

Channing, Walter, "An American Language and Literature," *North American Review and Miscellaneous Journal* (September, 1815), I:307–314.

Gaine, Hugh, *The Journals of Hugh Gaine,* edited by Paul Leicester Ford, New York, Dodd, Mead & Co., 1902, 2 vols.

"Leaf from the American Magazine—Literature of the Last Century, A," *Atlantic Monthly* (April, 1860), V: 429–438.

Lewisohn, Ludwig, *Expression in America,* New York, Harper & Brothers, 1932, 624 pp.

Pattee, Fred Lewis, *A History of American Literature,* rev. ed., New York, Silver, Burdett and Company, 1903, 475 pp.

———, *Sidelights on American Literature,* New York, Century Company, 1922, 342 pp.

Instead of using one continuous list in alphabetical order, many writers prefer to classify their sources according to books, magazines, newspapers, and other sources. In this type of arrangement, the individual sections are headed with appropriate captions, such as *Books, Periodicals,* and *Newspapers.* The entries in each group are listed alphabetically.

Bibliographical items may also be classified under the headings of *Primary Sources* and *Secondary Sources.* Under the first caption would be listed all original sources from which data had been borrowed. For example, in a paper on early American literary magazines published in Philadelphia, the periodicals themselves would constitute primary sources. Comments that the writer of the paper borrowed from historians and critics of early American writing would be classed as secondary sources.

Exercises

1. List four of your textbooks in bibliographical form.

2. In the card catalogue of the library, find items of the type indicated below and prepare bibliographical entries for them.

    A. Three books by one author.
    B. A book by more than one author.
    C. A work consisting of more than one volume.
    D. An edited or a translated text.
    E. A revised edition.

3. From an encyclopedia or other work indicated below, select an item of the type specified, and prepare a bibliographical entry for it.

    A. An unsigned article in an encyclopedia.
    B. A signed article in a special reference work.
    C. A signed article in a magazine.
    D. An unsigned article in a magazine or in a newspaper.
    E. An essay, a play, or a poem selected from an anthology.

4. Prepare a bibliography listing two books by each of the following authors, and either one book or one magazine article about each of the writers.

    A. Dr. Samuel Johnson.
    B. Sir Walter Scott.
    C. Oliver Wendell Holmes.
    D. William Ewart Gladstone.
    E. Edward Arlington Robinson.
    F. Robert Frost.
    G. Henry L. Mencken.
    H. Carl Sandburg.

Footnotes

The source of every quotation and of every paraphrased or summarized passage must be individually ac-
knowledged in the term paper. Specific identification of
each borrowed item gives authority to the writer's discussion, and permits readers to verify the accuracy of his
research. For this identification of sources, footnotes are
used.[2]

Position. Footnotes are generally placed at the bottom
of the page containing the citations to which they refer.
They are separated from the text by a short line. Each
one is single spaced, and a double space is left between
successive footnotes.

Index Numbers. The relation between a passage in
the text and a footnote referring to it, is indicated by index numbers placed at the end of the passage and at the
beginning of the note.[3] These numbers are typed or
written slightly above the regular line.

Footnotes are usually numbered consecutively on each
page, the first reference on a page being identified by
the figure 1. Some writers number them consecutively
throughout the whole paper; or, in longer articles containing several chapters, there may be a separate series—
beginning with the figure 1—for each chapter.

Form. Any method that adequately identifies sources
is satisfactory. Whatever form is employed, it should be
used consistently throughout the whole paper.

Italics and Quotation Marks. Titles of books and magazines are underscored. Captions of articles and parts of
complete works are set off in quotation marks.

---

[2] Footnotes may also be employed for various other purposes,
such as defining special terms; giving supplementary data; presenting the writer's additional comments that are not essential
to the text; and indicating cross references to other parts of the
paper.

[3] Instead of numbers, some writers use daggers, asterisks, and
similar devices; but this system becomes awkward and complicated when many footnotes are necessary.

First Reference to a Source. 1. In a paper that does not contain a final bibliography, the first footnote reference to a source should give full bibliographical details. Specific reference to page and volume (if there is more than one volume in the work) is included.

Reference to a magazine article:

¹ Vladimir M. Zenzinov, "With an Exile in Arctic Siberia," *The National Geographic Magazine* (December, 1914), XLVI:714.

Reference to a book:

¹ Robert Jones, *Theory of Music*, New York, Harper & Brothers, 1936, p. 16.
² H. O. Taylor, *Thought and Expression in the Sixteenth Century*, New York, The Macmillan Company, 1930, vol. II, p. 36.

2. In a paper that contains a final bibliography, the first footnote reference to a source may include only the author, title, and page reference. Other information is given in the complete bibliography (see page 371).

¹ Robert Jones, *Theory of Music*, p. 16.
² H. O. Taylor, *Thought and Expression in the Sixteenth Century*, vol. II, p. 36.

Subsequent Reference to a Source. After the first reference to a source, subsequent citations from the same source may be indicated by the following abbreviations:

1. *Ibid.* (From the Latin *ibidem*, meaning *in the same place.*) When no other footnote appears between the first and the subsequent citation, this abbreviation followed by the page reference is sufficient identification.

¹ Robert Jones, *Theory of Music*, p. 24.
² *Ibid.*, p. 31.

2. *Op. cit.* (From the Latin *opere citato*, meaning *in the work cited.*) When subsequent references to one source are separated from the first citation of that source

by intervening footnotes to other works, the author's surname followed by *op. cit.* and the page reference may be used.

⁵ Jones, *op. cit.*, p. 39.

3. *Loc. cit.* (From the Latin *loco citato,* meaning *in the place cited.*) For references like those in 2, *loc. cit.* is sometimes employed instead of *op. cit.*

⁵ Jones, *loc. cit.*, p. 39.

4. Neither *op. cit.* nor *loc. cit.* can be used if two or more works by the same author are cited in the paper. In that case, the title of the book must be repeated.

Other Abbreviations. In addition to the abbreviations given in the foregoing section, the following words and phrases are usually abbreviated in footnotes:

chapter	ch. (plural chaps.)	no date	n.d.
		no publisher	n.p.
circa (about)	c. (or ca.)	note	n.
column	col. (plural cols.)	page	p. (plural pp.)
		section	sec. (plural secs.)
compare	cf.		
following page	f. (plural ff.)	thus	*sic*
here and there	passim	verse	v.
line	l. (plural ll.)	volume	vol. (plural vols.)
new series	n. s.		

Exercises

Prepare correct footnote forms for the following items. Assume that the footnotes will appear in a term paper in the succession indicated here:

1. A quotation from page 403 in The Winged Horse, by Joseph Auslander and Frank Ernest Hill, published in 1927, by Doubleday, Doran & Company, New York.

2. A reference to page 386 in the same book mentioned in the preceding item.

3. A reference to page 201 in Thomas H. Dickinson's An Outline of Contemporary Drama, published at Boston in 1927 by the Houghton Mifflin Company.

4. A notation on page 627 in The Oxford Companion to English Literature, compiled and edited by Sir Paul Harvey, and published at the Clarendon Press, Oxford, in 1932.

5. A quotation from page 147 in the book cited in the third item above.

6. A paraphrased passage from page 78 of F. W. Howay's article, A Ballad of the Northwest Fur Trade, in the New England Quarterly, volume I, for January, 1928.

7. A quotation from p. xii in The Winged Horse Anthology, compiled and edited by Joseph Auslander and Frank Ernest Hill, and published in 1929 by Doubleday, Doran & Company, New York.

Specimen Term Paper

(Title Page)

VERSATILE

NOAH WEBSTER

By

Horace Camdon

English II

May 1, 1942

(Text)

VERSATILE NOAH WEBSTER

Today we think of *Webster* and *dictionary* as virtually synonymous. It is proper that we should do so, for Noah Webster was the greatest of lexicographers. His work was largely his own and was greater in scope than that of earlier dictionary makers, including Dr. Samuel Johnson. Webster originated many of the forms now common in lexicons and established the basis of modern comprehensive dictionaries.[1]

Although now known principally as a lexicographer, in his own day Webster was intensely interested in many things other than dictionaries. It is the purpose of this paper to point out some of his various projects, other than his dictionary, in order to show that he was a remarkably versatile man.

I. A Brief Sketch of Webster's Background

Born in 1758, Webster spent his boyhood toiling on his father's farm near Hartford, Connecticut. There he was taught to apply himself industriously to whatever tasks he undertook. This early training influenced his entire life, for he continued to apply himself diligently until he died in 1843 at the age of eighty-five.

The preparation for his busy life began in a district school, where his assignments included mainly studies in Dilworth's *Spelling Book* and in the Bible.[2] In 1774, at the age of sixteen, Noah entered Yale. While in college, he studied divinity, which was the principal subject in the curriculum, and other subjects, such as English, Latin, Greek, geometry, and geography. Even though his college work was interrupted at various times by the American Revolution, he completed his courses and received his diploma in 1778.[3] At his Commencement Webster gave the Cliosophic Oration in English, an honor which indicated that he was in the first quarter of his class.[4]

---

[1] *Encyclopedia Americana*, vol. 29, p. 151.

[2] E. E. F. Ford, *Notes on the Life of Noah Webster*, vol. I, p. 14.

[3] Horace Scudder, *Noah Webster*, p. 2.

[4] Harry R. Warfel, *Noah Webster: Schoolmaster to America*, p. 33.

Following his graduation, Webster returned to his father's farm. He wanted to continue his education by studying law; but his father, who had already mortgaged the farm to pay Noah's expenses at Yale, could no longer give him financial assistance. One day the senior Webster gave his son an eight-dollar bill in Continental currency, then worth about two dollars in silver, and said, "Take this; you must now seek your own living; I can do no more for you." [5]

Disappointed, though not ungrateful, the young man retired to his room, where he spent three days in meditation and in reading Dr. Johnson's *Rambler*. Those weighty essays produced a deep and permanent influence upon him. The teaching of the great moralist made Webster resolve that, whatever his fate in life might be, he would "pursue an exact course through life" and "perform all moral and social duties with scrupulous exactness. . . ." [6]

II. Webster's Interest in Education

Thus armed with a college diploma, a very small amount of money, and a resolution, Webster began his many-sided career. To earn his living he taught in various places for several years, and then in 1782 opened his own school in Sharon, Connecticut. While teaching, the young schoolmaster came to the realization that textbooks used by American children were inadequate. Most of the books were published in England and failed to meet the particular needs of boys and girls in the newly established republic.

Webster, therefore, motivated by patriotism, took upon himself the duty of writing suitable textbooks. In 1783 he brought out *A Grammatical Institute of the English Language, Comprising an Easy, Concise, and Systematic Method of Education, Designed for Use of English*

[5] Ford, *op cit.*, vol. I, p. 38.
[6] *Ibid.*, vol. I, p. 39.

*Schools in America. In Three Parts. Part I. Containing a
New and Accurate Standard of Pronunciation.* Within a
year he completed the second part, entitled *A Plain and
Comprehensive Grammar.* The third part, *The Necessary
Rules of Reading and Speaking,* was published in 1785.

In the preface of the first part, Webster remarked that
before the Revolution Americans adopted with avidity
not only the virtues but also the errors and follies of Englishmen.[7] After the war his countrymen changed their
view, and Webster believed that it was their duty to examine especially the English system of education used
in America. His point of view is clearly expressed in the
following excerpt:

"While Americans stand astonished at their former
delusion and enjoy the pleasure of a final separation
from their insolent sovereigns, it becomes their
duty to attend to the *arts of peace,* and particularly
to the interests of *literature;* to see if there be not
some errours to be corrected, some defects to be
supplied, and some improvements to be introduced
into our systems of education, as well as into those of
civil policy. We find Englishmen practising upon
very erroneous maxims in politics and religion; and
possibly we shall find upon careful examination, that
their methods of education are equally erroneous
and defective." [8]

As his first contribution toward the improvement of
American education, Webster sought to establish a
standard of spelling and pronunciation by presenting to
the people a set of simple, accurate rules. Believing that
his countrymen needed to master their language in order
to protect their hard-won liberties from the encroach-
ments of civil and ecclesiastical tyrants, he wanted to
teach Americans the basic principles of grammar and the
art of reading.[9]

[7] *Grammatical Institute,* p. 3.
[8] *Ibid.,* p. 4.
[9] Warfel, *op. cit.,* pp. 57–60.

III. Webster's Interest in Law, Government, and Economics

As previously mentioned, the schoolmaster and author of textbooks wanted to be a lawyer. In addition to teaching and writing, therefore, he studied law. So diligent and resolute was he in his study that by April, 1781, he was admitted to the bar.[10] At that time, however, people were too poor to hire lawyers; Webster, consequently, kept on teaching for several years. Meanwhile he continued to read law in the office of John Canfield.[11] After his marriage in 1789, he settled in Hartford, where he finally began to practice law.[12]

Industrious as Webster was between 1782 and 1789, he also found time to write pamphlets on subjects relating to legal problems, governmental policy, and economic questions. In a forty-eight-page pamphlet, for example, he set forth his arguments in favor of a strong central government for the United States.[13] Another pamphlet, entitled *An Inquiry into the Excise Laws of Connecticut*, treated the question of . . .

(The student finished the development of this topic, and proceeded to discuss his other points. Since the form of the term paper has been adequately illustrated in the part thus far reproduced, only the concluding paragraph is given after the list of headings for the intervening material.)

IV. Webster's Interest in Journalism

Contributor to magazines and newspapers. (Four paragraphs.)

Editor of *The American Magazine*. (Two paragraphs.)

Editor of *The American Minerva*. (Two paragraphs.)

[10] Ervin C. Shoemaker, *Noah Webster: Pioneer of Learning*, p. 21.

[11] Ford, *op. cit.*, p. 45.

[12] Shoemaker, *op. cit.*, p. 21.

[13] This pamphlet was published on March 9, 1785, under the title, *Sketches of American Policy*. For a complete analysis of its content, see Warfel, *op. cit.*, pp. 112–118.

V. Webster's Interest in Science

Author of articles on diseases. (Four paragraphs.)

Author of articles on animal husbandry. (One paragraph.)

Author of articles on the weather. (Two paragraphs.)

(Concluding paragraph)

From the foregoing discussion it is plain that Noah Webster labored all his life for the benefit of his countrymen. As an author of textbooks and a champion of education, he was, as Warfel calls him, the "Schoolmaster to America." His knowledge of law enabled him to write pamphlets that helped to establish the form of government that has made our country great. He fought constantly against injustice and ignorance. Being a practical man, he gave much thought to ways of improving the health and the general welfare of the people. Always, whether as essayist, magazine editor, scientist, or lexicographer, he worked for his country. Of Noah Webster it may be said that he was indeed a versatile man, who applied his talents industriously and unceasingly to the advancement of Americans.

Bibliography

Ford, Emily Ellsworth Fowler, *Notes on the Life of Noah Webster*, edited by Emily Skeel, New York, privately printed, 1912, 2 vols.

Mathews, M. M., *The Beginnings of American English*, Chicago, University of Chicago Press, 1931, 181 pp.

"Noah Webster," *Encyclopedia Americana*, New York, Americana Corporation, 1929, Vol. 29.

Read, Allan Walker, "Noah Webster's Project in 1801 for a History of American Newspapers," *Journalism Quarterly* (September, 1934), 11:258–275.

Russell, T. W., "Webster, Word Arbiter for 100 Years," *New York Times Magazine*, April 15, 1928, p. 11.

Scudder, Horace E., *Noah Webster* (*American Men of Letters Series*), Boston, Houghton Mifflin Company, 1909, 302 pp.

Shoemaker, Ervin C., *Noah Webster: Pioneer of Learning*, New York, Columbia University Press, 1936, 347 pp.

Smith, G. Hubert, "Noah Webster, the Archaeologist," *American Anthropologist* (October, 1931), 33:620–624.

Wagenknecht, Edward, "The Man Behind the Dictionary," *Virginia Quarterly Review* (April, 1929), 5:246–258.

Warfel, Harry R., *Noah Webster: Schoolmaster to America*, New York, The Macmillan Company, 1936, 460 pp.

Webster, Noah, *The American Magazine*, edited by Noah Webster, New York. Published from December, 1787, to November, 1788.

———, *An American Selection of Lessons in Reading and Speaking*, 3rd. ed., Philadelphia, Young and McCullock, 1887, 377 pp.

———, *A Brief History of Epidemic and Pestilential Diseases*, Hartford, Hudson & Goodwin, 1799, 2 vols.

———, *A Collection of Essays and Fugitiv* [*sic*] *Writings*, Boston, Thomas and Andrews, 1790, 414 pp.

———, *A Grammatical Institute of the English Language*, Part I, Hartford, Hudson & Goodwin, 1783, 119 pp.

———, *Miscellaneous Papers on Political and Commercial Subjects*, New York, E. Belden & Co., 1802, 227 pp.

Winslow, C. E. A., "Epidemiology of Noah Webster," *Transactions of the Connecticut Academy of Arts and Sciences* (January, 1934), 32:21–109.

Suggested Subjects for Term Papers

1. Nutrition and physical fitness
2. Women in business

3. Oriental rug patterns
4. Conquest of cancer (or other disease)
5. Moving pictures and education
6. American music (art, poetry) in the South
7. The Isthmian games
8. The literary style of ———
9. Recent trends in interior decoration
10. Satire in the novels of Sinclair Lewis
11. The fight for women's suffrage
12. The origin of language
13. New methods of fighting forest fires
14. Thomas Jefferson's democratic principles
15. Scholarship in relation to success in business
16. A recent discovery in science
17. The Federal Reserve System
18. Our trade with South America
19. Recent improvements in farming
20. The modern comic section
21. Natural resources in Alaska
22. The manufacture of pottery (or some other product)
23. The construction of the Grand Coulee Dam
24. Medicinal uses of insulin
25. Exploration in the Antarctic Circle
26. The city manager in municipal government
27. Safety education in industry
28. The Pan-American Conference
29. Forms of propaganda
30. A modern sewage disposal plant

BUSINESS LETTERS

Business letters are normally typewritten on paper 8½ × 11 inches in size. For special purposes a smaller sheet—for example, 7¼ × 10½ inches—is sometimes preferred.

The letter is usually single spaced, with double space between paragraphs and between groups such as the inside address, the salutation, etc.

Block and Indented Form. Either the block form or the indented form may be used.

BLOCK FORM

Heading	1628 Rood Avenue
	Skokie, Illinois
	April 5, 1942

Inside address Raymond and Price
483 Main Street
Evanston, Illinois

Salutation Gentlemen:

Body Two years ago I signed a three-year lease on my apartment in the Lakeside Building at 1628 Rood Avenue. The price was $85.00 a month.

Since the lease was signed, there has been a general decline in rents throughout the city. Apartments like mine in this building are now being rented for $75.00 a month on a yearly basis, and I understand that some concessions are being given even at this price.

In view of these facts, I should like to have you consider a reduction on my apartment. Although I am bound by the lease for another year, it seems only fair that, as a matter of equity, some adjustment should be made. As you know, the lease provides for a general overhauling of the apartment at the beginning of the third year. If a satisfactory reduction in rent is given, I am willing to forego this decorating.

Complimentary close Yours truly

Signature M. C. Kramer (hand written)
M. C. Kramer (typed)

In the block form, there are no indentions in any group; each successive line begins directly under the preceding one.

In the indented form, the first line of each paragraph

is indented from five to ten spaces; and each successive line in the heading, inside address, and signature is indented five spaces more than the preceding line.

Even when the paragraphs are indented, however, the heading, inside address, and signature are frequently typed in block form.

INDENTED FORM

Heading
1628 Rood Avenue,
Skokie, Illinois,
April 5, 1942.

Inside address
Raymond and Price,
    483 Main Street,
        Evanston, Illinois.

Salutation Gentlemen:

Body

    Two years ago I signed a three-year lease on my apartment in the Lakeside Building at 1628 Rood Avenue. The price was $85.00 a month.

    Since the lease was signed, there has been a decline in rents throughout the city. Apartments like mine in this building are now being rented for $75.00 a month on a yearly basis, and I understand that some concessions are being given even at this price.

    In view of these facts, I should like to have you consider a reduction on my apartment. Although I am bound by the lease for another year, it seems only fair that, as a matter of equity, some adjustment should be made. As you know, the lease provides for a general overhauling of the apartment at the beginning of the third year. If a satisfactory reduction in rent is given, I am willing to forego this decorating.

Complimentary close
Yours truly,

Signature
M. C. Kramer (hand written)
M. C. Kramer (typed)

Parts of the Business Letter

The business letter has six standard parts:

Heading	Body
Inside address	Complimentary close
Salutation	Signature

Heading. When a letterhead is used, the heading con-sists only of the date. This is generally placed at the up-per right-hand corner of the letter, two or three spaces above the line on which the inside address begins; or it is sometimes centered two or three spaces immediately below the letterhead. The name of the month is spelled out.

Correct: December 10, 1942
Not Good: Dec. 10, 1942
Not Good: 12/10/42

If a letterhead is not used, the address of the writer is typed above the date at the upper right-hand corner.

Correct: 1438 South Oak Street
Adelphi, Indiana
August 5, 1942

Inside Address. This consists of the name and address of the person or firm to whom the letter is written.

It may have closed or open punctuation.

In closed punctuation, a comma is placed after each line except the last one, which ends with a period.

In open punctuation, the comma and the period are omitted at the ends of lines.

CLOSED PUNCTUATION	OPEN PUNCTUATION
Ames and Marcy,	Mr. A. C. Barry
1622 State Street,	645 Monroe Avenue
Springfield, Illinois.	Chicago, Illinois

In open punctuation, however, a period follows an abbreviation at the end of a line.

Mr. A. F. Jackson, Jr.

Open punctuation has been growing in favor in recent years, and now is used more widely than the closed form.

Note. The form—open or closed—employed in the inside address should be followed consistently in the heading, inside address, complimentary close, and signature.

CLOSED	OPEN
Yours truly,	Yours truly
A. C. Badger.	A. C. Badger

In the salutation the colon is retained even when the other parts have open punctuation.

A courtesy title, like *Mr., Mrs., Miss, Dr., Professor,* etc., should always precede the name of an individual in the inside address.

Mr. R. P. Quinn	Professor C. M. Atwood
Mrs. C. D. Adams	Colonel M. R. Thatcher
Miss Anna Price	Honorable Charles E. Brown
Dr. A. H. Nichols	The Reverend John R. Craig

Titles indicating the position which a person holds in an organization may follow the name or may be placed on the following line, with the name of the organization.

Mr. Conrad Davis, Treasurer	Mr. Theodore M. Waterbury
Ohio Utility Company	Secretary, Hall and Price
Adams, Ohio	Montgomery, Delaware

Salutation. The most common salutations are:

Dear Sir:	Dear Madam:
Dear Mr. Raymond:	Dear Mrs. Raleigh:
Dear Dr. Fremont:	Dear Miss Sutton:
Dear Professor Atwood:	Ladies:
Gentlemen:	

Dear Sir, Gentlemen, Dear Madam, and *Ladies* are formal. *Dear Mr. Adams* and *Dear Mrs. Phillips* give a more personal note to the letter, and are preferred where the relationship between the correspondents warrants this personal element. As a matter of fact, these forms are growing in favor, and are often used even when there has been no previous interchange of letters.

For unmarried women the salutation is *Dear Miss ——. Dear Madam* is used only in letters to married women.

Body. The body is the main part of the letter. It carries the message. The general principles of good writing —paragraphing, sentence structure, and punctuation— should be observed here as in other types of composition.

Complimentary Close. The more common forms of the complimentary close are:

Yours truly	Sincerely yours
Yours very truly	Cordially yours
Very truly yours	

Sincerely yours and *Cordially yours* imply a personal relationship between the writer and the recipient of the letter.

Notice that only the first word of the complimentary close begins with a capital.

Signature. In its simplest form, this consists of the written signature alone. Frequently the name is also typed beneath the written signature in order to insure complete legibility.

John A. Stevens (handwritten).
John A. Stevens (typed).

When the letter is from a business firm or other organization, the signature may be:

1. The firm name—typed.

ADAMS AND LOCKWOOD

2. The firm name—typed, followed by the writer's signature and his position in the firm.

ADAMS AND LOCKWOOD

F. B. Peters	(handwritten)
F. B. Peters	(typed)
Treasurer	(typed)

General Principles

Abbreviations. As a general rule all words in a letter should be spelled out, with the exception of a few standard abbreviations which are in regular use, such as, *Mr., Mrs., Dr., Jr., Sr., Inc., Esq.,* and academic degrees like *A.B., Ph.D.*

Not Good: Mr. George A. Tyler, Treas.
Correct: Mr. George A. Tyler, Treasurer.

Words in addresses and dates should not be abbreviated.

Not Good: 1225 Main St.
            Aurora, Ill.
Correct: 1225 Main Street
            Aurora, Illinois

Not Good: Jan. 4, 1942
Correct: January 4, 1942

Stereotyped Expressions. Commercial jargon should be avoided. The letter should be natural and direct in style.

Jargon: Your esteemed order of the 10th inst. is at hand, and we wish to thank you for the same.
Natural and Correct: Thank you for your order of June 10.

Jargon: Goods were shipped as per your order of recent date.
Correct: The goods were shipped as you specified in your order of May 8.

Participial endings for letters are not good form.

Stereotyped: Trusting that we may hear from you soon, we remain
Improved: May we hear from you soon?

When the pronoun *I* is needed in a sentence it should be used. Prejudice against *I* led the old-time correspondent into various evasions. Sometimes he dropped the subject of the verb or he adopted the awkward substitute, "the writer."

Not Good: Expect to be in Chicago next week and will see you then.

Not Good: The writer expects to be in Chicago next week and will see you then.

Better: I expect to be in Chicago next week, and will see you then.

Other objectionable stereotyped expressions are:

Attached hereto	Subsequent to
Beg to say	Take the liberty to
Contents noted	Valued favor
Enclosed herewith	We wish to say
Party (for *person*)	We would say
Previous to (for *before*)	

Exercises in Business Letters

A. Write the proper heading, inside address, salutation, complimentary close, and signature for the following letters. Indicate the body of the letter by two straight, horizontal lines. Place the other parts in their correct positions.

1. You are Mary E. Bower, unmarried. You live in Albion in Indiana, at 645 Plainfield Boulevard. You are writing a business letter to F. B. Paynter, who is superintendent of the Morgan County Hospital at Paris in Indiana. You do not have a letterhead.

2. You are J. B. Carlton and are writing as secretary of the firm, Ashton and Franklin, to J. B. Sable and Company, whose office is in the city of Blandon in Illinois at 756 South Walker Street. You are writing on a letterhead.

3. You are Frank S. Brown. You live in Rockland in Illinois, and are writing to A. C. Bernard, who is dean of Mid-

land University, which is in Hanover in the state of New York. You do not have a letterhead.

B. Write the following letters:

1. As a prospective freshman, write to the personnel director of the college, asking him about opportunities for working your way through college. Tell what you can do and how much work you need. Give any other pertinent information.

2. Write a letter to the dean of the college, asking about scholarships for freshmen. Give any information that will enable him to determine tentatively whether you might be eligible for a scholarship.

3. As business manager of your college paper, write a letter to the advertising manager of a business house in your city which has not been advertising in your paper. Try to show him that he should advertise.

4. Write a letter to your favorite magazine, asking that it be sent to your new college address instead of to your home address.

5. A month ago you bought a suit, dress, or other article from an out-of-town firm. The article isn't satisfactory. Write a letter explaining the difficulty and asking that an adjustment be made.

INVITATIONS AND REPLIES

Formal invitations and replies are written in the third person, and all words are spelled out except the street number and a few standard abbreviations, such as *Mr.*, *Mrs.*, *Dr.*, *Jr.*, and *Sr.* The heading, inside address, salutation, complimentary close, and signature of the ordinary letter are omitted.

FORMAL INVITATION

Mr. and Mrs. Charles E. Bryan request the pleasure of Mr. Albert N. Johnson's company at dinner on Saturday evening, August the sixth, at seven o'clock.
1864 Bronson Avenue
August the first

FORMAL ACCEPTANCE

Mr. Albert N. Johnson accepts with pleasure the kind
invitation of Mr. and Mrs. Charles E. Bryan to dinner on
Saturday evening, August the sixth, at seven o'clock.
285 Marshall Avenue
August the third

FORMAL REGRET

Mr. Alfred N. Johnson regrets that he is unable to accept
the kind invitation of Mr. and Mrs. Charles E. Bryan to
dinner on Saturday evening, August the sixth, at seven
o'clock.
285 Marshall Avenue
August the third

INDEX

(Symbols in bold face refer to sections; light-face figures to pages.)

ARTICLE AS A WHOLE	Broad Subject **A1**	Poor Title **A2**	Incomplete Analysis **A3**	Group Related Ideas **A4**	Illo Arrang **A**
PARAGRAPH	Unity of Thought **B1**	Topic Sentence **B2**	Informal Topic **B3**	Weak Ending **B4**	Arrang **B**
GRAMMATICAL CORRECTNESS	Agreement— Verb **C1**	Case— Pronoun **C2**	Case— Relative Pronoun **C3**	Case— Possessive **C4**	Ten Sequ **C**
SENTENCE— THOUGHT CONTENT	Fragment— Subordinate **D1**	Fragment— Co-ordinate **D2**	Choppy Sentence **D3**	Unrelated Thoughts **D4**	Ram Sent **D**
SENTENCE— CLEARNESS	Related Parts Separated **E1**	Misplaced Modifier **E2**	Split Infinitive **E3**	Misplaced Correlatives **E4**	Parti Misp **F**
SENTENCE— CLEARNESS (*Cont.*)	Omitted Verb **F1**	Omitted Connective **F2**	Omitted Article **F3**	Faulty Comparison **F4**	Ve with Sub **F**
SENTENCE— EFFECTIVENESS	Conciseness **G1**	Effective Short Sentence **G2**	Variety **G3**	Awkward Repetition **G4**	Effe Repe **G**
DICTION	Correct Word **H1**	Exact Word **H2**	Colloquial- ism **H3**	Slang **H4**	Tr **H**
PUNCTUATION AND MECHANICS	Comma **K1**	Semicolon **K2**	Colon **K3**	Dash **K4**	Per **K**
	Apostrophe **K9**	Hyphen **K10**	Italics **K11**	Spelling **K12**	Syl bifica **K**